Summer Fields

THE FIRST 150 YEARS

Summer Fields

THE FIRST 150 YEARS

EDITOR **GAVIN HANNAH**

THIRD MILLENNIUM
PUBLISHING, LONDON

MGH *ma.* (OS)

GAH *mi.* (OS)

cunctis maioribus
heredibusque

© Summer Fields and Third Millennium Publishing Ltd
First published in 2014 by
Third Millennium Publishing Limited, a subsidiary of
Third Millennium Information Limited
2–5 Benjamin Street
London
United Kingdom
EC1M 5QL

ISBN 978 1 908990 21 1

British Library Cataloguing in Publication Data
A CIP catalogue record for this book is available from
the British Library.

Managing Editor: Susan Millership
Designer: Helen Swansbourne
Production: Bonnie Murray and Debbie Wayment
Reprographics by Studio Fasoli, Italy
Printed by 1010 International Limited, China
Front and back cover photography © Ralph Williamson

PHOTOGRAPHIC ACKNOWLEDGEMENTS
pp30 (play programme), 76 Brian Straton-Ferrier;
p43 (bottom) © Jeremy Sutton-Hibbert/Alamy;
p58 Francis Chute; p60 Martin Knowles; pp93 (maths
set), 110 (motto), 118 (cap), 166 (open prayer book)
Constantine Hatzis; pp104/5, 116 (rugby badge) Richard
Guinness; p124 Edward Guinness; p133 (top) Lady
T. Clarke; p156 Harold Macmillan by Bryan Organ
© National Portrait Gallery; p182/3 Bentley
Photographic, www.bentleyphoto.com, Tel. 01206
395888. Archival team photos from Gillman and Soame
and Hills and Saunders.

Contents

Introduction

David Faber, Headmaster

David Faber as a boy at Summer Fields

It has become something of a Summer Fields tradition to mark significant anniversaries with commemorative publications. For the school's centenary celebrations in 1964, Richard Usborne OS compiled a volume of Summerfieldiana, *A Century of Summer Fields: An Anthology 1864–1964*; the anecdotes and memories it contains remain as vivid, compelling and amusing today as they were fifty years ago. Twenty-five years later, Nicholas Aldridge published his authoritative *Time to Spare? A History of Summer Fields*. This new book owes a great debt of gratitude to the two that have gone before, and to Nick in particular – his memory looms large in all our minds in this, our 150th anniversary year.

Although Nick never taught me (my years as a boy here coincided with his own brief spell away from the school) I got to know him well over the years, especially in his post-teaching role as the school archivist. Sadly, Nick died during my first year as Headmaster and, although our time working together was all too brief, his impact on me was pronounced. I could always rely on his encyclopaedic knowledge of all matters relating to Summer Fields, either when researching a book of my own or when checking on some aspect of the school's history or a particular old boy. All those who were there will remember his moving funeral at Worcester Cathedral, followed by the beautiful and packed memorial service in his beloved school chapel.

A Century of Summer Fields begins with an apologia, in which Geoffrey Bolton is quoted lamenting the non-existence of a school archive, in turn preventing any serious attempt to write a history of the school (GB also, quite mistakenly, claimed that 'there's not a book in it'). In his later years, Nick tackled this dearth of organised resources, dedicating himself assiduously to the task of creating and sustaining the archives from which much of the material in this book is sourced; that work has been continued (and technologically improved upon) by our current Librarian and Archivist, Laurence Dardenne.

This new volume, however, is not a history book, even though it is Gavin Hannah, for thirty years the Head of History at Summer Fields, who has accepted the formidable challenge of editing and writing much of it (a project which quickly dispelled any hopes he may have had for an easy and quiet retirement!). Rather, this book is a portrait of Summer Fields drawn by those who know it best: its pupils and teachers, both current and past, whose recollections are intended neither to mimic nor to compete with existing school histories, but rather to complement them.

The process of researching this book has generated some wonderful new material, much of it in the form of memories, some of it actually tangible, which both balances and enhances the archival content. Having said that, this volume is not merely retrospective; in addition to prompting recollection, it also encourages us all to look to the future. We look back on the first 150 years of this famous and much-loved Oxford school, at the same time remaining confident that the next 150 years will see it continue to thrive in the tradition of excellence and diversity established by the first century and a half.

'Change and continuity are the counterpoised ingredients of a school's history,' Nick wrote in his introduction to *Time to Spare?* I was fortunate enough to inherit a school that was at the top of its game and to have the reins handed over to me by my predecessor, Robin Badham-Thornhill, whose own contribution to this book is rightly titled 'Change and Continuity'. Having known Summer Fields in a variety of guises (indeed, almost every guise possible), first as a pupil, then as an Old Boy, a parent and finally as a governor, I approached the challenge of maintaining that sometimes uneasy equilibrium with a uniquely personal perspective when I accepted the position of Headmaster. While Robin had been the first Headmaster to be appointed from outside Summer Fields, I, as the tenth, was the first to come from a non-teaching

experienced, others newly qualified in the teaching profession. All bring fresh ideas and new methods, but all continue to teach and look after the boys with that singular care and dedication that is a hallmark of life at Summer Fields.

At the 2013 Sports Day, just before the heavens opened, I was privileged to join with OS Olympian Lawrence Clarke in making a presentation to groundsman Roger King, in recognition of a phenomenal fifty years of service to Summer Fields; the Head Groundsman, Graham Person, is not that far behind having now worked here for forty-two years. Dr Felicity Fletcher-Campbell has been teaching the cello to Summerfieldians for thirty-seven years, while Johnny Bush is entering his thirty-fifth year of English teaching. There are currently thirteen members of staff, teaching and non-teaching, who have been at Summer Fields for more than twenty years.

For much of its history, the school was famously known for the 'three Cs: Classics, Chapel and Cricket (while many Old Summerfieldians remember an apocryphal fourth – 'cold baths'). Although those three aspects of the school's identity remain significant, it would now be hopelessly misleading to reduce life at Summer Fields exclusively to no more than that. The extraordinary variety of the academic curriculum, as well as sporting and extra-curricular activities, continues to grow, and current Summerfieldians go from strength to strength in terms of success both in the classroom and on the playing fields.

Supported by a dedicated, experienced and extremely able staff, the boys thrive in a vibrant learning environment, where the highest standards of academic excellence continue to be maintained, as they were in 1864. Following the successful ISI Inspection of 2009, further academic innovation led to glowing praise of the school's teaching and academic success after the most recent Inspection in early 2014. In the age of the public school pre-test, entrance to the most popular schools becomes ever more competitive, year on year; yet Summer Fields continues to fulfil its aim of preparing boys for Common Entrance and scholarships to those very schools. Eton remains the destination for the single largest cohort of boys each year, followed by the other few remaining all-boy schools: Winchester, Radley and Harrow. However, our leavers now move on to a far wider range of excellent public schools and continue to perform strongly in the entrance exams.

The boys enjoy an increasingly diverse programme of lectures and workshops which supplement their curricular learning with engaging activities. The English department welcomed its first ever Writer-in-Residence in 2012, children's author Lauren St John; the writer's residency is now an annual event, and our 150th birthday will be marked by a visit from Anthony Horowitz. Similarly, an annual week-long visit from an

background. My own somewhat unconventional route to the headmastership is well documented, and I recall vividly sitting in the Headmaster's study on 1 August 2010, a deserted school around me, wondering just how on earth this job was going to compare to my previous life as a politician and a writer.

Since my return to Summer Fields, I have had the pleasure of resuming acquaintance with many distinguished and long-serving members of staff, some of whom I had known as a governor or when they taught my son, and one or two of whom had even taught me. In recent years several long-standing staff, who have given years of service to Summer Fields, have retired from this hectic environment: Paul and Diana Cheater, who spent eighteen years at Summer Fields; Nigel and Linda Pearce after twenty years, and Gavin Hannah after exactly thirty years here. In their wake, a group of new teachers, Lodge parents and support staff have arrived at the school, some already

Artist-in-Residence has become a keenly anticipated yearly highlight, while the addition of specialist ceramics to the Art curriculum and the creation of a Portfolio Group to prepare boys for art scholarships have seen the standard of the boys' art hit new heights.

The school has been graced in recent years with some exceptionally strong mathematicians, many of whom have achieved success in national competitions and Olympiads. While the number of scholarships won each year is no longer the sole benchmark of academic success, as it once was, we remain extremely proud of the number of our pupils who win scholarships and exhibitions to public schools; between 2011 and 2014 alone the school won a total of fifteen awards to Eton, ten to Radley, five to Winchester and a handful to other schools. In 2011 the school won fifteen awards, the highest total for more than a hundred years: our founder would be particularly happy with the number of scholarships for Classics.

Sport, of course, continues to feature prominently in the lives of Summerfieldians. Above all, every single boy gets the opportunity to play in school matches as we put out up to eighteen teams across all age-groups on a busy Saturday. During the football season alone the school plays as many as 180 matches during the term. Certain sporting seasons are predictably more successful than others, but results have been steadily improving, from an already high level, over the past few years and there have recently been some outstandingly successful seasons in all three major sports. Highlights have included: the winning football 1st XI of 2011, statistically the most successful team since 1937 (the 1st XI went for almost three seasons without losing to another prep school); the 2012 1st XV, who won all their matches (the first such season since 1981 and only the second ever) and scored a record number of tries in the process; and, perhaps most successful of all over this period, the athletics team, which has broken numerous school records in the past few years and come away with a clutch of gold medals from successive National Prep School Championships. Boys have competed at county, regional and national level in a wide variety of sports including cricket, rugby, athletics, tennis, golf, squash, judo – and even kick-boxing!

2013 also saw a major redevelopment of the technical infrastructure in the Macmillan Theatre, generously sponsored by Rowan Atkinson, a former parent. The new sound and lighting equipment has significantly enhanced the school's productions, and has allowed many more boys to be involved backstage rather than under the lights themselves. Recent highlights have included: Dr Paul Dean's own adaptation of *Peter Pan* and an abridgement of *Twelfth Night*, Johnny Bush's production of the first act of *Hamlet*, Gareth Price's *The Hobbit*, and several stunning musicals from Pandy Stoop, including *We*

Will Rock You and, as part of our 150th anniversary celebrations, a sensational *Jesus Christ Superstar* with a cast of more than ninety boys; it was a production that would not have been out of place on a professional stage.

Music, too, is at the very core of Summer Fields life. Boys study it as an academic subject and more than 80 per cent of them learn an instrument, attending over 260 individual lessons every week. The school choirs perform widely: the Red Choir has sung in some of the most beautiful choral settings in the country, including several Oxford colleges (Magdalen, New College, Wadham, Exeter and Worcester), as well as in local and London churches and on tour in Rome (where they sang within

the generosity of a parent. The old pipe organ has found a welcoming new home in the village church of Warborough, south Oxfordshire.

This first step in a planned refurbishment of the chapel is only one element of Summer Fields' ambitious redevelopment programme, planned and launched to coincide with the school's 150th anniversary year. It is hoped that work will start imminently on Phase One of an £8 million three-phased development project that will transform the school over the next few years. A substantial new 'Pavilion' (not to replace the existing Red Pavilion!) will be built beside the swimming pool and sports hall, creating modern and spacious changing, showering and other facilities for the boys and visitors at ground-floor level. Upstairs will be a large open-plan, multi-use space with stunning views of the playing fields. Once Phase One is complete, we will move the changing rooms, showers and vins into the new building and start work on a complete rebuilding of the heart of the school, opening it up to create a spectacular and welcoming core space, together with new teaching and extra-curricular facilities.

All these developments are for the good of the boys. Boarding remains at the heart of Summer Fields' success (for the day boys, too, who derive equal benefit from all the boarding facilities). The welfare of, and opportunities for, each and every boy are central to everything that happens, and the quality of our pastoral care and facilities was once again warmly praised in our most recent Inspection report. This school, born when a Classics scholar and her husband took on the challenge of educating a handful of their friends' children, has grown and developed over 150 years to become one of the most successful and unique establishments of its kind in the country. Summer Fields is exceptional among prep schools for its longevity and its autonomy: few other comparable institutions remain wholly independent from associated senior schools, and it is to the credit of all Summerfieldians, current and past, that we have retained our distinctiveness and our strong sense of identity for a century and a half.

I began this introduction with a nod to Nicholas Aldridge, and it seems only fitting that I should conclude it with one as well. In the opening pages of *Time to Spare?* Nick referred wistfully to '[his] successor in 2014', correctly anticipating a future publication to mark the next anniversary; right up until his death, I think he rather hoped that it would be him undertaking the task one last time. It was not to be, but Gavin Hannah and his team have done a truly wonderful job and I very much hope that you will enjoy reading this book, and recognise some of the many memories contained within its pages.

DAVID FABER

the Vatican) and, latterly, Vienna. As part of our 150th anniversary celebrations in 2014 the whole school, with an orchestra and choir enhanced by parents and Old Boys, put on a truly memorable concert in Oxford's Sheldonian Theatre. We were privileged to perform the world première of the late Sir John Tavener's *A New Commandment*, specially commissioned for Summer Fields, in the presence of Lady Tavener and his family. This moving work was one of Sir John's last compositions before his untimely death in November 2013. The choir's spiritual home remains the Summer Fields Chapel, which at the beginning of this anniversary year had a new digital organ installed, specially designed for Summer Fields, thanks to

Editor's Preface

I was honoured to be asked by David Faber to produce this book as part of the school's 150th anniversary celebrations.

No one can work on the history of the school without paying tribute to the pioneering studies of Nicholas Aldridge. It has been humbling to follow in those illustrious footsteps. At the end of the Introduction to his history of Summer Fields, *Time to Spare?,* published in 1989, Nick writes that his chapters may be 'bristling with the most obvious mistakes'. I am sure that some of what follows will 'bristle' in a like manner. If so, the responsibility is entirely mine. Nick also hopes that his words will help 'my successor in 2014'. Well, that turned out to be me, and Nick may rest in peace, assured that his words have been not merely helpful, but invaluable. May the present work be of similar use to the writer in 2064!

Allow me to make three points. Firstly, this book is meant to be dipped into and enjoyed, but it is *not* a history of the school; much is omitted and the selection process is of course subjective. Secondly, it is not intended to offer 'a generally cosy and congratulatory chorus' of Summerfieldian triumphalism. Inevitably most of the observations are positive, as people asked to contribute to a celebratory volume usually have nice things to say – but there are some negatives. Thirdly, this is not *my* book. It is *yours*, especially if you are an OS. I have endeavoured to let the evidence speak for itself, allowing OSS voices to sing out clearly. My task has been to orchestrate the various themes by providing some linking text.

It has been an interesting undertaking and I can safely say that I have learnt more about Summer Fields during these months of research and writing than in three decades of haunting its corridors, fields and classrooms. I have also come to appreciate the sheer quality and diversity of Summerfieldian achievement. All who belong to the place enjoy a rare privilege, and one that should be for ever cherished.

GAVIN HANNAH
Summer Fields
Lady Day 2014

Acknowledgements

Many people have had a hand in the production of this book, and I am grateful to them all. In particular, my thanks go to Laurence Dardenne, Librarian and Archivist at Summer Fields, for her unstinting work in locating and arranging both pictorial and written material. Without her, I should have been lost! Sustained help and encouragement have been received from Daphne O'Connell of the Summer Fields Development Office. I should also like to express my sincere gratitude to the following for their specific contributions: Robin Badham-Thornhill (Summer Fields 1997–2010); Christine Berry (typing up Willy Pryor's thoughts and reading draft texts); Andrew Bishop (fives); Charles Churchill (ski trips, archival photography and reminiscences); Dr Paul Dean (Summer Fields 1864–1975); David Faber (Introduction); Deborah Ives (Buzzer); David Kidd-May (for a wealth of Summerfieldiana); Rob Lagden (ski trips); Judith Lane (Art); David Langdon (Music, Choir, sailing); the Rev. Robin Lapwood (Chapel); Rupert McNeile (ICT); Dominic Price (additional photography, ICT and Olympians); Gareth Price (Music, Choir); Joe Porter (Sport); Nigel Talbot Rice (Summer Fields 1975–1997); Rachel Williamson (Art).

Photographs have been specially commissioned and provided by Ralph Williamson. Winchester College Archives are to be thanked for the inclusion of the portrait of Wavell as a young scholar. Further illustrations of Wavell appear by kind permission of the Wavell Estate.

I should like to thank the publishers for all their professional guidance, expertise and support over the past months, notably: Susan Millership, managing editor; Dr Neil Titman, publishing director; Helen Swansbourne, designer; and the whole team at Third Millennium Information.

Finally, but by no means least, my sincere thanks go to my wife, Ann, for her patience, tolerance and forbearance as her place of work invaded even her home!

Editorial Note

This book is arranged in broad themes. Two chapters of general narrative offer some context for the various reminiscences. Dates in parentheses after a name refer to the time when that person was at Summer Fields, whether as a boy or a member of staff. At Summer Fields, the custom remains of referring to staff by their initials. However, in this book, full names have been used in the interests of clarity for the reader.

Summerfieldiana

Bate (obs.) – anger. To be in a bate, whether master or boy

Bish (obs.) – error or mistake

Black Book – a book kept in the Headmaster's study in which boys are entered for serious misconduct. Malefactors later receive an appropriate detention

Black Hole – Staff Common Room

Bolton – classroom block named after Geoffrey Bolton (GB)

Booty (obs.) – the Clerk of Works; any member of the maintenance staff

BOSFAM – acronym for Boys of Summer Fields and Masters

Broomstick Match – annual cricket match played at the end of the Summer Term between a Masters' XI and the 1st XI. The 'broomstick' refers to the shaved bat used by the adults

Buzzer – toy shop

Congo – congregational practice

Congregagger-pragger (obs.) – congregational practice

Ego (obs.) – I do, me (cf. Quis?)

Far Fields – playing fields over the cycle track

Gapper – a male gap-year student, usually from abroad (mainly from Australia, New Zealand or South Africa, where SF has built up links) who works at SF for one year, usually January to January

Gapper-matron – a female gap-year student working in a similar way to a gapper

Gut (obs.) – tuck, food

Guzz (obs.) – tuck, food

Hay Feast – traditional jollity at the end of the Summer Term. Picnic and games held in the fields by the Cherwell

Hobson's – surgery; sanatorium, named after Dr Hobson, school doctor 1927–59

Kipper Mine – cellar with the main heating boilers under the Lobby

Leagues – founded in 1926. Each boy is placed in one of four Leagues: Case (red), Congreve (yellow), Maclaren (green), Moseley (blue)

Lodge – the Boarding House in which a boy sleeps. The Lodges are: Borva, Cottage, Front Lodge, Mayfield, Newton, Savage's, Upper House

Macmillan – the Macmillan Hall, formerly the old gym

Near Fields – fields on the near side of the cycle track

New Bug (obs.) – a new boy

OS – Old Summerfieldian

OSS – Old Summerfieldians

Pax (obs.) – please stop doing that!

Quis? (obs.) – who wants this? (cf. Ego)

Reds and Blues – A boy may be awarded a 'Red' or a 'Blue' in one of five categories: Work, Games, Music, Organisation and Conduct. A Red is a plus point, a Blue is a minus point, counting towards, or against, a boy's League score. In the termly inter-League competition, cups are awarded to the League with the highest total in each category. The League with the largest overall total wins the League Cup and the League Feast (lately termed the League Treat)

SF – Summer Fields

Shadow – a new boy under the guidance of an old hand (his 'substance') deputed to show him the school routines during his early days

Squish, the (obs.) – school train, later a dedicated carriage, on a train from Paddington to Oxford or Oxford to Paddington

SUB – Show Up for Bad. SUBs are awarded for work of unacceptable standard. The Director of Studies orders the work to be redone and gives Work Blues. SUBs are detrimental to a boy's League Score of Reds and Blues

SUG – Show Up for Good. SUGs are awarded for excellent work. The Director of Studies examines the work, praises it, signs it and rewards the boy with extra Reds. Each term, a cup is given to the boy winning the most SUGs

Substance – a senior boy partnered with a new boy (his 'shadow') to show him the school routines

Vins – lavatories

Vol – voluntary; as in 'Vol In' or 'Vol Out'; as opposed to 'All Out' – indicates when boys are allowed indoors

Wavell – teaching rooms for ICT, Art, Design and Technology and Science, named after Field Marshal the Earl Wavell OS

Wagger-pagger (obs.) – waste-paper basket

Quo Vado?
First Impressions

My heart pumped more quickly than usual for that of an eleven-year-old boy as I stood in front of the main gates of one of the most well-known prep schools in England. With trembling feet I reluctantly walked through those gates. Not knowing what boarding is like, I finally made the decision to walk into Front Lodge with tears running down from my eyes.

Surprisingly I found that I was very warmly greeted by a kind couple who were the people in charge. After being welcomed I was soon engaged in conversation with other boys who immediately became good friends. I now felt relieved, acknowledging that boarding in a school was not torture.

When Lodge matters were sorted out I was guided by a 'substance', who looked after me for a week, to meet my form master. Then I ate an unbelievably tremendous supper and played games of tag with my new friends. When the clock struck 8, my friends and I returned to Lodge absolutely shattered. I fell asleep immediately, after a shower. My heart was now pumping normally. My feet didn't tremble. I wasn't crying.

ADRIAN YAM (2011–13)

It was the beginning of the Lent Term 2011, slightly chilly outside, probably not the best weather for a first day at school. For some reason I wasn't all that nervous. My mother wished me all the best of luck and dropped me off at the school gates. I was completely ignorant about boarding. I had never before encountered such a concept. Before, I had always been in a day school in Russia. This school was busy, but so were Russian schools. The difference was that the English were 'relaxed' busy, rather than plain busy. By that I mean that everyone was doing something but they were not at all in a hurry, and indeed Summer Fields has an air of pleasant relaxation that keeps you energised.

BORIS KHALIMOVSKIY (2011–13)

Nerves surrounded me. I was trapped in a fear bubble at my first boarding school. However, an immediate impression of warmth was soon imprinted on me. All of a sudden, I felt part of the school, almost as if I had turned on a switch. From being shy and lacking in confidence, I then felt as if I were part of the school community. I immediately knew that this school was right for me.

FINLAY WATT (2009–13)

There was a great sense of climax leading up to my first day at Summer Fields. After a week of packing and trying on the school uniform, I thought that it was about time for the summer holidays to end and for me to start at my next school.

When we arrived, I asked my father where we were. We had gone down a side street behind Marks & Spencer with no school entrance in sight. My parents gathered the luggage and made the long trek to Borva Lodge. The house was different from anything I had seen so far. The concept of a large room with more than two beds was alien to me. It was there that I met my first friends at Summer Fields. Next was the part I was dreading the most, as I had to say farewell to my parents. At this stage, I had never been away from my parents for more than the odd sleepover at a friend's house. On the stairs of Borva, I said goodbye and told my mother that I would ring her every day for the next week to tell her how things were going. I watched them walk out of the house and down the path, all the time waving at me, until at last, they were out of sight.

After a short lecture from the Housemaster, we all gathered our books and pencil cases and made a mass exodus to the school building, where our form masters were waiting. After a welcome from our form master, it was supper, our first meal at Summer Fields. The kitchen had prepared spag-bol as a good starting meal. Supper was followed by a game of football on the AstroTurf. Suddenly the bell rang, another new concept for me, and we all made our way back to our respective Lodges. The evening was filled with nervous excitement, as we were about to have our first night at boarding school.

As the lights went out, I lay wondering what this school might bring me.

WILLIAM BRUDENELL (2008–13)

I'll never forget my first full day at the school in early September 1997. I had arrived the day before with my older brother off a plane from Washington DC, where my father had been posted by the FCO the previous year, feeling not just emotionally homesick but also, as it turned out, physically so. My breakfast ended up on the floor of the corridor outside the school chapel well before the first-day's proceedings were under way. Thankfully, Mrs Badham-Thornhill was good enough to save me any embarrassment by hastily sending me back to my Lodge while several kind members of the cleaning staff were tasked with cleaning up the mess I had made. That afternoon, I also managed to get struck by a stream of hot water mistakenly tipped over my back by a member of the kitchen staff whilst tea was being served in the Sports Hall gallery. It was Mr Darling who came to my rescue as he picked me up and hurled me into one of the nearby showers after turning on the cold water. Unfortunately, his efforts didn't prevent me from reproducing my supper, most likely due to nerves once again, right into a bowl laid out for Mrs Bishop's breakfast, that evening after being taken to my Housemaster's lodgings to be comforted after a tumultuous first day.

FRANKIE PARHAM (1997–2002)

I enjoyed a fabulous five years at Summer Fields. I was so eager to join the school when I was seven, a term earlier than originally planned, that I completely forgot to say goodbye to my parents and had to be reminded to do so. Mercifully, I did not suffer from homesickness.

MALCOLM YOUNG (1965–70)

I went to Summer Fields in the autumn of 1963, the evening of the Harold Macmillan government and the dawn of the swinging sixties. My first memory was of visiting the then school outfitter Billings & Edmonds off Hanover Square, and the hours spent by my mother and housekeeper sewing on Cash's tapes, with name and changing-room number. On arrival at school, the first rite of passage was the removal of the rubber under-sheet from one's dormitory bed, which showed one was grown up and had settled in.

NICHOLAS SANSOM (1963–8)

My first impression was of a welcoming matron who, on our arrival direct from Bahrain, weaned me away from my mother in such a fashion that, whilst she remained distraught, I did not, at least not for long.

PETER FLETCHER (1958–63)

My first memory of the school is bidding farewell to my mother in the Headmaster's dining room. In those days there was no contact (except through censored letters) between home and school so I knew I was in for a long stretch. At that moment, Mum seemed more upset than I was. But the full horror of my situation dawned on me as we sat down to tea (I had never had a hot drink before) and I saw my father's name on the honours board on the wall. I suddenly realised that home was very far away. Like many boys in those days I was bitterly homesick for the first two weeks, and it didn't help when suddenly the dormitory door was thrown open, all the lights were turned on and there was a long, long silence before the assistant matron (who had a terrible stammer) could get out the words: 'WHO WAS TALKING?'

EDWARD MYNORS (1955–60)

It was my first full day at Summer Fields and we had gone outside for the mid-morning break. No sooner were we outside than there were shouts of 'Oiks Tallyho!, Oiks Tallyho!' from excited boys. We all rushed towards the public footpath which ran along the side of the playing fields, picked up conkers and threw them at the Oiks. Just one part of an education for a seven-year-old, but never forgotten.

JOHN GLEDHILL (1955–60)

My very first memory was of being left at the school by my mother and suddenly feeling very lonely. I was helped massively to get over this by hearing quite a few others of the new boys that term 'blubbing' in their beds after the lights were turned off. Lesson: If others are lonely, then one is not alone.

TIMOTHY NOBLE (1952–6)

So there we are, sipping a genteel cup of tea in the Headmaster's drawing room. My Mum and Dad, of course, are old hands, having previously put my three elder brothers through this hoop. And I'm trying to be inconspicuous, and thinking, 'As soon as Mum and Dad go, these gents are going to eat me.'

Suddenly conversation is stopped by the shrill announcement from the hall, in the broadest Lancashire accent, 'Mi muther's be'ind wi butter an eggs it' bag,' and into the room sweeps a pair of pre-National Health giglamps perched on the nose of one George Richard Phillipson (1947–52), son and heir of a Bolton building contractor. The rattling of John Evans' and GB's teacups is heard loud and clear on the Banbury Road – what on earth were they taking on?

But they had no need to fear. Phillippi, as he soon became known, was a model Summerfieldian who went on to be very grand at Harrow. We were good friends throughout – we studied together and played together in all the teams, including the rugby team which beat the Dragon for the first time ever.

RICHARD GUINNESS (1947–52)

I was one of the shy ones. My parents had first brought me through the portal to the Headmaster's study, Ticky [John Evans] had rubbed his hands and smiled his reassurances, and I had seen my mother glance back uncertainly before I watched the empty space where she had been. Next, I was ushered away by matron. From then all encouragement failed. I sat alone on the shoe lockers and I sobbed. I remained dewy-eyed until Saturday night, when the extraordinary unfolded in New Room...

RICHARD WHITE (1946–51)

I went to school with a quarter of a pound of sweets to last 13 weeks and remember standing in line every Sunday to receive just one sweet from that packet.

Not surprisingly, never having been away from home before, or even subject to the daily visit to school, I was very homesick. Of course, I was not allowed the toy monkey which I had always taken to bed with me and which in my imagination had accompanied me on many an adventure. But I must have coped.

I remember on the first night Matron came into the long dormitory, with probably 10 beds down each side, and told us where we would have to go for our early-morning cold bath. Whatever the weather, we were never excused the cold bath throughout my time at Summer Fields.

SAM LEGERTON (1945–50)

I lived in North Wales during the Second World War. I used to play on the neighbouring farms and the farmers' children used to speak both Welsh and English. One day, I asked Nannie what the F word meant, what did the B word mean and several other words. I was told not to worry as these words were only Welsh.

I then went to Summer Fields in May 1944 when Mrs Terry-Bevan was Matron. She was Welsh and asked me that as I lived in Wales did I speak any Welsh. Quite innocently I let fly a great list of four-letter words. Matron was somewhat surprised and quickly said that that would be quite enough Welsh, thank you!

PETER MAITLAND (1944–8)

Going away to school at the age of eight was the first really major event of one's life. In 1939 the shock was accelerated by the start of the term being brought forward ten days, because of the war. It was all a bit of a blur. But I recall that one major worry was tying one's tie and doing up one's shoes quickly and accurately, indicative perhaps of too sheltered a life. But learning is based on confidence and one has to start somewhere.

DENYS MOYLAN (1939–45)

I found my way to the Vinery, as the conveniences at Summer Fields were known. Rather to my surprise, they were in a kind of garden. To my consternation they had no doors. There was no privacy to be found in these privies. My morale sank to my boots. I wandered disconsolately back towards my form room, the tears coursing slowly down my cheeks.

JULIAN AMERY (1928–32)

My Dear Mamma,

I cannot tell you how much I like this place. Indeed, it cannot be called a school; it is more like a home. All the boys, and especially the Macmillans, are very kind to me, and as for Mrs Mac-Laren [*sic*], I never saw so nice a lady. We spend nearly all our playtime in the garden.

I was delighted with my little bedroom; there are seven pictures in it besides other ornaments. When I got up at 7.30, we all went down to the bath room and had a nice cold bath. For breakfast we had eggs and toast and coffee or tea. For dinner, we had two enormous helpings of dough pudding and roast beef. Then, as the rain had given over, we went in the garden and amused ourselves till afternoon school. The girls' guinea pigs, rabbits, cocks and hens are all very nice. Indeed, there is only one animal I behold with aversion and it is a vicious-looking beast of a donkey, which seems fond of squeezing itself through the railings, and browsing on the apricot trees.

EDWARD MIERS (1866–8)

part one
History

chapter one

1864–1975
Foundation, Growth, Maturity

Paul Dean

In 1864, Summertown – now a busy suburb north of Oxford city centre – was little more than a collection of small houses and cottages, interspersed with a scattering of villas. It was in one of these that Archibald Maclaren, a noted Oxford gymnastics instructor, and his wife Gertrude (destined to be known simply as 'Mrs'), whose father was the printer to the University Press and who had a mastery of classical languages, agreed to take the two sons of their friend Shirley Brooks (editor of *Punch*) to board and be educated. By 1865 nine more had joined them – including two boys with the name of Macmillan – and so began what was

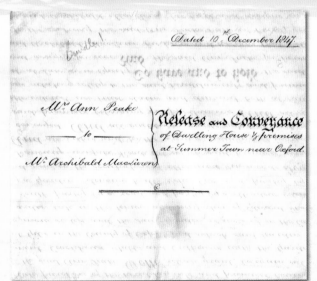

Previous pages: The Hay Feast, 2013

Left: The exchange of property between Mrs Ann Peake and Archibald Maclaren, 1847

Right: The villa now, with New Room to the right, photographed in 2013

called, until 1891, 'Summerfield'. Before long, a steady stream of boys was deposited by hansom cab at the terminus of the Dew Drop Inn, just next door (a coincidence for which generations of teachers have been duly thankful). Later, a designated carriage, nicknamed the Squish on account of the cramped seating conditions, took boys on the train to and from Oxford and London at the beginnings and ends of terms. Later still, most Summerfieldians arrive and depart by car.

In keeping with the educational philosophy of the day, the curriculum taught by 'Mrs' was largely Latin and Greek, with some Mathematics, French, Music, and Drawing taught by assistants. Non-classical subjects were not highly esteemed. When G. W. ('Bam') Evans joined the staff in 1884, 'Mrs' asked him what his responsibilities were. He replied, 'To teach the boys French.' 'You won't!' was her brief and, as he later admitted,

accurate retort. (The fixation on Classics prevailed for many years. In the 1920s, they occupied twenty-three of thirty-eight one-hour lessons per week, with eight allotted to Mathematics, and the remaining seven to everything else.)

Mrs Maclaren, Summerfield, Oxford, is the scholar and maker of scholars. My Geordie went to her knowing nothing. He got, last August, an Eton Scholarship. This was obtained, not by cram, but by sound education.

Alexander Macmillan (1869), on his son George

'Mrs' was an excellent teacher, and numbers rose rapidly; the earliest school photograph, taken in 1876, shows fifty-eight pupils. In 1866 the first scholarship was won, by Maurice

Mrs Maclaren ('Mrs') (1833–96), SF 1864–96

Gertrude Isabel Frances Maclaren was the daughter of David Talboys, a bookseller in Bedford, who later moved to Oxford, branched out into publishing and translation, started the Oxford Classical Texts and became printer to the University. Talboys had a working knowledge of several languages, including Latin and Greek. Gertrude's mother was a certain Mary Wheeler, whom Talboys had married as his third wife. Gertrude (later universally known as 'Mrs') was brought up in a busy household as one of nine children. She had two older sisters, each named

Charlotte (the elder dying in infancy) and three older brothers, Arthur, William and Henry. Her younger siblings comprised one sister (Marianne) and two further brothers (Edmund and James).

Gertrude was a bright and lively girl with a receptive mind, and she lived in a home where books and scholarship were highly valued. An image of her acquiring classical knowledge on her father's knee is perhaps more fanciful than realistic (she was only seven when he died in 1840). More likely her erudition stemmed from her mother or elder brothers and sisters.

On 27 August 1851, aged just eighteen, Gertrude married Archibald Maclaren, who founded the Oxford gymnasium which laid down the basic principles on which army physical training should be run. Archie had previously married Charlotte, Gertrude's older sister, in 1844, but she had died less than three years later. Thus Gertrude's marriage caused quite a stir at the time, technically illegal as it was according to *A Table of Kindred and Affinity* in the 1662 Book of Common Prayer.

Nonetheless, the union proved fruitful and 'Mrs' produced five children, Gertrude, Mabel, Alexander, Margaret and John Wallace. Mabel and Margaret were to marry future Headmasters of

Summer Fields, Dr Williams and 'Bear' Alington respectively.

Described as 'gifted' by Lady Burne-Jones, 'Mrs' was also brave, energetic, progressive and radical, traits doubtless inherited from her father. According to Dr Williams, she was 'a rare person of the mid-Victorian days' with a hitherto unexercised gift for teaching. 'Mrs' was also a person ahead of her times. Dr Williams thought that, had she been born twenty or thirty years later, she would have made a name for herself in the history of the women's movement.

In 1863, 'Mrs' began to teach Greek to Mabel (aged nine!), and this may have sparked the idea of offering her instruction to a wider world. At the same time, when Shirley Brooks, editor of *Punch*, appeared for a consultation with Archie Maclaren about the possibility of his two delicate sons, then aged about seven and nine, training at the Oxford gymnasium, 'Mrs', feeling that her talents and energy were running to waste, jumped at his proposal that the Maclarens take entire charge of the education of the two boys. Archie's initial objections were overcome, arrangements were duly made and Reginald and Cecil Brooks later began their studies under Mrs Maclaren's guidance. The school was born!

The first school photograph, 1876

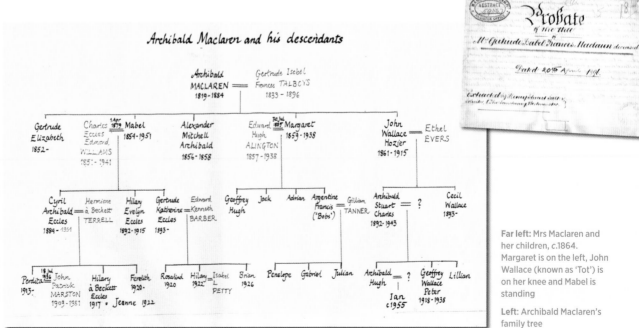

Archibald Maclaren and his descendants

Archibald MACLAREN 1819–1884 ══ Gertrude Isobel Frances TALBOYS 1833–1896

- Gertrude Elizabeth 1852–
- Charles Eccles Edward WILLIAMS 1851–1941 ══ 1 Apr 1879 Mabel 1854–1951
- Alexander Mitchell Archibald 1856–1858
- Edward Hugh ══ 30 Jul 1885 Margaret ALINGTON 1857–1938 1859–1938
- John Wallace Hozier 1861–1915 ══ Ethel EVERS

Third generation:
- Cyril Archibald Eccles 1884–1951 ══ Hermione à Beckett TERRELL
- Hilary Evelyn Eccles 1892–1915
- Gertrude Katherine Eccles 1893– ══ Edward Kenneth BARBER
- Geoffrey Hugh
- Jack
- Adrian
- Argentine Francis ('Bobs') ══ Gillian TANNER
- Archibald Stuart Charles 1892–1943 ══ ?
- Cecil Wallace 1893–

Fourth generation:
- Perdita 1913– ══ 18 Jul 1936 John Patrick MARSTON 1909–1981
- Hilary à Beckett Eccles 1917 ══ Jeanne 1922
- Ferelith 1920–
- Rosalind 1920
- Hilary 1922 ══ Isabel L PETTY
- Brian 1926
- Penelope
- Gabriel
- Julian
- Archibald Hugh ══ ? │ Ian c1955
- Geoffrey Wallace Peter 1918–1938
- Lillian

Far left: Mrs Maclaren and her children, *c.*1864. Margaret is on the left, John Wallace (known as 'Tot') is on her knee and Mabel is standing

Left: Archibald Maclaren's family tree

SUMMER FIELDS REGISTER

1960

1864

1 BROOKS, CECIL. One of the original two boys at Summer Fields. Went to Australia. *Brother of 2.*

2 BROOKS, REGINALD. Worked with his father for "Punch" and was called to the Table in 1881-1884. One of the two original boys at Summer Fields. Son of Shirley Brooks. *Brother of 1. Died 1885.*

3 HOETS, ALTON KINGSLEY. *b.* 1856. XI. Haileybury 1871. M.R.C.S. 1880. Practised as doctor in N.S.Wales. *m.* Ellen, *d.* of W. Grace, of Mogador, Morocco. *Brother of 7.* Died at Sydney 1908.

4 HUGHES, ROBERT HENRY WENTWORTH. *b.* . Wellington (Sch.) 1872-5, Prefect. Died 1876.

5 MACMILLAN, GEORGE AUGUSTIN. F.R.C.M., Hon. D.Litt. (Oxon). *b.* 1855. XI. Eton (K.S.) 1868. Hon. Fellow of Lincoln College, Oxford. Hon. Sec. British School at Athens. Hon. Sec. R.C.M. Director of Macmillan & Co. J.P. for County of London and N. Riding. Hon. Sec. and Treas. Hellenic Society. One of the original boys at the School. *Brother of 338.* Died 20 April, 1940.

†††6 MACMILLAN, MAURICE CRAWFORD. *b.* 1853. Uppingham ~~(Sch.)~~ ... ge, Cambridge 1871. Master ... Macmillan & Co. *m.* 1884 ... of Spencer, Indiana. *Brother* ... 892 *gt-grandfather of 2458.*

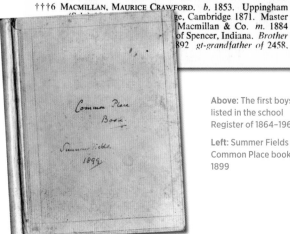

Above: The first boys listed in the school Register of 1864–1960

Left: Summer Fields Common Place book, 1899

Macmillan, to Uppingham; his father spoke warmly of the thorough grounding, yet with no element of cramming, he had received. In 1868 his brother George was the first of many SF boys to win a King's Scholarship at Eton. 'Mrs' was a motherly figure outside the classroom, kissing new boys ('my poppets') goodnight on the first night away from home. There was a family atmosphere, with the Maclarens' daughters, Mabel and Margaret, and some other girls, taught alongside the boys. Picnics, expeditions to Bagley Wood and fishing in the Cherwell were leisure occupations; games were informal until the school was large enough to organise teams. Discipline inevitably became increasingly strict as acquaintance with the character of the small boy grew. The Black Book for major punishable offences (still in use) originated after an angelically blond child had his hair covered in tar. The staff had to expand too: local clergymen, friends and relatives were roped in. Then, in 1874 and 1879, two full-time posts were filled by the Rev. Dr Charles Williams and the Rev. Hugh Alington, who later married Mabel and Margaret respectively, became Headmasters of the school themselves (Dr Williams 1896–1918 and Mr Alington 1918–1928), and have come down to posterity as Doctor and Bear.

Doctor and Bear

On the last night of term, we usually tried to raid the Doctor's study and capture a cane as a trophy. This was quite an operation of war. It needed a preliminary recce party to find out whether the Doctor was in or not. If he was out, you tried to make a silent attack in the dark without being heard from the sitting room.

Major Gen Harold Freedman-Attwood, DSO, OBE, MC (1910–12)

The atmosphere of the school changed after 'Mrs' retired. Doctor and Bear were austere personalities, inspiring more awe, and even fear, than affection. The precision of Doctor's classical training was legendary. His *Borva Notes* became the grammatical *vade mecum* for generations of boys, even being taken down to the air-raid shelter during alerts in the Second World War. He used to take the scholarship candidates (in straw hats with the school ribbon in the colours of Brasenose, his old college) up to Eton every year, staying at the White Hart, Windsor, and doing some last-minute revision round the breakfast table – at which fish was always served, Doctor believing it to be good for the brain. Sir Olaf Carōe (1903–6) recalled 'his clean features and ruddy cheek glowing with health, his silver hair, his more-than-silver voice' – a voice which, however, 'was silver with a sharp edge to it'. A mother once joked that she felt her son was not being beaten enough. Alas, Doctor failed to realise that this was a joke, with gloomy consequences for the child. On the evidence of his own daughter Kitty, he could be extremely obstinate. When the

Summerfieldian King's Scholars at Eton, 1909

The Black Book

The abolition of corporal punishment has rendered the Black Book the most serious penalty (short of being sent home for a period of time) imposed by the school today. During the 1920s, 'fetching the Black Book' was a process designed to inflict as much fear and humiliation as possible on the culprit. First, the march to Fifth Form Room; then the knock on the door (ignored), then a louder knock, then admission to face a harangue by 'Bear' Alington for distracting Fifth Form from its work. This sequence of events was repeated when returning the Book. But all this constituted a mere prelude to facing 'Bear' at four o'clock on the following Saturday afternoon, when the accused were assembled and offered a brief opportunity to plead their case. Sentence was duly dispensed according to the severity of the offence: learning some verses, a stinging cut with the cane on each hand, or, for the gravest crimes, a silent, two-hour wait before a visit to the Headmaster's study, there to receive 'whatever was coming to him on the seat of his trousers'.

Today, there is still an element of ritual involved in getting a Black Book. Firstly, the boy is sent to the Headmaster's study to collect it. This is a dreaded walk. However, it can serve as a 'cooling-off' period for both teacher and culprit. Often boys return, much relieved, to the study without their name being added. But if a Black Book is given, the boy takes it back to that same study in the knowledge that he will be there again soon to face a headmagisterial inquisition before sentence is pronounced – nowadays usually a lengthy detention and copying at a later date.

There are numerous stories concerning the Black Book. These often involved theft, as a tradition grew up of trying to steal it at the end of each term. During the First World War, an attempt by two boys (both, later, admirals) to take the Black Book during end-of-term prize-giving, was foiled by Matron, who caught them hiding in the cloakrooms. Alan Sykes (1969–73) even remembers stealing it and taking it home for Long Leave: 'My father insisted (wisely) that I took it back to school and return it.' During the 1920s a paraffin stove set fire to the Schoolroom floor close to where the Black Book was kept. However, universal joy was soon extinguished by GB, the Headmaster, who marched in and instead of attacking the fire, removed the Black Book to a safer place.

Fewer Black Books are given these days – usually for damage, broken windows or lights, lying and occasional 'accidental borrowing'. Are teachers becoming softer or boys better behaved? An analysis of the 'crime figures' between July 1946 and the end of the Lent Term 1955 reveals an average of 21.2 entries per term. The following selection gives the flavour of some of the offences: 'Deliberately walking into a snowdrift in his ordinary clothes', 'Describing a cricket ball as "bloody"', 'Plays with milk in prep, after warnings', 'Misbehaviour with a razor blade', 'Reading an American comic in form', 'Wearing another boy's shorts', 'Putting salt in the teapot', 'Illegally possessing matches and using same in the Vinery', 'Conspiring and fighting in the Vinery', 'Swinish behaviour', 'Behaving like a guttersnipe', 'Fooling about with the organ in chapel', 'Deliberate defiance and disobedience', 'Rebellion against prefects', 'Very serious disgrace' (what must this refer to?)... And so the list goes on.

chapel was built in 1896 in memory of 'Mrs', he insisted on designing it himself, only to realise after its completion that he had forgotten to include either a choir vestry or any provision for an organ. For staff, there were no formal contracts of employment, and when he thought a master had been at the school long enough, he often gave him the money to leave and buy a partnership elsewhere. Some, of course, never left at all. Among celebrated long reigns were those of J. F. Crofts (1883–1920), G. W. Evans (1884–1924), F. P. Penny (1893–1927) and C. E. Smyth (1897–1924).

> *The old Doctor was always very kind to me. I think we were all very fond of the old Doctor, although we may have been a bit frightened of him.*
>
> Admiral Sir Edward Parry, KCB (1902–6)

Above: Masters, 1889, with Doctor centre, Bear to his right

Lord Caccia, Harold Anthony Caccia, GCMG, KCVO (1905–90), SF 1916–19

Harold Caccia was born on 21 December 1905 in Pachmarhi, India. On leaving Summer Fields in 1919 he went to Eton and Trinity College, Oxford, where he gained a rugby Blue. He then pursued a distinguished career in the Foreign Office. In 1929 he was sent to Peking (Beijing). Returning for a short spell in London, in 1939, he was transferred to Athens. Driven out in 1941, he arrived in Cairo after a perilous journey via Crete. There, from 1943 he served in Algiers on the staff of another OS, the resident minister in North Africa, Harold Macmillan (1903–6).

In 1944 Caccia became the political adviser to the general officer commanding British land forces in Greece, before his appointment in the following year as minister at the Athens Embassy. Caccia went to Austria as ambassador from 1951 to 1954, before promotion to British Ambassador in Washington in 1956. He left the United States to take up the post of Head of the Diplomatic Service in 1962 until his retirement in 1965.

He was an energetic, efficient and popular man, traits which were said to have been honed at Summer Fields. Excelling in the classroom, Caccia also made his mark on the sports field. Playing inside left for the 1916 football XI, Caccia was

Harold Caccia in 1926 at SF

noted as a promising forward who always enjoyed a vigorous game. In the following season he scored seven goals, helping Summer Fields to victory in four of the six fixtures. Captaining the side in 1918, in a season interrupted by 'the great

flu', Caccia's approach to the game was described as 'the keenest of the keen'.

But such enthusiasm was detrimental to his performance with the bat. In the 1st XI of 1919, he averaged only 7.83 runs in seven innings, with a top score of 28. A report describes how 'he has not succeeded with the bat, being too eager to score'. Interestingly, he had previously made a century in a 2nd XI game against the Dragon. However, Caccia was rated as a very fine fielder, winning the George Barne Fielding Cup and 'well worthy of the company among whom his name will be engraved'.

Certainly no goody-goody, Harold Caccia was famous for his ability to belch on request. He also records how he was once in the Black Book for a record number of six times in one week. He managed to get out of it, as by a fluke he was given an afternoon's holiday out on Black Book Day. He counted this as his 'happiest memory of Summer Fields'.

Caccia's son and grandson attended Summer Fields. He was also delighted to keep up his contact with the school, albeit indirectly, when he held the office of Provost of Eton between 1965 and 1977.

Reflections of an old Pedagogue upon Preparatory Schools.

(Especially Summerfields)

1. Health.

This is the first matter to be considered, for without fairly good health the success of a Prep^y. School becomes impossible. Not only the worry & anxiety, the correspondence & the constant visits of Parents, make the lives of those in authority difficult & wearing, but the work of Forms, persistently being broken up & hindered by boys now going as invalids, now returning as convalescents, absolutely camust shows steady & definite progress. It is therefore of the utmost importance that the assistant Masters, as well as the Heads of the School, should keep (if only for their own sakes) a careful eye upon their classes' condition & should see that they do not sit in draughts in School time & that they obey orders, given daily, as to jerseys, greatcoats, & boots in cold or wet weather out of School. The fact of the School at Oxford being so large & situated in the Thames Valley is in the eyes of many Parents quite a sufficient handicap without this. —

Possibly the regular recurrence of Influenza and the want of fibre in "War boys" may be responsible for the cases, so frequent lately, of pneumonia & ear trouble: Certainly up to 1908 they were both almost unknown in the School, except when English Measles was complicated by whooping cough, as in 1900 — and Influenza was not unknown even

Leonard Strong,
1922

Cyril Williams

The new Headmaster, Doctor's son Cyril, had joined the staff in 1914 and was at the helm from 1928 to 1939. He was not as colourful as his predecessors, perhaps intentionally: one of his colleagues pithily said that Cyril was an example of 'working with the staff, not the staff working for the Head'.

Bear became as fabled as Geoffrey Bolton (GB) was to be later. His nickname is self-explanatory (but meant that his wife had to endure being 'Mrs Bear' and his son 'Little Bear'). Shakespeare's famous stage direction 'Exit, pursued by a bear' must often have been in the boys' thoughts. We hear of his explosions of temper, his harsh punishments, and his lack of sympathy with those who found learning difficult or daunting. These traits were suspected by many to compensate for shyness, a point made by Leonard Strong in his brilliant obituary notice of Bear for the *Magazine* in 1939, arguing that he was the prisoner of his Victorian moral code. 'He loathed fault-finding, and it was his constant duty to find fault.'

His explanation of the facts of life to the leavers, on their last Sunday – known as 'Blub Sunday' because some manly tears were condoned – was said to be a masterpiece of obfuscation, concluding with a prayer and with the injunction always to put one's coat back on after playing games, because: 'We had a boy here who, when he grew up, didn't, and died.' His son A. F. ('Bobs') Alington (staff 1922–37; governor from 1965), writing in Usborne's anthology, acknowledges his 'conviction that the best way to teach boys was through fear' and admits, 'I was afraid of him, too, when I was small,' but he also points to aspects of his father which the boys never saw – the simple, childlike religion, with a real horror of sin:

> In his old age he used to go to a special Communion service for the aged, which he would repeat aloud very slowly during the whole service at the same time as the priest (who always waited for him to catch up). During the Confession his voice was blurred with sobs... He was a humble, upright, downright, lovable old man, and I was devoted to him.

When Bear was ordered to retire by his doctors, his reaction was, 'Thank God that I need never beat a boy again.' It was a pity, Strong thought, that by the time he became Headmaster he was too old to enjoy the job, as happened later with Geoffrey Bolton.

He invited Bobs Alington to become a partner (not until 1955, when the first governing body was established, did SF cease to be privately owned). In 1930 Doctor and Bear relinquished their partnerships and were replaced by John Evans, GB and Roger Jacques. There was a hidden agenda here: John and GB had told Bobs that they intended to leave to seek promotion, and since Cyril and Bobs disagreed violently over the importance of Classics, Bobs felt he must secure some independent support. The partnerships were a means of inducing John and GB to stay. This was not managed without difficulty, much of it emanating from Doctor who, like King Lear, assumed that he would continue to reign even though he had abdicated.

In 1926 bad blood had been created by Bear's wife, who attempted, unsuccessfully and without his knowledge, to turf out the existing staff from Cottage, including John Evans, in favour of the newly married Bobs and his wife. Just at the time when Cyril took over, Evans was scheduled to go into hospital for a routine operation: it was plain that Bobs hoped he would not return. Bobs seized the chance to force an immediate,

Cyril
Williams,
Headmaster
1928–39

The Leagues

The four Summer Fields Leagues, modelled on the public-school House system, were first introduced in 1926 to provide some *esprit de corps* among the boys which, it was felt, had been previously lacking. The idea was the brainchild of 'Bobs' Alington. There was little difficulty in finding names. *Maclaren* (green) commemorates the school's foundress, Gertrude Maclaren. *Case* (red) was named after William Sterndale Case, a distinguished and much-loved Summer Fields music master, who trained for his profession both in England and Germany.

Congreve (yellow) and *Moseley* (blue) were OSS who gave their lives in the First World War. Billy Congreve won a VC. Henry Moseley was a physicist of more than ordinary promise, who, in his short life (1887–1915), revolutionised the natural sciences through his work on X-rays, leading to the formulation of Moseley's Law.

The whole school was divided into the four Leagues and remains so today. When numbers increased in the 1950s, GB suggested a fifth League, possibly to be called Wavell. But the boys hated this idea, their chief objection being that some of them would have to give up their current League and move to the new one.

Originally marks were given for every conceivable school activity, including work, sport, PE and all the Arts, or deducted for poor work or 'unbecoming behaviour'. These days, League rivalry continues through the award of Reds (good) or Blues (bad), with League Cups attainable for Work, Games, Music, Organisation and Conduct. The winners of the overall League Cup get their Feast with games in New Room (outdoors in the Summer Term), followed by a special supper. Recently, the idea of a 'League Treat' has been introduced whereby a special outing (such as ten-pin bowling) replaces the New Room games.

The names of the winning Leagues, together with their leaders or prefects, were first inscribed on raised wooden panels around New Room. When space ran out, the list was continued around the dining room.

Junior boys in their league colours at Christ Church, Oxford

SUMMER FIELDS, OXFORD.

EASTER 1930.

Our respective fathers, the Rev. Dr. Williams and the Rev. E. H. Alington, are now definitely retiring from active participation in the management of the School.

It will therefore interest our parents and friends to learn that three of the present masters are joining us as partners in their stead. These are Mr. J. F. Evans (M.A., Keble College, Oxford), who has been with us for fifteen years; Mr. G. Bolton (M.A., University College, Oxford), for ten years; and Mr. R. A. K. Jacques (M.A., Brasenose College, Oxford), who was a boy at Summer Fields himself. With such experienced men to support us permanently in the supervision and conduct of affairs, we may look forward with confidence to the continued efficiency and well-being of the School.

CYRIL WILLIAMS.
A. F. ALINGTON.

Above: Notification of the retirement of Dr Williams and 'Bear' Alington, 1930

Right: 'Bobs' Alington, Leonard Strong and Roger Jacques, 1924

drastic reduction in the timetable allowance for Latin and Greek. Even that was not enough, and he eventually resigned as a partner in 1937 over the issue. He was unmourned by Doctor, who wrote balefully from St Leonards of his 'modernside ideas and hatred of Classics'. Bobs deserved better. He had greatly improved the French teaching and his drama productions were justly admired. In 1926, he also invented the League system, which has proved his most lasting memorial.

Peter (Solomon) Benenson (1921–2005), SF 1930–5

Peter Solomon, better known as Peter Benenson, who, after Eton, Oxford, intelligence work during the Second World War and a career as a barrister, founded Amnesty International in 1961, arrived at Summer Fields in 1930. In later life, he adopted his mother's maiden name, Benenson, and in the SF Register he is listed as Peter Solomon-Benenson.

At Summer Fields, Solomon was a bright boy who won the 10th Eton King's Scholarship. He appears regularly in the SUG lists and excelled in Maths and History. He took prizes in the Townsend-Warner History Competition in 1934 and 1935 and his interest in History continued throughout his time at Eton. He entered Balliol as the Rosebury History Scholar. Solomon also handled authority well, as a League Leader for Moseley and a school prefect during his final two terms.

Keenly interested in drama, he took the lead part in *Julius Caesar* in Michaelmas Term 1933. His portrayal of the doomed emperor was deemed 'most effective' with his lines 'well spoken'. In the following year, he appeared as Pistol in the school's production of *Henry V*.

Solomon also enjoyed sports, passing his swimming test in the summer of 1933. There is no mention of any great achievement in cricket or

KING HENRY V.

By WILLIAM SHAKESPEARE.

CHARACTERS
(in order of appearance).

Archbishop of Canterbury	D. L. L. STEWART.
Bishop of Ely	H. C. THOROLD.
King Henry V	D. P. MACNEE.
Duke of Exeter	G. S. W. TALBOT.
Earl of Westmoreland	H. J. SHAW.
Duke of Gloucester	E. DE L. CAZENOVE.
French Ambassador	J. P. FANE.
Montjoy, *a French Herald*	R. M. SINCLAIR.
Bardolph	W. R. M. CRESSY-MARCKS
Nym	F. B. HARTSHORNE.
Pistol	P. J. H. SOLOMON.
Mistress Quickly	P. A. N. LAING.
Boy	R. A. RENDEL.
Lord Scroop	P. H. SHAW STEWART.
Earl of Cambridge	C. T. CUNNINGHAM.
Sir Thomas Grey	R. THICKNESSE.
Fluellen	T. R. MILES.
Governor of Harfleur	H. C. THOROLD.
Katherine, *daughter of the French King*	B. I. STRATON-FERRIER.
Alice, *her lady-in-waiting*	A. BROTHERTON-RATCLIFFE
Gower	R. THICKNESSE.
The Constable of France	D. L. L. STEWART.
Duke of Orleans	F. B. HARTSHORNE.
Lewis, *the Dauphin*	C. F. C. LEE.
	J. LYTTELTON.

football, but elsewhere it is a different story. As a boxer 'of the dashing type', he fought in the annual competition, winning the Boxing Cup in 1935. He also played golf in the Open Competition and, as an athlete, won awards for the high jump.

But rugby was his game. Solomon played as a forward in the XVs of 1934 and 1935. At first, he was seen as 'clumsy but energetic, who could be useful when his knowledge of the game improves'. Improve it did: 1935 saw the award of a Distinction Cap to a player now regarded as 'a most dangerous man within ten yards of the line', who scored what was described as the best try of the season in a side that won seven of its eight prep school matches.

Some of this early energy and drive may have underpinned his concern for the needs of others, particularly 'forgotten' prisoners of conscience; a concern leading to the formation of Amnesty International, now one of the world's largest and most influential non-governmental organisations.

Compassion

In spite of a tough regime, with the punishments not always fitting the crime, kindness, gentleness and sympathy were always on hand if a boy faced a genuine crisis, from homesickness to more serious matters:

> Mrs Williams (Hermione) made up for her husband's temper by being a kind Headmaster's wife who called us all by our Christian names. She invited all the new boys in my first year to her birthday party. I noted in a letter home in July 1939, 'It was a lovely tea of birthday cake, marangs [*sic*] and chocolate biscuits'.
>
> Peter Fullerton (1938–43)

> I remember being given one day off when my father died when I was nine. Matron, a large lady whose name I forget, tucked me up with a blanket on a chair in her room with *The Jungle Book* to read. She told me I had to behave like a soldier.
>
> Alastair Macdonald (1951–5)

Compassion was not unknown among the boys, too. Boys were often loyal to one another in the abortive schemes to run away, out of sympathy for the unhappy boy seeking escape. Summerfieldians also showed great personal kindness to their peers when disaster struck in wartime. Similar behaviour was also common when the daily round brought tragedy:

> There was a terrible national epidemic of polio while I was at Summer Fields. My memory of this has stuck in my mind ever since. In New Room there were several large six-place desks and we were each allocated one. I sat next to Charles Caröe (1945–8), who had become a friend. One day he was called to the Headmaster's study. He returned not long afterwards and quietly disclosed to me that he had been told that his mother had died of polio. I gave him some of my marbles and we just carried on.
>
> Sam Legerton (1945–50)

A letter from Hermione Williams to Julian Amery's mother, 1928

At the start of the 1930s a worrying trend appeared: numbers began to decline as the disunity of the partners – their inability to agree about the direction of the school – began to have repercussions. In 1934 there were fewer than one hundred boys, a situation unknown since the early days. Cyril himself was a divided character, wavering between the belief in authoritarian rule he had inherited from Doctor, and the kindlier temperament of his mother. He took refuge in a bluff manner which could lack tact and be interpreted as impatience. Hugh Stubbs (1926–30) wrote of his misjudgement of people and situations, his alternations between draconian punishments and culinary treats. It was difficult for boys and staff to know where they stood.

One person, however, could be relied on to smooth any ruffled feathers, his wife Hermione (who always called him by one of his middle names, Eccles, rather than Cyril). A mother-figure, in the tradition of 'Mrs', for the boys, and invariably charming to parents, she handled all the correspondence about personal matters, but kept her distance from the academic side of the school, so that the boys never associated her with work or discipline. There is a well-known story of a little boy who was so highly strung that he watched the fireworks display from a distance, holding her hand. That boy was Christopher Lee (1931–5), later to feature as Dracula in Hammer Horror films. Yet for every famous Old Summerfieldian there will be hundreds, unknown to the world, who remember Hermione's kindness as the most important thing about their time there.

Cyril's reign saw several innovations. The Eucharist was offered as an alternative to Mattins on some Sundays, a custom which survives. More subject specialisation by the teachers was introduced. Drama became more ambitious, with Shakespeare prominent. However, the buildings and accommodation remained sparse. Cecil Day-Lewis, on the staff in the academic year 1927–8 and a frequent visitor in later life as Poet Laureate, recalled rooms doubling up for classes, freezing winter weather and a gamut of smells, 'ink smells, chalk-duster smells, smells of mud and mown grass, and the mousey smell of little boys'. One notable improvement was the complete refurbishment of the boys' lavatories (known as the Vinery or Vins from their place of origin). They had long been regarded with aversion – and were memorably described by Thomas Shaughnessy (1925–8) as 'a slanted continuous sewer in constant flow'. Even after renovation, no doors were provided.

Summer Fields, St Leonards ('Summers *mi.*'), 1903–66

In 1903 the possibility of a seaside branch of Summer Fields, to cater for boys of delicate health who might suffer from the notoriously damp Oxford climate, became a reality with the purchase of Bohemia House in St Leonards-on-Sea, East Sussex. It lay within half a mile of the sea and was capable of accommodating between forty and fifty pupils. The house was surrounded by fine grounds and much woodland, forming a paradise for young boys. Doctor, who had bought the property, retained overall control of 'Little Sum' or 'Summers *mi.*', as it came affectionately to be known – and commandeered it every year for his summer holiday – although it had its own Headmasters, the first being E. D. Compton who was already on the Oxford staff. He was accompanied by eleven boys, seven from the Oxford site, and by Wallace Maclaren, son of Archibald and Mrs, who had been the first OS member of staff. Relations between the two schools were sometimes uneasy, and attempts by Ken and Kitty Barber (Doctor's daughter) to buy out Doctor's interest in the undertaking in order to pass on the school to their son, Hilary, led to friction as Cyril and Hermione Williams, now firmly established in Oxford, rather hoped that their son, also named Hilary, would become at least a partner at St Leonards.

St Leonards boys tended to be more aristocratic than academic, and for some years if a Sussex boy showed any sort of scholarly promise he was transferred to Summer Fields, Oxford for his final grooming. Potential Summers *mi.* scholars occasionally found that their health had mysteriously improved and were recalled to Oxford, while September 1940 brought the entire southern contingent there – the Barbers and thirty-four boys – as evacuees to Oxford seeking sanctuary from German bombs. Ken Barber found John Evans uncongenial, not least

Above: 'Summers *mi.*', 1907 and 1966

Left: A classroom, 1932

when he suggested that, if the St Leonards school reopened when peace came, it should be called something else. However, it retained the name and relations between the two schools improved considerably.

The end, though, came quickly in 1966 when Bohemia House was subjected to a compulsory purchase order for the construction of a civic centre. Some of its pupils then moved to Oxford, as did their Headmaster, R. A. L. (Ran) Ogston, who taught Latin and became Librarian, remaining until 1979. In these days when prominent public schools have outposts in the Middle and Far East, the place of 'Summers *mi.*' in the school's history should not be underestimated on account of its distant location. Several hundred boys were educated there, including three who were to play significant roles in the political life of their countries: Prince Rainier of Monaco, who was a pupil in the mid-1930s, Crown Prince Hassan of Jordan in the mid-1950s, and Crown Prince (later King) Jigme Singye Wangchuck of Bhutan, who arrived only in 1965.

Above: St Leonards staff, 1953

Above right: The Hay Feast tradition continued at St Leonards

Right: Prince Rainier of Monaco, left in picture, in the 1930s

Below: Bohemia House, St Leonards-on-Sea

I went to Summers mi. *first, and my first 'school' memory is of rushing over the railway arches in south London on a dark September afternoon, watching the sparks from the overhead electric wires. At Hastings, we were picked up by taxi and taken up to a house at the end of a drive, lined with enormous cars, each with a chauffeur and footman. This was Summer Fields St Leonards, the House of Lords as we called it when we got to Summers* ma. *The peacocks on the lawn chirped loudly and the atmosphere of Summers* mi. *was only semi-scholastic.*

Selwyn Cobb (1926–30)

GB and JFE, an Improbable Partnership

Geoffrey Bolton arrived at SF in 1919, aged twenty-six, in time to experience the regime of Bear, and stayed for forty-one years. When one reads his recollections of the pranks that he and other young masters used to play on older, more staid colleagues, especially F. P. Penny (1893–1927), one struggles to picture the lugubrious, wraith-like figure of later photographs indulging in such horseplay. (Penny deserves immortality if only for his habit of walking down the corridors with a clenched fist outstretched in front of him, for boys running round corners to bump into. Late in life he amazed everyone by getting married.)

GB's was a complex character. The son of a London solicitor whose Westminster chambers still thrive, he had gone from Repton to Oxford in 1912, but his studies were permanently derailed by the outbreak of war. He served in the Royal Sussex Regiment and was hospitalised to England ten days before the Somme, with an illness which some later said was due to gas and others to shell-shock. His brother Billy was killed in the Dardanelles and, as Nick Aldridge says in his biography, 'Almost certainly something in GB died in the war that killed so many of his friends.' His inflexibility, his

moroseness and his furious temper, so reminiscent of Bear (whom he adored), suggest psychological scars. He returned to the front in 1917 and to Oxford for a final, hedonistic term in 1919. His chance meeting with Geoffrey Alington led to his appointment at SF, where John Evans, later Headmaster, had also recently joined the staff.

Above: The masters, 1921. Three Headmasters appear here. 'Bear' Alington, seated, dominates the centre. On the ground immediately in front of him sits John Evans. GB stands in the centre of the back row.

Below: GB at the Hay Feast, 1960

GB was a bit of an enigma to us. He was a kind Housemaster in Cottage. His shout of Surgite! at 7am got us out of bed fast and straight into a cold bath. He went to great trouble to look after our needs for toys and stationery in the 'Bazaar'. He was keen on every kind of sport and always on the touchline for matches. He also ran the library and encouraged us to read widely. But he was fiercely demanding as the Fifth Form Master. He was a fine Classics teacher and maintained a steady output of scholars every year. I owe my scholarship to Radley entirely to him.

Peter Fullerton (1938–43)

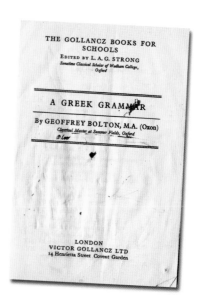

It was always said, and it was for many years true, that life at the school was based upon the three Cs: Classics, Chapel and Cricket. All were practised with a devotion which some found stifling. The youngest boys began Latin in the charge of two formidable sisters, called governesses, Rhoda and Mildred Hill ('Miss Hill *ma.*' and 'Miss Hill *mi.*', collectively if incorrectly called the Miss Hills), who taught from 1903 and 1905 respectively until 1946, staying on loyally to see the war through to its end when they would much rather have retired. Their pupils could probably have passed the current Common Entrance before they were nine!

At the other end of the age range, GB made some minor changes to *Borva Notes*, but Doctor's method of teaching Latin was in general rigidly adhered to, because it continued to produce winners of Eton scholarships, even though it was felt to be flawed by better scholars than he had been. Grammar was taught by more practical methods too. If a boy made a venial slip GB would cry 'Tweaks!' as a signal to the boys on either side of the offender to pinch him. A real howler prompted the command 'Roots!' which, far from being an injunction to look up the etymology, was an instruction to everyone within reach to pull the boy's hair as hard as they could. Greek was sacred: when an interview candidate unfortunately mentioned the use of its alphabet in mathematics, GB fumed against the 'prostitution of a noble language'.

An extract from Geoffrey Bolton's memoirs

IV

Look Back – in Gratitude.

If now I look back on the Summer Fields of 40 years ago, there is no doubt much to criticize. But I should like to make it clear that then I accepted everything uncritically and that I was supremely happy – happy not only in being out of the Army, but happy in my relationships with boys and masters. Moreover, I had a deep affection and respect for Uncle Hugh and realized how lucky I was to serve under him. Nothing therefore that I write here can or should be ascribed to malice. Objectively, I can see that Summer Fields had its faults; subjectively, I have condoned nearly all of them.

Left: William Case, 1919

Below: The Sussex Martlets cricket team, 1919

Miss Hill mi. *wore her hair like earphones. She was alleged to have been knocked over by a wave when bathing and 'never to have been the same again'. They were officially known as governesses, but they were much, much more than that. They taught the bottom two forms and brought their Latin up to such a high standard that they would have scorned the modern Common Entrance papers. Their firm foundations supported the whole fabric of the work of the school.*

Patrick Savage (1939–75)

Chapel was pretty much beyond alteration, at that time anyway. It took place twice on Sundays, in addition to a session of Bible study and congregational choir practice. Thanks to Bear's memories of his own childhood, the Victorian Sunday lasted long into the twentieth century at SF, as boys had to remain at their desks for two hours during the afternoon. On fine summer Sundays they were allowed to sit on the field instead, but any attempt to move was checked by Bear, who would bawl through a megaphone he kept in his study.

If we may suspect GB of being no wild enthusiast for chapel, the same cannot be said for cricket. He wrote the official history of the Oxford University Cricket Club, and a book about the Sussex Martlets, of which he was president for many years. One of the few photographs in which he is smiling shows him with C. B. Fry. He also added his own enthusiasms, prominent among them P. G. Wodehouse, whose novels he used to read to the boys in the evenings, and Gilbert and Sullivan (he claimed to identify closely with Jack Point, the tragic jester in *The Yeomen of the Guard* – surely a telling self-projection). The cult of Wodehouse continues, with two devotees currently on the staff: Johnny Bush and Andrew Bishop.

Such out-of-hours sociability had not always been the norm. Relationships with the boys were one of the many things which divided the younger masters from the older when he arrived. The veterans held that, unless one were teaching, taking a game or on duty, one should not fraternise with the boys at all. The exception to this was William Sterndale Case, the Music Master (1910–22). He had a broader and more cultivated background than his colleagues, and had been a music critic for *The Times*. Young at heart and playful of nature, he ignored what he considered to be stuffy attitudes, and was the only person who ever stood up to Doctor – once, indeed, calling him a 'bloody old fool' to his face at breakfast, a remark for which anyone else would surely have been sacked. His early death in 1922, from a sudden blood clot to the heart, was universally mourned. He would have looked benignly upon the Anti-Authority League,

formed by rebellious pupil Julian Amery a few years later (slogan: 'Gott Straff Authority'), whose object was to induce the old guard on the staff to treat the boys with more consideration.

GB taught English, History, Geography, Mathematics, Scripture and French in addition to Classics, and helped with football and cricket (rugby was introduced in 1920). He did not concentrate on Latin and Greek until he became Master of Fifth Form – the name still given to the Scholarship class – in 1927. This was a distinct privilege, for that form had previously been the preserve of the Headmaster. GB had to work hard to keep up; these great figures whose scholars won so many awards were not necessarily great *teachers*. They instilled knowledge unforgettably, but rarely drew their pupils to love their work. Toby Eady (1948–54) made the interesting distinction between Jimmy Bell, 'a teacher', and GB, 'an enforcer of knowledge'.

And what of GB? Does that titanic personality baffle all description? Never in fact or fiction have I come across so magnificent a teacher, one who touched nothing that he did not illume. In class or out of it, he talked to us as a man of the world, talking to men of the world.

Hugh Stubbs (1926–30)

Julian Amery, Baron Amery of Lustleigh (1919–96), SF 1928–32

Julian Amery was born on 27 March 1919 in London. He went to Eton (1932–7) and Balliol College, Oxford (1937–9). He first arrived at Summer Fields in the Lent Term of 1928, as a lively, confident boy, who wore his hair brushed straight, without a parting. He was a diminutive figure, usually attired immaculately in green, tweed plus-eights with hardly any leg or stocking showing. His individuality led to ruthless teasing:

> One moment I remember with amusement concerns Julian Amery, who was a diminutive but very aggressive little boy. Having teased him one afternoon into a white heat of frenzy, we left him upside down in a tall litter basket on the playing field, into which he fitted precisely. I have often wondered how he got out.
>
> John Reay-Smith (1924–8)

In part, this teasing was caused by his refusal to conform to the 'herd' instinct and join the other boys. He was said to be 'outrageously different' and loathed any form of compulsory exercise.

In the classroom, Amery was not exceptionally brilliant nor did he exert himself, taking little interest in competing for the ordinary school prizes. His own memories of Summer Fields are clear. The best was the Hay Feast with 'the pleasures of warm weather, strawberries and cream and unlimited licence to attack all in authority'. The worst was Monday lunch in winter, eating 'a small portion of lukewarm, grey meat, known as "cat's meat"'.

Amery was bad at games and valiantly resisted any attempts to make him tackle low in rugby. He refused also to comply in football, but he enjoyed some cricket. He often played golf, with some distinctive equipment, which John Henderson (1930–3) recalls:

> He had an enormous golf bag, with thick straps and large pouches and a spectrum of brand-new clubs. Heavy the whole thing must have been. We were always very much aware when Julian was playing golf. There was a panache, if lack of precision, about his swing which matched his accoutrement and his clothes.

Julian Amery also wrote a play, in French, *Le Casque à Point*. This had nine characters, lasted for about twenty-two minutes and was produced in the summer of 1932. It tells the story of a French peasant's revenge on a German officer who had maimed and killed his daughter in the First World War. In the reviewer's opinion, there was too much action and too little dialogue, despite a performance 'of great gusto which had its moments'.

At Summer Fields, Amery showed a passionate interest in politics. Sometimes he could be seen standing on top of the lockers haranguing a none-too-respectful audience on the iniquities of the Tories – an interesting line for a future member of the Conservative Party!

Julian Amery (on right) at the Hay Feast with Robin Reade, *c*.1930

He always seemed up to date with Britain's domestic and foreign affairs, reading *The Times* avidly in preparation for conversations with his political father, Leo. He debated fiercely, often turning the current feeling of the floor and delivering his views 'with the gravitas of an elder statesman'.

The year 1950 was a good one for Julian. On 26 January 1950 he married Catherine, younger daughter of Harold Macmillan (1903–6), and he was elected to the House of Commons as MP for Preston. His political career now had lift-off and a string of offices followed: Junior Minister at the War Office (1958), later at the Colonial Office; Secretary of State for Air (1960–2), later Minister for Aviation; Minister of State at the Ministry of Public Building and Works (1970), at Housing (1970–2) and at the Foreign Office (1972–4). Having given considerable service to his country, Amery retired from the House of Commons in 1992 and was granted a life peerage, as Baron Amery of Lustleigh. He died on 3 September 1996.

A page from Julian's writing exercise book

John Evans at the Hay Feast, 1930

GB cannot really be discussed without John Evans, who preceded him as Headmaster (1939–56) and with whom he worked for nearly forty years. When Cyril Williams retired, Roger Jacques gave up his partnership, so that for the first time the Headmaster had no connection with the family of the founders. John Evans is a mysterious character about whom one would like to know more. He had been appointed by Doctor in 1914 in a letter containing the immortal words, 'I hope you are a Communicant, and that you play Bridge.' Commissioned in October 1914, he survived the war despite 'being laid out' by a sniper's bullet in Delville Wood two years later during the Somme campaign. At Summer Fields, he preserved a Roaring Twenties atmosphere, smoking Turkish cigarettes, cultivating a roguish air which involved addressing all and sundry, adults and boys alike, as 'my dear', and disbursing the masters' salaries at the end of term in brown-paper envelopes, murmuring deprecatingly as he handed them over, 'My dear – here's twopence-halfpenny.' Any new-fangled educational ideas about, for example, the value of the plastic arts or the designing of posters as prep, were dismissed as 'raffia-work in the nude'. Any boy of less than polished manners was labelled a 'Yahoo'. Together with Liz Lysaght, the Chaplain (1914–49), he maintained a liberal Catholic tradition in chapel, taking as his motto, 'We offer as much as possible, we force as little as possible.'

He and GB were in many ways incompatible – indeed GB described him as 'very difficult to work with' – but they parcelled out the duties between them, John Evans doing (and sometimes neglecting) the administrative and social jobs while GB concentrated on the academic and sporting side. Evans'

teaching was, one feels, not a vocation. He heard the translations the boys had done for prep in the next morning's lesson, marking orally as he went round the class, and apparently not realising, or not caring, that the boys who had not yet construed altered their versions in the light of errors that had just been exposed. The last boy to be heard invariably produced an admirable rendering.

John Evans had a long history of nervous collapses; taking up the headship in 1939 cannot have helped, since it meant that for years he would have to struggle against falling rolls, cramped conditions and the poor state of the premises. His health deteriorated further, and from 1943 onwards he had several breakdowns, forcing recognition of the fact that there was no line of succession to two bachelors, and prompting the reorganisation of the school as a charitable trust. A final collapse in 1956 marked the sudden end of his tenure, although he lived on until 1972, becoming a governor and so having a chance to return to the school periodically.

The Headmaster, Evans, was deeply neurotic and always seemed anxious that things were going to go badly wrong, even when they weren't. He was sycophantic to the parents in proportion to their social standing, and though it didn't seem too odd at the time, he gave a half-holiday to celebrate the release of Lady Mosley, who had two Guinness sons in the school, from Holloway.

John Jolliffe (1944–7)

GB thus became Headmaster, the post he had long dreamed of, but which he enjoyed (and one could not even really use that word) for only four years before the school doctor – seconded by Oxford's Regius Professor of Medicine, who had been co-opted as an authority with whom even GB might not argue –

forced his retirement on health grounds. Hating the idea of ceremonies and speeches, he got up at 4.30am on his last day and drove off to his Sussex home.

He had made some changes: less oppressive chapel services, a reining-in of prefectorial licence and, improbably, an annual dance with the girls of Greycotes School. There were some building projects, and greater attention was paid to the grounds than before. A major fundraising appeal was launched in 1957. But he increasingly looked, and felt, like a survivor from another era. He died three weeks after the Centenary Dinner which illness cruelly prevented him from attending. The mingled fear and awe he inspired were brilliantly summed up by Denys Jameson (1931–4), who wrote, 'I know just why the ancient Greeks kept out of the way of their gods.'

A dance with the girls of Greycotes School, 1964

The letter from GB and John Evans on the reorganisation of the school as a charitable trust, 1955

SUMMER FIELDS NEAR OXFORD
TELEPHONE NO. 58340.

OCTOBER, 1955.

The difficulties which confront the independent schools have in the last ten years grown so rapidly and so formidably that we have felt it essential to take what steps we can to ensure the future of Summer Fields. We take it as axiomatic that parents and old boys wish to see the School going forward in the same beliefs and traditions which have guided it for ninety years, whatever external changes may take place.

With the object, therefore, of making things as easy as possible for our successors, when their time comes, we have turned the School into a Trust Company, with a Board of Governors chosen, with one exception, from old boys of the School; their names, we feel, are a guarantee to parents and O.S.S. that, as long as independent schools survive, there need be no fear for the future of Summer Fields.

The Chairman of the Board, unanimously elected at our first meeting on September 19th, is the Bishop of Exeter. He alone of the Board is not an old boy, but his connection with the School has long been so close that we are proud to think

Patrick Savage: the First Modern Headmaster?

The appointment of Patrick Savage to be Head Master (he always insisted that it should be two words) in what we can see, in retrospect, to have been the momentous year of 1960, was a symptom of change to come. In classic SF fashion, there was also continuity, for his imagination had been kindled by stories of the school told by a contemporary of his at Westminster who was an OS, and the fire was fuelled by another OS friend, Francis Egerton, MC (1927–31) at Christ Church, Oxford, who took him to meet John Evans in 1939. He was engaged as a teacher at a salary of £60 per term (John Evans had started at £40 thirty years earlier, so nobody was in it for the money). Within weeks of his arrival he was called up, and when he returned in 1945, he had spent four years in a prisoner-of-war camp, a period which, however rarely it was mentioned, must have coloured his whole approach to the exercise of authority and discipline. Many boys recalled his approachable, mischievous manner, far more informal than was the custom, and the apparently genuine regret with which he meted out punishment when necessary.

In the fifteen years between his demobilisation and his taking charge, Pat Savage saw the old guard gradually depart. John Evans and GB, of course, were constants: the former boyish and approachable ('Are you having *fun*, my dear?'), the latter grim and unnerving, with his odd fads and prejudices (onions and cats were anathema) and his unvarying routines (bed at ten o'clock and lights out at 10.27).

Mr Bell was brilliant at reading aloud, and produced the school play. He struggled hard to make me sound gloomy enough, as Macbeth's aged retainer, for my only six words, 'The queen, my Lord, is dead.'

Julian Reade (1949–52)

When John Evans had to retire, Pat Savage became Deputy Headmaster, and when he succeeded GB he nominated two senior masters, Jimmy Bell and Pat Marston, as his assistants. Jimmy Bell (1927–32, staff 1938–78), fabled bon viveur and theatre-goer, stoically taught Classics to the lower Common Entrance forms, even continuing to take one for eight years

Left: Patrick Savage, Head Master 1960–75, in 1965, and **above**, at the Hay Feast, 1970

Jimmy Bell in 1978, **right**, and **below**, at the Hay Feast, 1930s

I remember Pat Marston, the Ogre, who, if he was in a bad mood would wear his blue and white tie, especially on Mondays. If he wore a rose in his lapel, it cancelled out the warning that he was in a bad mood.

The Rt Rev. David Jennings (1952–7), current governor

Pat Savage felt that he was looked upon as a reformer in 1960 but as a reactionary in 1975 when he retired. He saw himself as a pragmatist, responding to situations rather than implementing policies. His governing body had a free hand since, unlike all his predecessors, he did not personally own the school. Finance was an immediate priority, with appeals launched in 1957 and 1970 and fees increased – a potentially awkward coupling. Salaries were put on a proper footing for the first time. Numbers rose: there were 180 boys on the roll by the end of his time, all of them boarders – compared to just over 240 today, of whom about 40 are day boys. New buildings appeared: extra form rooms, a new kitchen, a splendid new library converted from 'Cubicles', the old dormitory in which, GB once reckoned, he had read about twenty million words aloud to the boys before 'lights out'. The curriculum broadened: Bobs Alington said to Pat Savage, 'If I could have done what you've done, I should still be here!' There had been distinguished English teachers before (Strong, Day-Lewis); now the subject became more literary. Visiting speakers abounded, extracurricular clubs and activities flourished, with the boys encouraged to take a greater part in running them.

after his official retirement. He produced a stream of school plays, which he maintained should last no longer than ninety minutes – about twice as long as is common nowadays. Pat Marston (1918–22, staff 1931–70) – 'the Ogre' as he was called, and indeed called himself – married Perdita Williams, Cyril's daughter, in 1936 (the prefects being allowed champagne at the reception) and so revivified the ancient lineage. He was an outstanding cricketer and golfer, and presented the school with new fives courts to replace those which Doctor had designed and which (one is tempted to say 'therefore') became quickly unusable. He would helpfully wear a particular tie (the 'bate tie') to indicate a day when he was in a bad mood. He and Pat Savage retained the old pronunciation of Latin to make it sound like English, and took quiet satisfaction in pointing out that the Prime Minister, Harold Macmillan (1903–6), did just the same.

Verses to Perdita

(or attempts at them)
composed one night at Borva when
I could not sleep
1914

En! mea cara, veni! Laete mihi carpe capillos,
Tum capiti reddas tegmina rubra meo.
Aspice! dum curru insidet pulcherrima virgo
Sancta dies quod adest, sol sine nube nitet.
Ut puer incepit formam laudare venustam,
Imprimit in cameram* virginis ora suam,
Ast etiam in Borva, qua me dormire juvavit,
Aure bibo ut mire mane puella vocat.
Te tamen interdum non saepe, benigna, videmus:
Aspicere ut liceat saepius ora mihi!
Te fuerit forsan superans, ast, mater, honore
Femina nulla tuo gratior esse potest.
Perdita pulchra, etsi cunctis sis semper amanda,
Carior es cunctis, tempus in omne, mihi,
Da veniam, quaeso, quod tam mala carmina dixi,
Ast laudare decus qualiacunque juvat.

VISCOUNT RUNCIMAN OF DOXFORD, O.B.E.
1912–14

Greater use was made of Harold Clayton's multi-volume *Natural Approach to Mathematics* – the 'New Maths' – and Science became more practical. Art and Music were expanded. More was done to make the school look attractive to visitors, with displays and mounted photographs. Above all, the boys felt more involved in the life of the place. They appreciated Pat's bonhomie and encouragement of their interests.

Pat Savage was due to retire in 1976. With this in mind, in March 1974 the governors appointed Nigel Talbot Rice, who had been on the staff for a decade and was already Pat's deputy, to be the eighth Headmaster (one word again) of Summer Fields. They were keen that an internal appointment should be made if possible, to avoid upheaval and to offer continuity, with an already familiar face. They also felt that the next incumbent should be married. Nigel Talbot Rice fitted the bill exactly.

Pat Savage subsequently wrote to the governors informing them of his wish to retire a year early, namely at the end of the 1974–5 academic year. The Bursar and the School Matron were also due to leave then, and he thought it would be sensible for his successor to begin with a fresh team in Michaelmas 1975. 'It is always better to stop something a little too early rather than a little too late,' he added. 'I *am* getting a bit weary, I'm afraid… It is because of my *love* for the school that I have reached this

conclusion.' Pat Savage observed that Nigel Talbot Rice was 'entirely *different* from me' which was all to the good, since the only thing Headmasters needed to have in common was 'their fondness for the school'.

So it has ever been: so may it ever be.

The library today, and **below**, in 1973

The Coat of Arms

It was under Pat Savage that Summer Fields acquired something special – something indeed to give it identity. Ever interested in heraldry, Savage collaborated with Sir Anthony Wagner, Garter King of Arms, and designed a coat of arms for the school which was officially recognised in 1964. He took the red-white-red-white-red of the flag as the basis, upon which to add the three bezants (gold coins) symbolising St Nicholas, to whom the chapel was dedicated, and three lilies to honour the school's long connection with

The school crest prior to the acquisition of the coat of arms

Eton. The wreath is the usual representation of the twisted scarf, worn around the helmet partly to hide the fastenings by which the crest was attached. From the wreath tumbles the mantling, a cloth hanging over the back of the helmet and body armour to protect them from the heat of the sun. The red ox, taken from the arms of the City of Oxford, is placed outside the city gate to show that Summer Fields is not within the walls, but 'near' Oxford. The green mound represents the 'Summer Fields' which are appreciably higher than the centre of Oxford.

The arms of Summer Fields are officially described as follows:

SHIELD: Gules two Bars Argent between in
chief three Bezants and in base three
Lily Flowers proper.
CREST: On a Wreath of the Colours On a
Mount Vert before a Porte between two
Towers Or an Ox passant Gules.

Hugh Fearnley-Whittingstall (1965–), SF 1973–8

Hugh Fearnley-Whittingstall arrived at Summer Fields in 1973. After Eton, Oxford and a short spell at the River Café, he has become a truly national phenomenon through his iconic River Cottage on the Devon–Dorset border. Millions of television viewers are charmed and entertained by his articulate enthusiasm for a 'back to basics' philosophy of 'real food' cooked from locally sourced ingredients.

At Summer Fields, Fearnley-Whittingstall was a bright and active boy. He won prizes in Fifth Form and took his share of general responsibility as League Prefect for Case and, finally, Head Prefect. He was a fair athlete, his speciality being the 100m, although he also won cups for the discus and golf. He enjoyed Drama and acted in several plays. He gave 'a bold, but restrained' performance as Richard Burbage in No Bed for

Bacon, a 'historically unsound play' set in Shakespeare's England, and in 1976 took the part of Donalbain in Prep School Shakespeare – Ugh!, a cut-down version of Macbeth.

The authority, confidence and humour so evident in Fearnley-Whittingstall's TV appearances were already noted at Summer Fields, particularly

in debates. In a joint venture with the Dragon School, he spoke against the motion that 'This house believes that science is more of a curse to mankind than a blessing'. His speech was 'explicit and precise, stressing the importance of science in medicine'. It led to victory by 45 votes to 20, with 6 abstentions.

His literary talent is also apparent in several pieces of prose and poetry published in the Summer Fields Magazine. And, yes, there was a nascent curiosity about food and cookery. In Mayfield, he was a founder member of the Cookery Club which blossomed under the watchful eye of Jimmy Bell and, later, Charles Churchill. Summer Fields stimulated an early interest which has since become a passion and a way of life. It thus played an important part in shaping his career.

Food

For many decades, meals at Summer Fields were formal affairs: boys sat at designated tables by year group, overseen by a master or under-matron sitting at each end. In recent years meals have become fully self-service, overseen by the Domestic Bursar, Ann Hannah. Prefects and a select few sat on 'Top Table', as the High Table is still called, and it was from there that the Headmaster or duty master controlled each meal. Kitchen staff brought round the food. From one end of the table the main course was dispensed; from the other, the pudding. A cheese course was a privilege for those at the table ends. Breakfast, lunch and supper were each sandwiched by a Latin Grace read by a senior boy or, occasionally, by the duty master.

During the 1930s food swapping and barter were general practices. Sunday usually brought sausages or boiled eggs, the latter carried around the tables in wire-cage baskets. Servicing the dining room were 'Addle-egg' Alelaide (who often carried round the eggs), Nellie and Priest, 'the priestess of the High Table'. 'Severe and aloof', she was renowned for her ability to pour beer from a high-held glass jug 'with unerring aim, weaving her way to and fro across the dining hall from master to master till all were served'. The joints were carved for the maids by the school carpenter, Charlie Payne (1897–1931). Some claimed that the need for a carpenter to do the job suggested tough meat...

Throughout the Second World War, Summer Fields managed to feed its boys, who did not lack for much even though many meals were dull, if wholesome. Intermittently, luxury items appeared. However, unacceptable food often met with protest, occasionally verging on rebellion. The so-called 'Cat's Meat Rebellion' of 1926 was a universal protest against the manner in which the meat was carved and served; twenty-four years later, there was a major disturbance over sausage rolls.

Hunger was the issue behind the Great Sausage-Roll Rebellion in the summer of 1950. One supper dish was sausage-rolls, or more likely a single sausage-

roll, a cold cylinder of bland conglomerate surrounded by soggy pastry. It usually came once a week, and was not popular. One week it came twice, on successive days, and then on the third day there were sausage-rolls again. After supper we went out to the playing fields, and GB was on duty. He stood on the grass, looking outward, and we became aware that something dramatic was about to happen. At that moment a very brave boy named Gray, [most likely Peter Gray (1946–51)] walked up to GB and

We had fish for break-fast this morning it was so nice we generally have jam twice a week. All the slops at football have to go for a walk on Tuesdays an...

addressed him. GB straightened and virtually levitated in surprise but became aware, as he returned to earth, that Gray was backed by a deputation of all the senior boys of the school. GB did not listen gracefully but he listened. Next day we were informed that in future we should not have sausage rolls more than once or possibly twice a week.

Julian Reade (1949–52)

Tea outdoors: **top**, 1938; **inset**, 1929

Right: Kitchen preparations in the 1960s

Left: Extract from a letter home in 1894 by Geoffrey Arbuthnot, later Admiral Sir Geoffrey Arbuthnot, KCB, DSO (1894–1900)

Below: The dining room today, and **inset**, in the 1930s

Occasionally food and sweets (ever a valuable currency at Summer Fields) could bring out some elements of entrepreneurial originality from some boys. With a mixture of pride and embarrassment, your editor recalls the early antics of a Summerfieldian now successfully involved in global business transactions... On the corner of Summerfield Road, where Savills now stands, was another kind of establishment:

My favourite memory of Summer Fields is starting my first ever business, aged just twelve, by setting up an undercover fish-and-chip-shop run. I worked out that as a day boy I had a good reason to be out of school grounds, in Summertown, at unusual hours when most boys were bound to their Lodges. I collected money from pupils usually after leave weekends. My peers would wait in the music block keeping watch on Summerfield Road at night for me, while I ran into Summertown and ordered up to seventeen portions of cod and chips. I'd fill my pockets with tomato-ketchup sachets, then run back, if necessary dodging any wandering masters.

In those days it was £2.50 for a large portion. I would charge £3.50 per pupil making a £1 profit on each order. This became quite lucrative and lasted for around four months with twice-weekly runs. I spent my profits on sweets to augment the weekly sweet rations! Having returned with the goods, we ate them in Mr Bennett's or Mr Langdon's music tuition rooms in the dark. We then hid the wrappers inside the lids of the pianos. In the end I was 'busted' and caught red-handed. After an investigation by Mr Talbot Rice and Mr Johnson, I lost the privilege of wearing my Leavers' Guernsey for several weeks, as well as being handed multiple Black Books!

Giles Hannah (1991–6)

chapter two

Summer Fields at War

Summer Fields itself suffered no material damage on account of war, but international conflict affected the school in several ways. Some staff made the ultimate sacrifice while serving their country; others lost sons. Old Summerfieldians, in the course of military duties, were killed or wounded. The two World Wars upset the school's daily routine to a greater or lesser degree and from the turmoil of war there emerged individuals distinguished by their millitary expertise or heroism.

Anyone undertaking serious study of those OSS and masters killed in war should consult Chris Sparrow's book *No Time to Spare* (2006). This volume offers brief accounts of the military careers of each, together with details of the context in which they died. Only a few may be considered here. As Chris Sparrow points out, it was not only in the two World Wars that OSS were lost. The first Old Boy to die in action was Lieutenant Thomas Griffith (1867–70), the twentieth boy on the Register, killed in January 1879 at Isandlwana in the Zulu War. The Boer War accounted for nine more, who are commemorated by a window in chapel. The last to be killed in action was Captain Herbert Richard Westmacott, MC (1960–5), who died in a covert operation against the IRA in May 1980. Not on military service, but working as a freelance photographer for the *News of the World*, was Ed Henty (1967–72), killed in 1993 as a massive IRA bomb ripped through the heart of the City of London. However, it is the First World War which brought the first great losses to the school.

Detail from the Memorial Brasses to Old Summerfieldians killed in the First World War

PP-FISHER. ~~YOR~~

WORCESTERSHIRE REGT.

GOWER. COLDSTREAM GUAR

K.R.RIFLES.

NORFOLK REGT. M.V.O.

LE K.R.RIFLE CORPS.

Above: The school, 1915

The First World War

In the fiftieth year of the life of the school, the First World War broke out. Long years of increasing European tension, militarism, fear, the politics of imperialism, all overlaid with a web of international alliances, unleashed four years of bloody conflict which claimed the lives of nearly one million men from the United Kingdom alone. No fewer than 139 of them were from Summer Fields. Throughout the conflict, the *Magazine* recorded the school's casualties. In a section entitled *De Aestivis Agris*, the Roll of Honour is noted. In July 1916, the editor comments that 'with the "Big Push" in progress, our casualty lists are growing longer each day and it is impossible to keep them perfectly accurate'. It was at this time that the great offensive on the Somme began, on the first day of that month.

In fact, despite the so-called 'Big Pushes', the figures suggest that, after an initial slaughter, the increase in the number of those killed remained steady as the war progressed, with a slight acceleration during the final eleven months of the conflict. Measured from December to December, the annual increase in OSS mortality is as follows: forty-five (1914–15), twenty-seven (1915–16), twenty-seven (1916–17), thirty (1917 to November 1918). Three main reasons may be suggested for this. First, to counter the initial heavy losses, officers (and the majority of OSS combatants were junior officers) were ordered into combat dressed more like other ranks, thus becoming less of a target for watchful snipers. Second, officers remained closer to their men when leading attacks. Third, the shock of what was to contemporaries a novel kind of warfare wore off, and experience led to new approaches to fighting which marginally improved the chance of survival.

Nonetheless, it is a sobering statistic that of the twenty-eight new boys who arrived at Summer Fields in 1897, no fewer than eleven (39 per cent) would be victims of the war. Neither Doctor nor Bear was spared the loss of a loved one. Hilary Williams was killed in 1915, and Geoffrey Alington, an Old Boy

Below: Letter from Charles Eccles Williams to Brigadier General Austin Anderson (1879–83) about Hilary Williams' death

TELEGRAMS, SUMMERTOWN.

SUMMER FIELDS, NEAR OXFORD.

Oct 9: 15

My dear Anderson,

My wife & I are much touched by your remembrance of us in our sorrow & by having found time, with all your other work, to write to us about him. Thank you from the bottom of our hearts. It was good of you to go over, & I wish he had [...]

A visit to the Commonwealth War Graves Commission cemetery at Ypres, 2010

who had returned to teach at the school (and who had dispatched Latin prose from the trenches for the boys to translate) in 1916, but not before he had met and impressed Geoffrey Bolton, whose future at SF was thereby determined. Bear's nephew, Winford Alington, who like his father had been a master at the school, died a mere two days before the ceasefire in 1918. His ghost was seen by Leonard Strong in Cottage in 1921. This fascinating story is recounted in Strong's *Green Memory* (1961) and quoted in Nick Aldridge's *Time to Spare?* The ghost remained attached to Cottage, and had to be exorcised in the 1990s.

One effect of the First World War on life at school was that the boys became heavily infected with 'spy-mania'. A particularly enthusiastic anti-espionage coterie grew suspicious of anyone who looked the slightest bit shady, or who spoke with any sort of foreign accent. This led to some amusing and embarrassing scenes resulting from cases of mistaken identity. Howell Davis (1914–18) recalls how the spy-hunters once noticed 'an elderly gentleman with pince-nez glasses' who walked daily down what is now the cycle track, often pausing to

Captain the Hon. Julian Grenfell, DSO (1888–1915), SF 1898–1901

Julian Grenfell was born at 4 St James's Square, London, on 30 March 1888, the eldest son of William Grenfell, first Baron Desborough. He attended Summer Fields from 1898 to 1901. His sporting talent was soon apparent, and he won his place in the 1st XI in his final year, opening the batting in several high-scoring matches. He moved on to Eton and Balliol. Grenfell was not a Scholarship boy but, nonetheless, possessed an intelligent and original mind. Arriving at Oxford in Michaelmas 1906, he was described as 'a splendid figure of a man, over six feet high, with two greyhounds, a famous Australian stock-whip, and an immense enjoyment of life'. At Balliol his 'animal high spirits' occasionally descended into rowdyness. He took as 'a sincere compliment' his nickname of 'Rough Man' or 'Roughers', often using his stock-whip on people he did not like, notably Philip Sassoon.

Grenfell, like his father, was renowned for his athletic and sporting prowess. He boxed middleweight for the University, rowed at Henley and won the College steeple-chase. But his greatest passion was for hunting with his favourite dog, Slogbottom, the subject of his poem 'To a Black Greyhound' (c.1912).

In December 1909 he suffered a breakdown. When only just recovering from this, he fell in love with Pamela Lytton, wife of the second Earl of Lytton. Their relationship was curtailed when Grenfell joined the Royal Dragoons, and was sent to India and later to South Africa. Bored with military life, Grenfell planned to leave the army. However, events overtook him, and in 1914 he was sent to France with his regiment. He wrote home, early in November: 'It is all *the* best fun. I have never, never felt so well, or so happy, or enjoyed anything so much. The fighting and excitement vitalise everything, every sight and word and action. One loves one's fellow man so much more when one is bent on killing him.'

A fortnight later he shot three Germans during sorties on the enemy lines, employing stalking skills learnt on Scottish moors to crawl in daylight to within feet of their trenches. He entered these 'kills' in his game book. Directly after '105 partridges', the entries read: 'November 16th, One Pomeranian; November 17th, Two Pomeranians'. It was during the latter expedition that he spotted signs of an imminent German attack, and for warning the authorities of this, he was awarded the DSO.

Grenfell's Trench Diary from 1915 offers glimpses of a different kind of soldier. Nerves and fear had kicked in. One entry records: 'Heard noise of bomb dropping on top of dug-out. Petrified. Lost self-control – lay still, clenching my hands, for 20 secs. Asked what it was. "Rum jar, Sir, thrown away!" came the reply.'

Nevertheless, his love of combat survived, and on 29 April 1915, during the Second Battle of Ypres, Grenfell wrote the poem 'Into Battle', for which he is best known. The entry in his diary for that day is typically modest. 'Tuesday 29th: Moved off about 8.00 am towards Pop. Brigade rested in field. Rested all day, and got back to our farm at 7.30 pm. Pork chops for dinner. Wonderful sunny, lazy days – but longing to be up and doing something. Slept out. Wrote poem, "Into Battle".' This piece is a statement of his creed, namely that combat is intrinsic to life, and that the warrior is closest to nature. The poem enjoyed immediate success after its publication and remains one of the most anthologised poems of the First World War.

On 13 May 1915 Grenfell volunteered to run messages during a heavy bombardment, and that afternoon he was seriously wounded by a shell splinter to the head. He died in the military hospital in Boulogne on 26 May. The next day 'Into Battle' was published in *The Times*, on the eve of

Grenfell, back row, third from the right, in a production of *Queen Bridget and the Dragon*, by Geoffrey Alington, 1911

the author's burial in the military cemetery above Boulogne. The following month Billy Grenfell (1899–1903), Julian's younger brother, was also killed in action in France.

Julian Grenfell was a complex character. His skills as a poet and as a boxing Blue well illustrate the combination of aesthetic sensibility with man's primitive instinct to fight. Winston Churchill's verdict was both positive and laudatory. 'He was all that you could have desired and all that our race needs to keep its honour fair and bright.'

Into Battle

The naked earth is warm with Spring,
And with green grass and bursting trees
Leans to the sun's gaze glorying,
And quivers in the sunny breeze;
And Life is Colour and Warmth and Light,
And a striving evermore for these;
And he is dead who will not fight;
And who dies fighting has increase.

The fighting man shall from the sun
Take warmth, and life from the glowing earth;
Speed with the light-foot winds to run,
And with the trees to newer birth;
And find, when fighting shall be done,
Great rest, and fullness after dearth.

All the bright company of Heaven
Hold him in their high comradeship,
The Dog-Star and the Sisters Seven,
Orion's Belt and sworded hip.

The woodland trees that stand together,
That stand to him each one a friend.
They gently speak in the windy weather;
They guide to valley and ridge's end.

The kestrel hovering by day,
And the little owls that call by night.
Bid him be swift and keen as they,
As keen of ear, as swift of sight.

The blackbird sings to him 'Brother, brother,
If this be the last song you shall sing
Sing well, for you may not sing another;
Brother, sing.'

In dreary, doubtful waiting hours,
Before the brazen frenzy starts,
The horses show him nobler powers;
O patient eyes, courageous hearts!

And when the burning moment breaks,
And all things else are out of mind,
And only joy of battle takes
Him by the throat, and makes him blind –

Through joy and blindness he shall know,
Not caring much to know, that still
Nor lead nor steel shall reach him, so
That it be not the Destined Will.

The thundering line of battle stands.
And in the air Death moans and sings;
But Day shall clasp him with strong hands,
And Night shall fold him in strong wings.

watch the cricket. Thinking that he had sinister intentions – 'Who but a German would wear such glasses?' – a plan was hatched to surround him and drag him to Doctor for interrogation. The unfortunate man was duly accosted and bundled towards the ha-ha in front of the main lawn. Out came Doctor. Wise in the foolishness of small boys, he handled the matter with great tact. After an apology to the shocked old man, the spy-hunters were summoned to the study, where they eyed the cane, fearing the worst. However, after some tense moments, they were dismissed, Doctor believing they had 'acted with best of patriotic motives, and that their conduct should be overlooked'.

A pre-war Flying Club on Port Meadow, a couple of miles or so to the north-west of Summer Fields, had been converted into an aerodrome used for training, from which flimsy, box-like planes regularly flew 'startlingly and exhilaratingly low' over the school fields. Howell Davis remembers how, one day, some boys kicked their footballs at one such airframe, considering that 'they were not far below his wings'. Sir Denys Buckley (1914–19) relates how even these flying machines further fuelled the spy-fever:

> One day, a monoplane came flying low over the farm buildings. As it did so, the farmer came out of a doorway and raised his hands to his eyes. We were convinced that we saw him remove a mask from his face so he could be recognised by a fellow spy in the plane, to whom he was signalling.

For a German boy at Summer Fields, the immediate consequences of these neurotic suspicions were only too apparent. Henning-Bernd von Arnim (1911–16) became the centre of attention, 'not alas, because of my charm, but because I spoke the Kaiser's, rather than the King's English. My guttural

Masters, 1917, with Doctor seated centre

Left and above: William La Touche Congreve and his memorial at Corbie

Right: Extract from the school magazine of 1917

ANOTHER V.C.
CAPTAIN T. R. COLYER-FERGUSSON.
NORTHAMPTONSHIRE REGIMENT.

WE have in this number of the School *Magazine* chronicle with deep but proud sorrow the death another Old Boy who has won the great honour a V.C., but alas! who never lived to know it. Ri Colyer-Fergusson came to us in May, 1905, th youngest of three promising brothers—grandsons of th famous Professor Max-Müller—all of whom passed o to Harrow in due time. Unassuming but always quietl determined and absolutely reliable, he was the typ of English schoolboy who makes no fuss but faces hi duty bravely—how bravely in this instance is shown b the following extract from *The Times*:

'Captain T. R. Colyer-Fergusson has been awarde the Victoria Cross for most conspicuous bravery, skil ful leading, and determination in attack. The tactica situation having developed contrary to expectation, was not possible for his company to adhere to th original plan of deployment, and, owing to the diffi culties of the ground and to enemy wire, Captai Colyer-Fergusson found himself with a sergeant and five men only. He carried out the attack nevertheless, and succeeded in capturing ' dis posing of the

pronouncements, complete with rolling Rs, resulted in tremendous and continual ragging and since I was easily aroused to complete fury, there were many fights and the inevitable tears.' To his surprise, he further noticed that with the onset of the war, his 'von' suddenly disappeared and his name 'got among the As on the lists instead of the Vs', as indeed it remains, in the school Register.

Although some boys complained of food shortages, on the whole normal school fare continued, with the usual marmalade and sausages for breakfast, 'a wonderful mixture when eaten together'. It has been suggested that the boys may have received worse medical treatment, the best doctors being away in France, or coping with the ever-increasing numbers of wounded admitted to English hospitals, but there is little to support this assertion. There was a rigorous blackout 'with blinds and brown paper to cover every crevice', and boys also undertook potato-weeding expeditions as part of voluntary war work.

Judging by the final tally of military honours, OSS fought bravely for their King and Country. The list comprises two VCs, forty-six DSOs and sixty-four MCs (three with bar). Including men from St Leonards, 179 OSS were Mentioned in Dispatches. Many others were wounded, some several times, but still they returned to the fray, like Major Roger Fenwick (1907–12), thrice wounded before his death in action in 1918.

Two OSS who, for their valour and heroism, received the Victoria Cross in the First World War were 'Billy' Congreve and 'Rivs' Colyer-Fergusson. William La Touche Congreve, VC, DSO, MC, *Légion d'honneur* (1902–4) was the first OS to be awarded

the Victoria Cross (there have been three in total). Serving on the Somme with the Rifle Brigade in July 1916, a Military Cross already to his name, as well as a DSO, for capturing a crater containing four German officers and sixty-eight men, Congreve was already noted for personal courage. Indeed his VC resulted from 'most conspicuous bravery during a period of fourteen days preceding his death in action', rather than from a single act of heroism. His medal is rare in this respect. Congreve had consistently tended the wounded under heavy shell-fire, moving them to safety as and when he could. Shot by a sniper on 20 July 1916 while on a forward reconnaissance mission, the manner of his death epitomises the adventurous daring of 'the bravest and most gentle fellow in the world'. The school noted, 'with a proud sorrow', his imperishable record of 'resource and courage that cannot be surpassed'.

Thomas Riversdale Colyer-Fergusson, VC (1905–9), killed on 31 July 1917 during the Third Battle of Ypres, bravely faced his duty. With only his sergeant and five men he attacked and captured a German trench, 'disposing of the garrison'. Having successfully resisted a counter-attack, he then, alone with his sergeant, captured two enemy machine guns, successfully turning them on any assailants, before succumbing to a sniper's bullet. For this 'amazing record of dash, gallantry and skill', he was posthumously awarded the Victoria Cross. At Summer Fields, Colyer-Fergusson was 'quietly determined and absolutely reliable'. When he joined the school, no one could foresee that he was destined for a life so short and so distinguished.

Colyer-Fergusson as a young lieutenant

Lieutenant Arthur Rhys-Davids, DSO, MC and Bar in his SE5a

Among the twelve OSS to die in the air, we should note Arthur Rhys-Davids, DSO, MC and Bar (1909–10) of the Royal Flying Corps. RD, as he was known to his flight, achieved a total of twenty-five 'kills' before crashing behind the German lines after a fast and low pursuit of two German planes, at the age of only twenty. Renowned for his 'fearlessness and dash', RD was a magnificent fighter, never failing to locate enemy aircraft and invariably attacking, regardless of the numbers against him. The rareness of his character is displayed by his speech at the dinner to mark his DSO. Having voiced respect for the 'fine examples of bravery and courage' shown by the enemy, he called for a toast to Baron von Richthofen. Rhys-Davids' portrait hangs in the Imperial War Museum.

At sea, two OSS died during the First World War. Acting Sub-Lieutenant Raymond Portal (1906–10) went down with Admiral Hood and his flagship, HMS *Invincible*, at Jutland on 31 May 1916. *Invincible* took several hits, and then such was the force of the explosion when her powder magazines ignited that the vessel was blown in half, her stem and stern rising high out of the water 'around her seething death-bed'. Only six of her complement of about one thousand men survived.

Lieutenant-Commander George Cholmley (1893–4) took command of British submarine *E3* in January 1914. In October of that year, *E3* slipped quietly out of Harwich to patrol the North Sea off the island of Borkum. Surfacing in a bay, Cholmley failed to notice an enemy submarine, *U27*. Stealthily, *U27* approached and from a distance of about 600 yards launched two torpedoes, sending *E3* and all her crew to the bottom. An OS thus has the unfortunate distinction of commanding the first British submarine to be lost in action, the first to fall prey to another such vessel.

The Second World War

A remarkable six Old Summerfieldians were in Churchill's Cabinet when he became Prime Minister in May 1940, and two further members had sons at the school. Advances in warfare resulted in fewer UK deaths between 1939 and 1945 than during the First World War. Estimates vary but, in terms of British casualties, approximately 400,000 people died in the Second World War: 60,000 civilians, 35,000 members of the Merchant Navy and about 300,000 members of the armed forces, of whom 133 were Summerfieldians – a similar number to the school's losses in the First World War.

Lieutenant the Hon. Christopher Furness, VC (St Leonards 1922–4), commanding a Carrier Platoon of the Welsh Guards, found himself caught in the German blitzkrieg as it tore through Holland, Belgium and France in 1940. The British Expeditionary Force in Belgium became cut off and were ordered to 'evacuate the maximum force possible'. The 'miracle' of Dunkirk was about to follow.

Furness's battalion formed part of the garrison at Arras. From 17 May, he had been involved in constant forward patrols, 'imbuing his command with a magnificent offensive spirit'. On the evening of 23 May, Furness was wounded but refused to be evacuated. By now, German troops threatened the town on

three sides and Furness was ordered to cover the withdrawal of the transport to Douai. As the British vehicles began to depart, the Germans attacked. Trucks and lorries were shot up and the road became blocked. With little chance of halting the onslaught, Furness decided to attack the enemy as even the slightest hindrance to them would buy time for the British escape. He advanced with three Carriers and some light tanks. His tanks were soon put out of action and all the Carriers were hit, their crews killed or wounded. Nonetheless, he pressed on, reaching the German positions and inflicting heavy losses at close range. Finally, with his own Carrier disabled and its crew dead he engaged the enemy in hand-to-hand combat, until his own inevitable end. His act of self-sacrifice, against hopeless odds and when already wounded, forced the enemy temporarily to withdraw and the large column of British vehicles got away, unmolested. Furness won his VC aged just twenty-eight.

Of those serving in the Royal Air Force, twenty-eight OSS lost their lives. William Rhodes-Moorhouse, DFC (1922–7) was a Battle of Britain fighter ace with 601 Squadron. He had already demonstrated his skills in aerial warfare having five 'kills' to his name (thus an 'ace'), prior to the award of his DFC. Flying his Hurricane Mark I, he destroyed seven more enemy aircraft before being shot down, over Tunbridge Wells, on 6 September

The school, 1939, with Cyril Williams centre, GB second row, seated second from the left

Christopher Furness, VC

William Rhodes-Moorhouse, DFC

1940. On flying operations since November 1939, Rhodes-Moorhouse was noted for his displays of 'great courage and devotion to duty'.

At sea, nineteen OSS of all ranks, ranging from Vice-Admiral John Fitzgerald, CB (1898–1902) to Midshipman William Barclay (1933–7), died serving their country. Aged just nineteen, Barclay was on convoy escort duty aboard the destroyer *Mahratta*. Hit by a torpedo from a lurking U-boat, she sank in minutes, taking all but sixteen of her crew with her.

The impact of the war on Summer Fields itself was greater than in the previous world conflict. The first major effect concerned numbers on the roll. Nick Aldridge has pointed out that in this respect the Second World War 'saved Summer Fields'. Throughout the 1930s, numbers had been falling. By 1939, there were fewer than eighty boys in the school. Summer Fields was 'saved' as three schools were evacuated to Oxford. First, in 1939, came Mr E. K. ('Tubby') Stephenson and twenty-three boys from Farnborough. This amalgamation proved an instant success. It was supplemented in September 1940 when Ken and Kitty Barber brought the remnants of Summer Fields, St Leonards. These boys, seeking sanctuary, had already been evacuated to Alderwasley Hall, a small Roman Catholic school near Matlock, in Derbyshire. They stayed at Summer Fields until 1945. Then, in 1942, came Mr and Mrs W. J. V. Tomlinson with their family and twelve boys from St Cyprian's, Eastbourne (an institution savaged by George Orwell, who went there, in his essay 'Such, Such were the Joys'). They moved into Mayfield, which had been shut up at the beginning of the war. Thus, by 1943, numbers were back to normal and they consistently increased to around 155 by 1960.

Peter Nathan (1942–3), from St Cyprian's, although in Oxford only for five terms, generally enjoyed his war years at Summer Fields:

On arrival in 1942, we were housed in Mayfield, where Bill Tomlinson became Housemaster assisted by his delightful wife, Bud. My selection as Captain of Cricket for my first Summer Term was an embarrassment, but I was supported sympathetically and we won seven out of ten matches. I had not played golf before coming to Summer Fields, and I played more like a cricketer than a golfer. Plus-fours were worn by many boys, but the nearest I got was wearing trousers tucked into long, woollen socks. This did not stop my winning the Dudley Medal, still a prized possession.

St Leonards, 1940

SUMMER FIELDS, ST. LEONARDS-ON-SEA, is amalgamating temporarily with its mother-school, Summer Fields, near Oxford. Mr. and Mrs. BARBER will accompany their boys there next term, which begins on Sept. 25th. It is hoped to reopen at St. Leonards as soon as possible after the War.

SUMMER FIELDS, ST. LEONARDS-ON-SEA.—Mr. and Mrs. E. K. Barber intend to reopen the School in its own premises for the Summer Term, 1945.

at Summer Fields near Oxford

3 Sept

Farnborough School,
Holme Park,
SONNING,
Berks.

Dear *Mr Garland*

As War has now broken out, I am writing to say that it is not possible for Farnborough School to carry on here.

Mr. Borgnis has been recalled to the Navy. I cannot count on the services of Mr. Wall or Mr. Mansfield for more than a term, if as much. Amalgamations of Schools, their buildings and their STAFFS are inevitable, and I think our best course is to go whilst choice is open to us.

I have made arrangements to transfer Farnborough, lock, stock and barrel to Summer Fields, Oxford - a school whose reputation I feel sure you know well. Mr. John Evans, the Headmaster, has been a personal friend of mine for 25 years. Mr. Pendlebury, Mr. Thomson and I will accompany the boys.

You will find Matron here

The fees, which incidentally are the same, will remain unaltered.

I feel that this is not only the best course to take, but that we are extremely lucky, at short notice, to have been able to make this arrangement with a school of which I have the highest opinion, and I feel sure that you will be more than satisfied by this arrangement.

Mr. Evans feels that the boys are better - in present conditions - at School, properly supervised and employed and is opening on Thursday, September *14*

I warmly agree with this course.

Mr. Pendlebury, or Mr. Thomson or I will be at Paddington to take the boys to Oxford by the 4.45. If you wish to communicate with me, my address is Summer Fields, Oxford.

Yours sincerely,

E. K. STEPHENSON.

I hope you will send him as a Boarder - he can come before the 14th if desired.

Above: Boys in 1944

Left: A letter from the headmaster of Farnborough School, Sonning, regarding its evacuation to Summer Fields, 1939

as usual. The sun never seemed to stop shining that summer. We bathed frequently in the Cherwell, wallowing in the mud. We had our Hay Feast, and occasionally even had classes out of doors.

There were difficulties posed by constant changes of staff as younger men were called up to fight. Indeed, Pat Savage went off to war in 1939, sadly to spend most of it in captivity. During that winter, other members of staff were called up, one by one, to be replaced by undergraduates or older men. This led to the appointment of some 'rummish characters', as Pat Savage later wrote:

I remember a retired brigadier who wore spats and was alleged to teach his French forms the technical terms used in roulette. Also, a non-practising clergyman who wrote letters of protest to his colleagues in green ink. There was the excellent Miss Walford, known as 'Micky', but she was a master, rather than a mistress, as she did Duty [i.e. took overall responsibility for the welfare of the boys for a specified period during the working day]. A classic remark of hers comes to mind: 'Don't mock me Davis, or I'll shake the liver out of you.' Bob James had a smart military moustache, but was, in fact, a conscientious objector. He was married to a Viennese wife called Lisl, and they lived in a caravan down in the Farm Fields with their daughters, who had botanical names like Bryony and Erica.

John Jolliffe (1944–7) remembers some of these wartime staff as 'mostly a dismal lot left behind for one reason or another':

There was a ferocious (and very anti-English) young Irishman called O'Connor, a rather vague, quite well-meaning brigadier with grey spats called Dickins and a fussy squeaky little man called Clayton. More fun was Mr James, a leftish conscientious objector with sandals, who lived in a caravan and encouraged the use of the rather good boys' library.

There were staffing difficulties, too, on the domestic side. A shortage of 'maids' was a constant problem, but the school somehow kept functioning through the valiant efforts of Gardner, the butler, 'a shadowy, sinister figure', and Miss Bell, the housekeeper (1932–45), who coped admirably with the complexities of food rationing.

Tom Allsop (1935–78), the school carpenter, the whole maintenance staff, the gardener, the groundsmen, the butler, the Matron, Miss Bell and all the maids worked speedily and tirelessly to construct effective blackout arrangements. Air raids constituted the main disruption, at least in the short term, but real hardships were few and the war became more of an inconvenience than a danger. In 1938, an air-raid shelter had been dug in the old shrubbery on the site now occupied by the older part of Bolton. Peter Fullerton (1938–43) recalls that it

Another evacuee, this time from Farnborough, was C. J. Slade (1939–40), later the Rt Hon. Sir Christopher Slade, who became Chairman of Governors in 1978:

In September 1939, my brother Julian and I viewed the prospect of a transfer to a much bigger, strange school with some misgivings. We need not have worried. John Evans and GB could not have given us a kinder and warmer welcome. My first few months at Summer Fields coincided with the period of the 'Phoney War'. I occupied a week in the Sanatorium at Newton by composing anti-Nazi verses of greater passion than elegance. However, until Hitler entered the Low Countries we were not very conscious of the war, except when we saw masters departing to join the Services, or returning to visit us, like Jimmy Bell resplendent in uniform. When the 'Phoney War' ended, GB told us that he did not expect the French to hold out much longer. I remember regarding such pessimism as unthinkable and almost unpatriotic, but he was proved too right. John Evans and GB did their best to keep things going

Summer Fields,

near Oxford

December 1940

We have so far been very fortunate with the Blitzkrieg, and only the odd bomb in the comparatively remote distance appears to have been dropped as far as we have been concerned.

The sirens have however functioned on several occasions, generally shortly before the bigger boys bedtime.

With a number of other people's sons we naturally do not completely ignore these sirens, and those not already in bed have gone to the shelter for a short time rather than stay in one room like the Chapel or New Room, and then gone to bed if all is quiet even if the 'All Clear' has not gone, a few adults only remaining up and about in case of emergency.

One cannot lay down a hard and fast rule satisfactory to meet all contingencies, and a decision has to be made every time.

We feel that sleep and health are the most important things and that the risk of illness from continual leaving warm beds is greater than the risk of being bombed, and we are happiest about the boys when they are all in bed and asleep.

Although the shelter is a good one and the boys seem to like it, they cannot sleep there properly, and some alarms have lasted most of the night.

We hope to do what is best whatever may happen, but your views on this difficult point will be welcome.

J F E

N.B. EAR PLUGS You should apply to your A.R.P. Warden for your boy's Ear Plugs, which will be supplied free of charge.

If your boy's gas mask has not been fitted with the green contex, we advise consulting your A.R.P. Warden, who will carry out the fitting for you.

'was long and narrow, with wooden benches on each side, and a mighty steel door which shut with a loud clang. There was dim lighting inside and it was always cold and damp from the dripping walls.'

After initial periods in the shelter during night alarms, the boys were kept in bed unless things became too hot, which they never really did, 'the risk of their catching pneumonia being as great as their being hit'. Between 1940 and 1941, the siren often sounded at about 6pm. Then the boys trooped to the shelter. There, work carried on. The end compartment was reserved for Fifth Form, who patiently studied their *Borva Notes*, before the treat of a Wodehouse story. The alerts ceased after 1941 and the shelter was then hardly used. Oxford was reputedly on the list for the famous Baedeker Raids, but these never came to the city. Indeed, Oxford was lucky and only one bomb, and that a dud, fell within ten miles of the school.

Heating in school buildings wasn't up to much even pre-war. There was no central heating except in hall and chapel. There were coal fires in class rooms but these were not lit until November and coal rationing kept them small. 'We started fires on Monday morning (2 November 1942) and about time too! It is freezing here in the mornings. We are having only two baths a week.' None of the dormitories was heated at all. In the Lent terms many of us had chilblains on our fingers despite wearing mittens, which hurt when cold and itched like mad in bed at night. And we had perpetual runny noses and sodden cotton handkerchiefs – there were no Kleenexes!

Peter Fullerton (1938–43)

Packing Instructions for Hand-bag.

ALL TERMS.

1 pair Pyjamas.
1 pair Bedroom Slippers.
1 pair House Shoes.
1 Brush and 1 Comb.
Bible and Prayer Book.
2 Handkerchiefs.
Washing material in Sponge Bag.
Health Certificate
Ration Book.
Identity Card.
Trunk Keys.

7/41

TERM *Michaelmas*
Name KNOWLES. M.   No. 94

Summer Fields
OXFORD

CLOTHES LIST

MEMORANDA

i. Every article to be plainly marked with full name and school number with Cash's tape in red. Not only suits, linen, etc., but everything mentioned on the list—especially Boots, Shoes, Sponges, Combs—all of which generally require re-marking each vacation. Please do not use marking ink.

ii. Each boy is required to bring back with him a Hand-bag, containing sufficient articles for the first night.

iii. It is particularly requested that this list be adhered to and that *all* clothes may be sent back with the boys at the *beginning* of term. The clothes list must be included in the trunk.

iv. Knickerbockers are worn with Tweeds, and Long Trousers with Grey Flannels for the Two Winter Terms on week days, Long Trousers on Sundays. In the Summer Term Long Trousers are worn on Week-days and on Sundays.

v. It is requested that no sweets or eatables of any kind may be brought back to school, or sent to the boys during the Term. The only exception to this rule is a cake (not too rich) for birthdays.

The School Outfitters, Messrs. BILLINGS & EDMONDS LTD., 4, Princes Street, Hanover Square, W.1, can supply all the articles on the clothes list. All enquiries with regard to outfit, colours and patterns should be made to them.

In a paradoxical way, the war was good for the boys. It strengthened friendship bonds, bringing out the best in pupils' characters as they consoled each other in times of grief and maintained scrupulous levels of honesty.

Peter Fullerton (1938–43) wrote over two hundred letters home during the war, all of which were kept. They offer a clear view of its impact on school life. In the course of the following account he quotes from this correspondence, indicated by single inverted commas, with dates in parentheses:

For those of us at Summer Fields during the Second World War, the war itself had remarkably little impact on our daily lives. We were shielded by a school routine which barely changed. Other prep schools were not so lucky and were evacuated. We were joined successively by Farnborough, then our sister school Summer Fields, St Leonards and St Cyprian's. This kept our numbers up because about thirty boys left the school at, or soon after, the outbreak of war, most going to America. The boys who came in from other schools were of all ages. There was a bit of teasing about some of them being 'oiks' but no bullying, and we soon made good friends amongst our contemporaries.

There were no transistor radios in those days so we seldom heard the BBC news. But I shared a newspaper with Timothy Brinton (1939–42). We read, almost with disbelief, of the catastrophes of the early part of the war – the collapse of France, Dunkirk and the fall of Singapore. We then followed intently on our maps the long campaign in North Africa with its ding-dong succession of advances and retreats by the Eighth Army.

Some fathers were already in the armed services or were called up. I heard that one boy, one of my best friends, had lost his father, a Captain RN. He was brave about it and we did our best to console him. 'Last week we had an ARP drill. It was great fun and we are going to put our gas masks on in the next one' (8 October 1939).

Nothing then happened until June 1940, just before the beginning of the London Blitz. We could hear the wail of the air-raid siren in Summertown loud and clear. 'On Monday night, we had an air raid which lasted about three quarters of an hour. We were suddenly woken up by Father Gray. We realised at once what was happening. I must say everybody behaved very well and after waiting five minutes we all went down to the air-raid shelter. We were given an extra hour in bed next morning and missed first period. On Tuesday we also had an air raid which lasted nearly four hours! We all got terribly bored in the shelter and there was terrific cheering when finally the 'All-Clear' went. The next morning we were allowed to sleep until eleven o'clock! As we had missed breakfast we had a three-course lunch which was very nice. We have not had any more air raids this week thank goodness' (30 June 1940).

There were more air raids the following term in September and October. 'We had two air raids last week, one in the middle of work in the afternoon and one in the middle of the night. But we did not go down to the shelter because Mr Evans said that it would probably be unnecessary. The 'All-Clear' sounded half an hour later' (6 October 1940). We always cheered when we heard the long single high-pitched hum of the 'All-Clear' as opposed to the wailing warning siren. More air raids followed. 'We had three air raids last week, one in the middle of third period, the other in the middle of the night, and the last in the evening. We were doing choir practice at the time and we drowned out the sirens! It lasted an hour and a quarter. Several bombs were dropped round Abingdon and we could hear a lot of AA fire. We were going to have a Kinema that night but it had to be put off' (27 October 1940).

Oxford city was not bombed by the Luftwaffe but some bombs were dropped on the Cowley motor works. The German bombing in the Oxford area stopped at the end of 1940 when Hitler turned his attention to the Russian front. But the blackout at night continued right through the war, with strict attention to no chinks of light being visible outside the school buildings.

With many fathers on active service, Dunkirk was the worst time of the war for some boys. But most were safe, apart from one Old Boy unfortunately killed during the bombing of Rotterdam. There was general anxiety, but the school carried on. After Alamein, 'when we were allowed to ring the school bell, silent since Dunkirk', things began to improve. The

Normandy Landings of 1944 brought an expectation of victory. When it came, in May 1945, meringues were served on VE Day.

After the war, the air-raid shelter served as an exciting playground for the boys, as remembered by Charlie Palmer (1976–80). It became a place for great fun, although one day, 'Maggot hopped out of a game with a six-inch nail sticking up clean through his foot. "Oh dear, I do hope I don't miss the rugby season," he remarked to Matron.'

In general the war was experienced from a distance. John Jolliffe (1944–7) remembers the excitement of the summer of 1944, as he and others followed the fortunes of the Normandy Landings via the *Daily Telegraph*. However, there were a few occasions when the boys had first-hand glimpses of the conflict. For instance, on the night of 14 November 1940, they could have seen the glow on the horizon, as 515 German bombers, on Operation Moonlight Sonata, rained down upon Coventry first phosphorus markers, then nearly 600 tons of high-explosive bombs and thousands of incendiaries, causing massive destruction of buildings and the deaths of 568 civilians. In the summer of 1944, Peter Maitland (1944–8) remembers 'looking out of my dormitory window to see the planes and gliders flying over for D-Day', while Reggie Norton (1943–5) recalls 'being woken up by hundreds of bombers flying out to bomb Germany'.

However, it was in May 1941 that Summerfieldians had their closest experience of the war. This involved the aircraft type which had dropped the first RAF bombs on a German target. Peter Fullerton (1938–43) takes up the story again.

Last Sunday afternoon we had a very exciting time. A Whitley bomber crashed only a quarter of a mile away. The first I saw of it was that it was coming down at an angle of 45 degrees. It was only 500 feet when it started to dive and when it hit the ground there was an awful grinding noise and it went up in sheets of flame. Three of the crew of four were killed, but the rear gunner managed to jump out when it was 20 feet from the ground. He broke his leg but was otherwise uninjured.

In May 1943, Reggie Norton, a St Leonards boy who returned there when the school reopened in 1945, arrived at Summer Fields fresh from Gibraltar where his father worked. He nearly did not make it, 'as the next flight on June 1st was shot down by the Germans'. Reggie spoke three languages, Spanish, Portuguese and English, his weakest. As tales of

Above: Letter home from Martin Knowles (1941–5)

Right: The Second World War Memorial in the chapel

THEIR NAME
LIVETH

1939 - 1945

F. A. LEE-NORMAN
H. S. L. LEVESON
R. M. V. LYSAGHT
J. LYTTELTON
D. G. MADDEN
H. A. N. MANDER
J. N. McGRIGOR
N. S. MERPETT
B. H. MIDDLETON
A. W. D. MILLER
F. H. MORLEY
H. L. MOSSELMANS
R. D. NAPIER
H. C. NICHOL-
        SMITH
T. C. PETO-
        LINDSAY
J. PITMAN
L. C. PITMAN
N. H. S. RATHBONE
L. D. RAWNSLEY
W. G. READER

R. A. RENDER
G. REYS WILLIAMS
E. P. S. RUSSELL
J. B. RUSSELL
R. L. S. RUSSELL
S. H. M. RUSSELL
P. D. SANDBACH
P. H. SHAW STEWART
E. H. P. SLESSOR
E. K. SQUIRES
A. J. R. STEELE
I. A. L. STEWART
J. A. SWANSON
G. S. W. TALBOT
R. E. M. THACKERAY
H. E. R. TORIN
R. C. S. TRAILL
G. A. WELLS
F. H. WITTS
G. W. WADHAM
J. W. FAWCUS
R. H. GREGORY

German spies were again rife among the boys, Reggie, with his foreign accent, was regarded with deep suspicion and occasionally had a tough time:

> Summer Fields in wartime was a bit of a shock though I did write home that I liked the food! I think that for more than a week or two after arriving I cried myself to sleep as I really missed my family. However, the fact that my English was probably spoken with a Spanish accent resulted in my being bullied. I was called 'dago' and was generally given a bad time. But as I was nine and tough, I gave back as much as I got. I remember giving a boy a black eye after I'd thrown a conker at him! I also asked Mr Evans, the Headmaster, for my passport to show them I was British. I became more popular when I received large tins of Mackintosh sweets from my father and threw handfuls on the floor for the boys to scramble for!
>
> At night when we went to the dormitory I remember that at one point we thought a German parachutist might be landing on the school grounds. We looked out of the window to keep an eye on things. We did see someone, but it must have been a master. I also remember at night-time in the dormitory eating peppermint toothpaste. Once you had used up your sweet rations, this was the only thing there was!

The war inspired a number of incidents. Gregory Baker, who went on to Eton in 1943, remembers, in the summer of 1940, 'being herded by some thuggish thirteen-year-olds, into the cricket nets, along with most of the junior boys and beaten up with cricket stumps'. This brutish gang was the so-called 'Panzer Corps'. Denys Moylan (1939–45) also recalls this 'group of senior boys, not, I think, Scholarship material', who managed to herd almost the whole school into the 1st XI nets. GB came down like the wrath of God and they melted into the crowd. One member of the 'Corps' was 'a big lad for his age, with definite signs of a moustache.'

In 1945, except for VE Day, it was downhill all the way. Two very severe winters meant that one was freezing cold and hungry all the time. There were power cuts which made things worse and not surprisingly everyone seemed to be in a bad temper. The frequent bad temper of several of the masters was often infectious, and made the boys even nastier to each other than they would have been otherwise. One agreeable respite was community singing in the gym.

John Jolliffe (1944–7)

Field Marshal the 1st Earl Wavell, PC, GCB, GCSI, GCIE, CMG, MC (1883–1950), SF 1893–6

For most modern Summerfieldians, 'Wavell' immediately signifies not one of the most able military commanders of his day, but the place where they study Science, Art, Design and Technology and ICT in the teaching block bearing his name.

But as a soldier and administrator, Wavell enjoyed an impressive career. He was Commander-in-Chief in the Middle East (1939–41), where he conducted skilful campaigns against numerically superior German and Italian troops. He was Commander-in-Chief in India (1941) and Supreme Commander South East Asia (1942). From 1943 to 1947, Wavell served as Viceroy of India.

Just after his tenth birthday, Wavell arrived at Summer Fields. Educated by governesses at home, he had never been away to school before, but he showed little sign of homesickness. A correspondent noted:

> Aged ten, Wavell was a sturdy, quiet-mannered boy, a trifle small for his age, handsome and with a quick, shrewd gleam of humour in his eyes. He never gave the slightest sign of being homesick; indeed, there was a family legend that as soon as he had arrived at Summer Fields, he was introduced to a group of boys, and began to play with them, and after a few minutes strolled over to his parents, observing. 'You can go now. I shall be quite all right.'

John Connell, writing of Wavell at Summer Fields, notes that 'of his strong spirit of independence, there can be no doubt; nor of his intellectual ability; nor of his physical courage'.

Wavell excelled academically at Summer Fields under a spartan regime steeped in Classics. A school report shows him top of the class in Greek, Latin Translation, Latin Composition, Maths and English and second in French. His prodigious memory helped him. He always found it easy to remember huge swathes of poetry. Indeed, his anthology, *Other Men's Flowers*, consists entirely of the works he knew by heart. Wavell also had

Above: Wavell as a young Scholar at Winchester

Below: Wavell the Commander, Singapore 1942

powers of concentration and detachment rare in someone so young. He showed 'pluck', too, on the games field. He captained the 2nd XI at cricket. 'Very good at football,' said another report, 'most determined tackler; an indefatigable player and a pleasure to watch.'

Wavell was a reserved boy. Of himself, he wrote: 'I must have been an unattractive boy, very self-centred and rather bumptious, but clever enough to keep out of trouble and on the right side of people.'

A contemporary at Summer Fields, Robert Dundas (1894–97), later a Classics don at Christ Church, Oxford, wrote of Wavell in 1952:

> When I was ten he was my first and greatest schoolboy hero: a very solid little boy, with resolution and a low centre of gravity and very hard to knock over at football. He went to Winchester and came down a term or two after he had left SF. I stood at the door of Fifth Form and gazed at him in mute admiration. He observed, quite kindly, 'Young Dundas, I'm not a peepshow.' I retired a little dashed, but still mute and still adoring.

Wavell was placed seventh on the roll at Winchester. Dr Williams wrote to his father, 'I fully trust that, please God, he is going to make a good – perhaps great – man.' Wavell's view of himself, though, was pragmatic:

> I have always taken examinations easily and they have never worried me and I have therefore probably gained places above my

Wavell: man of letters, 1944

real merit. I was not popular with my contemporaries and rather lonely. There was too much ego in my cosmos.

In military terms, Wavell was overwhelmed both in North Africa by Rommel and by the Japanese in the Far East. It has been alleged that he lacked sufficient ruthlessness. However, there can be few commanders in history who have been given such gargantuan tasks without adequate provision of men and resources. Wavell's greatness lies in damage limitation. His relationship with Churchill always remained uneasy, but Wavell never blamed his men for any military reverse. As he wrote in 1943: 'I should like to pay tribute to the British soldier; he has shown himself in this war the finest all-round fighting man in the world.'

As Viceroy of India, Wavell did his best, acutely aware of the ebbing strength of the Raj. As a soldier, for all his misfortunes in the Second World War, his reputation at its end stood as high as those of any of his contemporaries. At Summer Fields, in 2014, Wavell's name is daily on the lips of virtually every boy. Thus he lives on.

The Second World War also inspired a good number of stories, many of them from the indomitable Willy Pryor (1947–52; staff 1969–99), who, of course, was not actually at Summer Fields during the war... The Earl of Kinnoull, as Viscount Dupplin (1971–5), remembers Willy

regaling us with stories of Summer Fields during the war when he had been there. The Battle of Britain film was very new and we all thought that the Luftwaffe Stukas must have attacked Summer Fields at some point. Later, when on a run with Willy in the Far Fields, I tripped over a lump of metal, which was then unearthed and identified as a piece of a Stuka by boys and Mr Pryor alike. Later that term, in the Sports Day exhibition, it was displayed and I was extra proud, being noted as the discoverer. I led my parents to it and we gazed at it in wonder. Then another parent behind said to his wife, 'Amazing... it looks just like a squashed bucket,' which of course it was, as we could suddenly see!

In general, the war years passed lightly over Summer Fields. But there was no light passing for those directing the conflict. One of its supreme directors was Field Marshal the Earl Wavell, educated at Sandhurst, Winchester College and Summer Fields.

Wavell's son, Major Archibald J. Wavell, MC (1925–9), joined the Black Watch and, despite having lost an arm in Burma, volunteered to go to Kenya when the Mau Mau conflict broke out. He was mortally wounded on Christmas Eve, 1953, while defending his camp under fire.

Summer Fields remains proud to have its Old Boys among modern military personnel. The spirit of service to the country continues, thus maintaining an important tradition. It is to be hoped, though, that no more will have to make the ultimate sacrifice in the line of duty.

Chris Sparrow pointing out Field Marshal Wavell's son, Archibald (SF 1925–9), at the National Memorial Arboretum, 2012

chapter three

1975–2014
Entering a New Age

Energy and Modernity

Nigel Talbot Rice, Headmaster, 1975–97

One of the advantages of becoming Headmaster from within the school is that you already have some idea of the priorities which need to be tackled in the next few years. For many years the Royal Mail had been requesting Pat Savage to remove the 'Near' Oxford in the school's address as this meant that our post would be included amongst that of outlying villages. Summer Fields being truly a part of Oxford, it was felt to be perfectly appropriate to comply, so this became the first noticeable but minor change of the new regime. Far more importantly, Nick Aldridge was persuaded to return to his old school where he had been so successful both as a boy and as a young teacher in the 1960s, and on Jimmy Bell's retirement in 1978, Nick took over as Assistant Headmaster and also the vital role of Master of Fifth Form.

Summer Fields had been very fortunate in the buildings that the Maclaren and Williams families had acquired or provided in the late nineteenth and early twentieth centuries, and they built on a grand scale. Little major building had been undertaken since then, so it was clear in 1975 that Summer Fields should not rest on its laurels but prepare for the twenty-first century in all areas of school life, not least through the provision of further first-class buildings. To this end, four appeals were launched in 1977, 1984, 1989 and 1994, as a result of which a formidable building campaign was undertaken, funded largely by the

The indoor swimming pool, opened by HRH the Duchess of Gloucester, 24 May 1985

wonderful generosity of parents and the school's own resources, including funds from the sale of Front Lodge and sixteen acres of farmland.

The old Front Lodge was a nineteenth-century villa situated just within the gates at the Banbury Road end of the school drive. This was an utterly charming house, pervaded by an atmosphere that must have been created over many years by the spirits of people at peace with themselves. It was a house which embraced you with a quiet calm as soon as you entered. Into this delightful place came Nick Aldridge, a young man who had just left Eton and was waiting to go up to Cambridge. He was lean and spindly, gangling but by no means gauche. He had an inherent charm and a sophisticated wit way beyond his years, but there was also an endearingly boyish quality about him.

David Kidd-May (1955–2000)

In 1974 there were 180 boys in the school, but this number was no longer financially viable – indeed the accounts for the academic year 1974–5 showed a deficit of well over £2,000, a not inconsiderable sum in those days. This situation could not continue, and I made a personal undertaking that there would be no more deficits during my tenure as Headmaster. By 1997, the numbers had increased from 180 to 256, including twelve day boys, with the appropriate new buildings and facilities in place to cope with this expansion.

Above: The school roll of 1974. The school numbered 180 boys

Left and below: The gymnasium in the 1930s and in the 1960s, prior to its extension and redevelopment

Famous old boy opens new hall

The most famous living old boy of Summer Fields School, Oxford, returned to his former prep school after 76 years to open a new complex named in his honour.

Mr Harold Macmillan, aged 85, unveiled a plaque in the Macmillan Hall which gives the 115-year-old school a theatre, cinema, assembly, music and gym facilities.

He spoke of "the high tribute" of having the building named after him, and considered it a greater honour than the Gladstone bag named after another prime minister — "some obsolescent form of luggage mouldering away in an attic."

Mr Macmillan told how Summertown was a little village surrounded by fields when he was a schoolboy and spoke of the horsedrawn bus which used to take him from Oxford Station to Summer Fields.

The two greatest changes in life since his youth were traffic and money, he said. The streets were once full of horsedrawn vehicles and coins were made of real gold and silver.

Many members of Mr Macmillan's family have attended Summer Fields. His great-grandson is due to start in a few years' time.

Above: Harold Macmillan opening 'Macmillan'. *Oxford Times*, 21 December 1979

Below: Orchestral practice in Macmillan during the 1990s

Some of the old guard felt that the school was becoming too large, but most governors realised that it was better to have too many boys than not enough! Some limits were imposed and then extended. During this debate I used to joke that I risked being the only prep-school Head to be sacked for having too many boys in the school! As a result of this increase, in the late 1980s and 1990s Summer Fields bucked the trend against eight-year-old boarding places and was still turning away first-year boarders as late as 1997.

Whilst facilities and buildings have become increasingly important to prospective parents, it is of course the quality of the staff and the school's general reputation that ensures its ongoing success. A thorough in-house review of academic standards was undertaken in 1976 and a personal tutorial system introduced to improve the overall pastoral care. Under the new regime discipline was tightened up, the working day slightly shortened and everyone, boys and staff alike, were expected to work harder. In 1978 some old stalwarts retired, including Jimmy Bell, Philip Johnstone and Harold Hartley, and new, young blood arrived, helping to reinvigorate all areas of school life.

Of course there is much more to a good prep school than excellent academic and sporting results, and far greater emphasis was given to Music (under David Langdon's brilliant organisation), Art (run by the inspirational Judith Lane) and Drama, which flourished under the many enthusiastic young staff keen to produce a wide variety of plays and musicals. Indeed, some production for juniors or seniors was put on nearly every term. Although I consider myself the most unmusical Headmaster in the country, the importance of good music facilities cannot be overstated. Thus in 1979, Harold Macmillan opened the converted and extended gym, which included a new music centre and twenty-two music practice and teaching rooms, as well as a theatre gallery. Now known as Macmillan, the building was further enhanced in 1994 by a full conversion into a complete theatre, with side galleries similar to those at the Swan Theatre in Stratford. Tiered and padded bench seating was also installed throughout, including the gallery above the music centre, so the original 1898 gym was transformed into a most attractive theatre and concert venue.

Another early change was the abandonment of sports jackets, ties and old-fashioned grey flannels for everyday wear. These were replaced by a more informal Guernsey, aertex shirt in the requisite League colour and corduroy trousers. The best outfit (No. 1s) was to be sports jacket (blazers for prefects) and

League ties, mainly worn for special occasions and Leave-Outs. These exeats had been introduced by Pat Savage to enable the boys to go home for a night, but they were now extended to two, or occasionally three. Later, new exeats, known as Single and Double Credits, were added, in order to increase the contact between home and school during term-time. All boys were entitled to Credits, although for serious misdemeanours they could be forfeited.

As contact between home and school increased, parents' evenings were introduced to give the opportunity for more personal communication between teaching staff and parents, who were no longer considered 'a necessary evil' (a description used by one Headmaster many years ago). Initially, the American habit of labelling parents and staff was resisted, but after witnessing some occasional confusion in distinguishing one from the other, badges were finally introduced.

The most significant difference between then and now was the triangular relationship between staff, boys and parents... Not only do the boys go home more often, but they are in constant touch, in person or electronically, with their parents, who are in everyday evidence at the school. In 1955 it would have been a very rare sight to see a parent at a match.

David Kidd-May (1955–2000)

I was the first married Headmaster since 1939 and in a community like Summer Fields the role of the Headmaster's wife is both vital and often unacknowledged. She must be ever there to support her husband in the demanding job of running the school. In this respect I was extremely fortunate and it is only fair, at this point, to pay tribute to Joanna for the central part she played. Much was involved and nothing specified: meeting and showing parents and visitors around the school, entertaining VIPs and governors, arranging flowers, liaising with Housemothers over a host of daily matters, reading to the First Years at Beech House, occasionally comforting staff in times of personal trouble and, often, just being a woman in a predominantly male world and an 'unschooly' figure to whom both boys and staff knew they could turn at any time if ever they felt the need. All this Jo took on at the age of only twenty-eight. She grasped the nettle without hesitation and over the ensuing years her contribution to the school made a world of difference to the quality of life there.

On becoming Assistant Headmaster in 1971, I was granted permission by the governors to build Beech House, and Joanna became Housemother there to ten of the youngest boys who lived in a homely atmosphere on the top floor. At that stage we

Beech House
in 1972

had two daughters, increasing to four by 1977 and followed by a son in 1982. When Helena was born in 1977, not even Nick Aldridge could work out when the last child had been born to a current Headmaster of Summer Fields, but Samuel's birth provided an excuse for celebrations as he was definitely the first son born to a Headmaster *in situ*.

Like most prep schools Summer Fields had traditionally been a very bachelor establishment, but gradually more staff married and eventually all Lodges except Lower House had married couples in charge and their wives did a tremendous job of making Lodge life more like home. Borva was soon turned from a sanatorium into another new-boy Lodge. Rupert and Di McNeile were appointed to run it, and in due course the house was extended to accommodate twenty-two new boys. Likewise Cottage, with David and Jo Kidd-May in charge, was extended to house another member of staff and a second staircase was added in the interests of fire safety. In time Newton and Mayfield were also modernised and a new Lodge (Front Lodge) added on to Old Lodge. House was gutted and a completely new staircase installed just off the Lobby. Two new classroom

Joanna and Nigel
Talbot Rice in 1968

Views of the school in 2003, **above**, and prior to the building of the Sports Hall, **right**

blocks, called Bolton *ma*. and Bolton *mi*. after GB, were built consecutively, which enabled all full-time teaching staff to have their own classroom and embellish it as they pleased with posters and examples of boys' work – a very welcome improvement all round.

One very generous parent, supported by an additional small group of other parents, enabled us to build a splendid indoor swimming pool which was a great asset throughout the year. The Wavell Centre, named after the famous OS Field Marshal and catering for Art, Science, Computing and CDT, was opened in 1991 by Douglas Hurd, then Foreign Secretary. This replaced the old carpentry shop and squash court. Compensation for the loss of the court was made in 1994 with the building of a new Sports Hall, which provided three squash courts, two Eton Fives courts, a rifle range and central area for basketball, indoor tennis, football and hockey, indoor cricket nets, as well as fencing and judo, which had become increasingly popular. This

Below left: The inauguration of the indoor pool, May 1985

Below: A letter to the school from Prime Minister Margaret Thatcher on the opening of the Wavell Centre, 1991

Sports Hall is a magnificent facility, sunk one level into the ground to lessen the external visual impact and meld with the existing architectural skyline. It has a stone amphitheatre and climbing wall at the Beech House end.

> *There have been, of course, enormous structural changes. When I arrived, there was no indoor or open-air pool. Swimming was in the river, in the Deep End, where there was a diving platform, and the Shallow End was where boys learnt to swim in a harness at the end of a kind of stout fishing-line and rod wielded by kindly Chippy.*
>
> David Kidd-May (1955–2000)

10 DOWNING STREET
LONDON SW1A 2AA

THE PRIME MINISTER

    I am delighted to send you, through Douglas Hurd, my greetings and congratulations on the opening of Summer Fields' new Science, Art and Technology Centre.

    I am especially pleased that it has been named after Lord Wavell. In Lord Wavell and Harold Macmillan, you have two old boys who were shining examples of men, outstanding in their own profession but whose knowledge, experience and sympathies went far beyond. Wavell was a first class soldier. But I like to think of Wavell, the young subaltern, tramping across the South African veldt or, later in life, riding across the plains of India, declaiming the poetry which he collected and bequeathed to generations of lovers of the English language. He was too modest in rating his own achievement because he did far more than gather other men's flowers. He put into that book his own love of literature, his experience and his wisdom and those qualities continue to shine through, half a century later.

    We need to equip ourselves for an age of high technology but all our recent experience has shown the value of breadth of knowledge as well as depth of knowledge. Your new Centre will provide that. I am sorry that I could not be with you at its opening but I wish it every success and success to all those who work and learn in it.

Left: Science labs in the 1970s

Below: The Wavell Technology Centre in 2006

The changing rooms in 1995

As the numbers increased it became necessary to enlarge the chapel, which was extended westwards with a gallery upstairs and a dayroom beneath which could be quickly converted to extend chapel seating as required. When the indoor pool was built the organ and vestry were moved from north to south to make room for new changing rooms, the Vins already having been rebuilt and modernised. The conversion and provision of sufficient married and bachelor accommodation, enabling nearly all staff to live on site – an enormous bonus for a boarding prep school – completes the alterations and building work undertaken from 1975 to 1997.

Right and below: The Farm before and after conversion

The chapel had always been at the heart of the school, and this emphasis continued. However, some changes were made. Weekday Evensong was abandoned, while the working day began with a brief form of worship – a hymn, Bible reading and prayers – and the boys themselves and various staff began to play a greater role in chapel services. During these years there were three Chaplains, Fred King (1975–80), Fergus Capie (1980–90) and Bryan Gadd (1990–2001), and we had frequent visiting preachers for Sunday services, including many public-school Headmasters. Willy Pryor (1947–52; staff 1969–99) sometimes preached, and it was a safe bet that he would contrive to mention at least one of his many relatives during his sermon. Confirmation, conducted for many years by Bishop Cartwright, a governor, continued to be offered to the senior boys, many of whom found the more intimate and personal preparation for this sacrament more appropriate at prep-school age.

There were many achievements both in and out of the classroom in the period 1975–97. On the academic front, very few failed at Common Entrance, despite most public schools, and Eton in particular, gradually raising their pass mark. Eton has traditionally been the destination favoured by SF parents. For example in 1997, thirty out of forty-nine leavers went to Eton, eight to Radley and the remaining eleven to Winchester, Harrow, Charterhouse, Rugby, Stowe, St Edward's and Fettes.

The number of scholarships steadily increased, with 1989 witnessing the longest list of public-school awards for sixty years. This was followed by three exceptional years, 1991–3, with seventeen awards to Eton alone. In fact, during the seven-year period from 1990 to 1997, Summerfieldians won top scholarships to Eton, Harrow, Radley and St Edward's, including a top music award to Eton. It is also worth noting that despite the perception that Summer Fields was an academic hothouse, those who really knew the school realised this was far from the case, recognising its mixed-ability intake and wide programme of extracurricular activities.

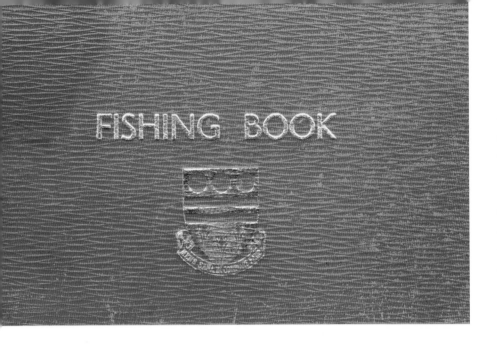

Sport certainly played an important, but not excessive, part in the life of the school and many boys represented SF in the major games: football, rugby and cricket. However, other sports such as athletics, hockey, golf, tennis, judo, fencing, squash, fives and shooting were also increasingly available. Encouragement was given to a wide variety of outdoor activities such as fishing, camping, gardening and orienteering, as well as a score of indoor clubs and societies. Debating was given a new lease of life and flourished on Saturday evenings, as was Scottish dancing which prompted regular, popular 'fixtures' with Tudor Hall. A summer-term Expedition Day was established in 1977, when the whole school and staff went off for the day to places of cultural or educational interest. This quickly became a well-established tradition. During the long summer holidays the school began a lucrative let to a non-residential language school, the proceeds of which helped over the years to provide at least one new classroom block and improvements to existing facilities.

It was the very generous gift of a parent who invited a group of senior boys to a shoot at their Gloucestershire estate. We arrived suitably wrapped up in wellies, wax jackets and flat caps, brimming with nervous excitement, nobody quite sure what to expect. I remember the safety briefing, 'Keep your eyes open!'; I remember petting the dogs and being told not to as they were working; I don't remember any birds actually being shot!

At the end of the afternoon we turned to head home. We piled into the school minibus and drove along the farm track towards the main road. After the day's rain, the track had become a quagmire and the minibus got stuck halfway up a hill, and started to slide. The boys jumped out and helped to push, thrilled with the drama of the spraying mud and tyre smoke.

Soon we were told to abandon the stricken minibus and instead we enjoyed an impromptu swim in the pool at the house, whilst a tractor was found. Sadly the vehicle was eventually freed and our hopes of having to stay the night in luxury were dashed!

Marcus Hannah (1987–92)

From the Reverend William Pryor.

October 1st 1998.

Elm Tree Cottage,
Summer Fields,
Oxford.
OX2 7EN

Dear Parents,

Once again we have got the Boys' Gardens re – allotted in record time in order to take in the new influx of New Boys, and are well ahead with the tidying up of the growth of the summer holidays, and well into the cultivation for next year. From now on is the best time for manuring, and planting biennials, perennials and even annuals in the flower gardens, so may I suggest a few for planting now for flowering next Spring and Summer. For Spring, Bulbs, Forget – me – nots and Wall flowers make a colourful display, but they should be interplanted with flowers that make a good show on Sports Day when all the competitions reach their climax, and the Boys' Gardens have their Open Day. . So Pinks, Carnations and Sweet Williams; Canterbury Bells both Biennial and Perennial; Lupins, Foxgloves, Delphiniums and even Lilies can steal the show. With our recent mild winters, normal annual seeds like Marigolds, Cornflowers and Escholzias have over – wintered successfully!

In my time as a boy here, Head Gardeners were despatched in chauffeur driven Bentleys to add

Gardening

Gardening has always been popular at Summer Fields. Roger Jacques took over the boys' gardens in 1925. They were started in 1914, when a strip of land was ploughed and divided into sixteen plots. Each plot formed a garden for two or three boys. It was suggested initially that flowers should be grown in the front parts, with radishes, lettuces and mustard cress sown in the back beds. Until recently (and long after his retirement), the gardens were run in his inimitable way by Willy Pryor.

Care of the gardens has since passed into the hands of Clare Pollard via Bill Bailey and Ollie Bishop. The boys continue to work their plots, which some unkind souls have likened to graves. However, there is no doubt that these 'graves' offer learning, exercise, satisfaction and relaxation for many groups of boys. Parental input to these horticultural activities is not unknown. An added incentive is winning the Bruce Cup (for beginners), the Purchas Trophy, or the coveted Silver Trowel and Fork, since converted into an intriguing tool called a 'spork', which annually mystifies the Guest of Honour at summer prize-giving when called upon to award it. Peter Fullerton (1938–43) lavished hours of attention on his garden, growing vegetables to support the 'Dig for Victory' campaign for home-grown food and competing for 'the garden prize at the end of the summer term – a consolation to those of us who were no good at cricket'. Edward Mynors (1955–60) remembers:

> The garden which my two older brothers had looked after during their time at the school was passed on down the family, though we mainly grew salad vegetables to supplement our diet. Mind you, we did plant our own vegetables unlike some of the gardens which were planted by chauffeurs at the beginning of term!

During the 1920s and 1930s, the criteria for garden excellence included 'brightness', 'neatness' and 'best laid out'. Although, in the words of Francis Bacon, gardening ought to be 'the greatest refreshment to the spirits of man' and 'the purest of human pleasures', at Summer Fields it could sometimes turn nasty!

Nobody would ever have expected the gardening club to be a *Mafioso* organisation, but I always remember shortly after winning the Bruce Trophy as a nine-year-old, two previous winners of the main Purchas Trophy and the Silver Trowel and Fork, approaching me like a pair of Krays and quietly threatening me with severe violence if I didn't back off and let them win it again. The conversation went like this.

M and B (the boys in question): 'So you're the boy who won the Bruce Cup eh?'

Self: 'Yes that's right.'

M and B: 'You like gardening, do you?'

Self (still thinking how kind of them to take the time): 'Yes, thank you I'm really enjoying it!'

M and B: 'Well I don't know who you think you are but we won the Purchas Cup last year and we want to win it again, so I wouldn't try too hard any more if I were you, or else – do you see what we mean?'

Self (reeling from the shock, but passions rising as these clearly experienced operators walked off): '&**&&*&$$' or something equivalent to a nine-year-old's version of the curses Captain Haddock utters in the *Tintin* books.

I am glad to say that this really made me more determined than ever. I then won the Silver Trowel and Fork for the next three years in a row – my only ever hat trick.

Dominic Parr (1981–6)

Wombling with Willy Pryor – formerly a popular hobby

Dancing

The dancing and Scottish dancing 'fixtures' 'against' schools such as Downe House and Tudor Hall generate great excitement among today's boys. Contacts are made or renewed with friends' sisters or friends of their friends. Senior boys giggle, huddle or tease one another in dormitories, corridors and even classrooms. There is nothing new in any of this. Before the First World War, dancing classes were held in the gym and boys were prepared, according to Evelyn Cobb (1909–14) 'under the astonishing direction of M. de Gautier whose antics in white gloves with fan would have surprised the modern Sylvesters'.

But there was a problem. It was GB who, completely untypically, started the annual fixture with Greycotes. 'Is the match against the girls' school at home or away this year, Sir?' The problem, of course, had been, no girls. For many years prior to this, as Nick Aldridge writes, 'Boys had been steering one another round the French-chalked dining-room floor on Thursday afternoons to the tinkling strains of the accompanist, while Miss Lane intoned, "And – left, right, together: right, left, together…", and now at last there seemed to be some point to it.'

Such was the status of dancing that no fewer than six 'Dancing Prizes' were awarded to boys in 1930!

The 'Squish'– the traditional escorted train journey to and from London at the start and end of term – ceased. The vast majority of parents came to prefer collecting and delivering their son by car, and it was clear that at Half Term and Leave-Outs a hired coach direct from the school to central London would be quicker and more convenient. More convenient, yes, but the potential for great drama was reduced. For some years, David Kidd-May (1955–2000) had the honour of being 'Master in Charge of the Squish' – what trials he endured, as he recalls:

> The scene is Paddington; the guard has blown his whistle commandingly and many a trembling hand on the platform holds a trembling lace handkerchief above a trembling lip. The chocolate-and-cream carriages are already on the move, when a foreign-looking figure is seen plunging through the barrier, gesticulating frantically. With a skip here and a leap there he jerks his way amongst the statuesque caricatures of grief-stricken mothers and scrambles at last onto the running board of the train.
>
> 'I go to Oxford!' demanded the intruder in a Teutonic accent. 'Not in here you don't,' replied your intrepid protector of Summerfieldian privacy, showing the interloper just what he means! John Evans later received a solicitor's letter from an irate German. But, as no oaths had been uttered nor blows struck, he ignored it and the matter went away.

On another occasion, the masters in charge almost missed the train, scrambling aboard as it gathered speed for Oxford. Imagine the resulting scenes of chaos with seventy boys running riot (not to mention the obsequious explanations to the Headmaster) had they missed it. Then there was the time that all the luggage was sent to London on an earlier train, resulting in boys' trunks being scattered all over Paddington Station and parents playing a giant game of hunt the thimble! Two drunks were once found on the floor of the boys' carriage and one 'Squish' actually caught fire! The official explanation was the inadequate application of grease to an axle, but David argues that the real reason was in fact, 'an act of Fate in placing the largest, the fattest, the heaviest Summerfieldian of our party directly over that axle-box'.

Extract from a letter home from John Straton-Ferrier (1932–5), 1933

Above: Dramatic productions featuring staff in 1995

Below: A 'French Experience' trip, 1994; David and Jo Kidd-May at breakfast at the Château du Perron

A further change at this time, minor but significant, was to move 'Bombers and Fighters' to a new place at the end of the Michaelmas Term. This annual event, a popular, lively game played by staff and boys, has provided a rich store of memories of extraordinary themes and equally extraordinary character-acting by members of staff.

In 1994 the French Experience was inaugurated whereby each form spent a week or longer speaking and studying French language and culture under the watchful eyes of David and Jo Kidd-May, after their retirement in 1993 at the end of thirty-eight years' devoted service to the school. It was a bold experiment which would not have been so successful without their care and dedication.

Two significant royal events fell during this time. In 1977 the Queen's Silver Jubilee was celebrated with a special supper, the whole dining room being transported onto the fields by the

Booty and other staff under the watchful eye of Bill Dixon, Bursar from 1975 to 1986. The evening began with a chapel service, including rousing renditions of 'Jerusalem' and the National Anthem. There followed a fine feast of roast suckling pig and roast ribs of beef. Charles Churchill, as the compère Eddie Waring, rounded off the celebrations with entertaining games between the four Leagues. A whole holiday in the Michaelmas Term celebrated the second royal occasion, the wedding of Prince Charles and Lady Diana Spencer in 1981. The entire school were guests at the USAF base at Upper Heyford, where they were treated to a truly spectacular fire-fighting demonstration among other things. Then it was back to Summer Fields for a celebratory lunch, with guest of honour 'HRH Princess Alice of Gutenburg', alias Felicity Fletcher-Campbell, a cello teacher in the Music Department when not in princess mode!

I remember the Bursar, who always wore a tweed suit and bow tie. He had been in the RAF. He sat at the head of the table at lunch. Only one thing made him angry: boys who showered their food with the salt cellar. 'Put it on the side of your plate in a neat pile!' These things stay with you for life.

Charlie Palmer (1976–80), on Bill Dixon

Another exciting event happened during these years, although the boys only found out about it afterwards. We had a request from the police to use one of the Newton dormitories as an observation post to keep watch on a house just across the Mayfield Road, being used as a base by suspected drug dealers. The surveillance lasted two or three days, culminating in a police raid and a chase as one dealer escaped, dashing across the school grounds in a vain attempt to avoid arrest.

Crazes

Over the years, a number of crazes have periodically gripped the school. Some are short-lived, while others rumble on quietly for years. In the late 1920s, crosswords, banjoleles, ukuleles ('not all tuned to the same key'), petrol-driven model aircraft with 'their few heady seconds of flight', all enjoyed their brief periods of ascendancy. At other times crazes have included darts, conkers, catapults, stamps, 'chariot-racing' in New Room, model cars, Dinky toys, wooden boats made by Chippy, football cards (modern 'Match Attax'), football trading stickers (rumour has it that our Headmaster, David Faber, still has his collection hidden away in an attic!), playing cards, tunnelling in the boys' gardens with the concealed channels soon becoming 'mantraps' for unwary masters, building a menagerie of snails in one's desk, making ink from elderberries, butter manufacture from cream taken from Hobson's, skateboards, roller blades, 'militarism' – the formation of private armies centred around the heroic leader of the moment and waging war with the ferocity of Attila the Hun – Rubik's Cubes, radio-controlled cars, pets and yo-yos.

> About 1932, the yo-yo craze was sweeping the country. I was lucky enough to acquire the dexterity to get it to do 'round the world', 'walking the dog', 'over the falls' and 'loops'. I became a minor celebrity at Summer Fields until yo-yos were superseded by the next craze.
> James Richardson (1931–5)

But three other particular crazes merit special comment. The first was the seemingly pointless fad for 'brick grinding'. Here, the idea was simply to grind together two common bricks until each had been reduced to a small pile of dust. Were fans of this activity on their way to successful careers as bureaucrats? Next came the desire to supplant the weekly sweet ration by consuming large quantities of Punch and Judy toothpaste which was found to taste every bit as nice as some of the sweets. Limitless toothpaste could be had from Matron. The gourmets considered banana flavour the best. But the sudden, notable increase in toothpaste consumption did not go unnoticed by Matron, and this craze died an early death at her hands. Finally, there was a surprise

Crazes may come and go, but chess remains a perennial favourite

for Summer Fields – knitting, yes, knitting! The arrival of a single boy armed with needles and a ball of wool led to slavish imitation. Parents were bombarded with requests for all sorts of knitting equipment and soon the school resounded to the 'click-clack' of knitting needles. Simultaneously, Summer Fields became littered with masses of jagged, multi-coloured scarves besprinkled with dropped stitches and holes. Where was the sporting hero now? As Anthony Cheetham (1951–6) remembers, 'Those who could not knit were regarded with disdain, while the boy who had mastered both plain and purl was admired by all.'

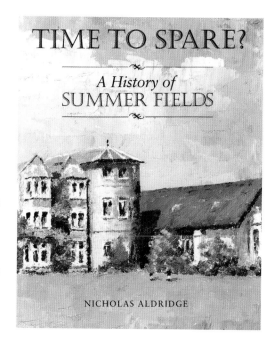

After the success of the 1977 appeal and the subsequent building programme, some parents suggested a celebration would be in order, and it was decided that this should take the form of a ball in summer 1979. With the support and hard work of a dedicated committee of mums, it was an unqualified success and became by popular request the first of many, held every three years. There were six during my time, always on the night before Sports Day and the Fathers-and-Sons cricket match. Somehow everyone managed to find the stamina to keep bright and fresh. The senior boys were highly impressive as waiters for drinks and at the dinner, wearing scarlet bow-ties and cummerbunds and using their charm and attentiveness to add considerable class to the evening.

The year 1989 marked the 125th anniversary of the foundation of the school. Celebrations were dignified and appropriate. Nick Aldridge published *Time To Spare? A History of Summer Fields*, his 'first foray into researching and writing history' and now a *sine qua non* for anyone studying or writing about the school's past. On 10 June, a special service was held at St Michael's Church, Summertown, conducted by the Rt Rev. Cuthbert Bardsley (1916–19), former Bishop of Coventry, who gave the address (as he had done for the centenary celebrations twenty-five years earlier). Back at the school, a grand reception was held in New Room and guests were able to marvel at the precision of the Coldstream Guards as they Beat

the Retreat on the Home Fields. It was a glorious spectacle specially arranged for us by Major General Sir George Burns DSO, OBE, MC (1920–4), Colonel of the Regiment. The following weekend saw a glittering ball, with its special '125 cocktail' and dancing far into the night.

During this period, Summer Fields became quite a training ground for Headmasters: Richard Gould (Twyford), Nigel Chapman (Lockers Park and Horris Hill), Stephen Cox (Solihull Junior School) and Henry Phillips (Hordle Walhampton). These were followed by Mark Johnson and Christian Heinrich at Cheam and Cumnor House respectively, with, finally, Adrian Floyd running a flourishing Finton House in London.

One aspect of the changes during these years was summed up in my valedictory speech, which I should like to recall:

> When I took over as Headmaster in 1975, Summer Fields was a very bachelor establishment, but over the years it became clear I was running a marriage bureau and finally a fertility clinic. Eight staff romances and weddings took place and twenty-one staff children were born between 1975 and 1997 – how times had changed in those twenty-two years!

So ended a time of considerable change and modernisation. The school now had buildings and facilities and the quality of staff to go with them ready to meet all the challenges of the twenty-first century: the curriculum had been broadened and scholarship and Common Entrance results were some of the best in the prep-school world. The predominantly male atmosphere had been superseded by a warmer, family-based environment. Sport, Music, Drama and Art were all in the ascendant. But in the end, the school's high reputation in 1997 could only have been achieved with the dedication and commitment of a truly professional staff. Some, looking back nostalgically over these years, have described them as a golden era for Summer Fields.

Summer Fields Summer Ball

Friday, June 20th, 1986
8.00 p.m. to 2.30 a.m.

Tickets £30 each   Black Tie

R.S.V.P. The Secretary, Summer Fields, Oxford   See over

8.00 p.m.   Cocktails on the Headmaster's Lawn: Music by the Tony Charles Steel Band.

8.45 p.m.   Dinner in the Marquee.

8.45 p.m.   Dance Band of the Scots Guards in the Marquee.

10.15 p.m.   Musical Entertainment by Summer Fields Madrigal Group.

Then: Dancing in the Marquee: Dance Band of the Scots Guards and the Tony Charles Steel Band.

Throughout the evening
     Dancing in New Room: Chatters Discotheque.

Dinner, Cocktails, Wines and Whisky & Lager Bar all inclusive.

Change and Continuity

Robin Badham-Thornhill, Headmaster, 1997–2010

Having been Headmaster of Lambrook, I arrived in 1997 as the first non-Summer Fields member of staff to take the helm of this great Oxford institution. I brought with me ideas developed outside the school. Also, I brought my wife Angela and a young family into the community. Angela was to play a vital part in the life of Summer Fields.

So, what was there to do, taking over a school regarded by many as one of the top prep schools in the country, from a Headmaster who had been one of the longest-serving and most successful in his field? The school was full. There had been an ambitious building programme over the previous twenty years. The academic record was outstanding.

Early on in my tenure, I made it very clear that I would be my own man. I should continue to strive for academic excellence and an all-round education, but would ensure that the school moved with the times, adapting and changing to meet the demands of the late twentieth century and the next millennium.

Top of my list of priorities was to ensure that the school continued to thrive as a boarding school and continued to gain academic success through the curriculum offered and the achievements of the boys. Alongside academics, breadth is a vital ingredient in any education provided, especially in the fields of Art, Drama, Music, Sport and the range of other activities outside the classroom. In a changing world the school had to develop its ICT provision, its international dimension and its links to the community outside Summer Fields.

Young Summerfieldians had to be equipped to become citizens of the future with the character and personality to relate well to everyone around them. Above all, they needed to understand that if they were going to do anything, they had to do it well. In addition, the school had to continue to develop its fine facilities and have the best academic and support staff in the country.

For many years, academic success at Summer Fields was measured by the number of awards gained at senior schools, especially Eton. From 1997 until 2010, boys won a total of 101 awards, many to Eton in increasingly competitive circumstances but, also, to a wider selection of schools including Winchester and Radley. As the millennium approached, independent schools became increasingly accountable to the world of inspection. Thus the role of the Director of Studies, working closely with the Headmaster, became extremely important. The outstanding results of the 2009 ISI Inspection were most gratifying. Changes had been made to the curriculum and more emphasis was placed on independent learning rather than just received teaching.

Although Summer Fields remained the leading feeder school for Eton, even after the introduction of its pre-Common Entrance test, the range of destination schools increased. Boys passed via Common Entrance into a broader field of schools including Oundle, Sherborne and Shrewsbury.

To emphasise the importance of academic achievement, a programme of classroom renovation was completed. Every room had a makeover. Interactive whiteboards were installed and, in accordance with new regulations, windows were placed in every classroom door. In addition, the library was refurbished over the period 2003–5 and a full-time librarian appointed.

As a leading boys' boarding prep school it was equally important to develop the boarding facilities and to continue to have small boarding units, which constitute one of the greatest strengths of the school. Following a successful appeal over two years, in September 2002, Sir Christopher Slade (1939–40) opened the new boarding house, Savage's, named after Patrick Savage. The building of Savage's released space in the other

Above: Some of the ceramic murals depicting life at Summer Fields, 2000

Below: Angela and Robin Badham-Thornhill, Headmaster 1997–2010

Bottom: Robin Badham-Thornhill (right) with Sir Christopher Slade (OS)

Buzzer

The school toyshop or 'Buzzer' remains ever popular with today's Summerfieldians. This little shop opens on half holidays, selling a range of stationery, models and toys. Currently, Buzzer's 'Custodians' are Housemothers Deborah Ives and Ann Snow. Its stock is an accurate indicator of any current craze. Today, 'Match Attax', Chattering Meerkats and Monkeys, as well as 'squeezy multicolour brains' are the best-sellers.

No one is quite sure how Buzzer acquired its name, the most likely explanation being that 'Buzzer' is a corruption of 'Bursar' from the days when Jack Alington fulfilled that role as well as running the toyshop. To the boys, he quickly became 'Jacky Buzzer'. Thus the name was born.

At first, Buzzer was merely a cupboard. From this small beginning it graduated in 1962 to a hut in the Rose Garden and then, when managed by

Buzzer: **above** in 1964, **below**, as it is today

the present editor and his wife, to smart new premises in the basement of the Sports Hall. From there, under the guiding hand of Sarah Sparrow, a new-look Buzzer, fitted out exactly like a shop, was relocated to its current spot behind the Matrons' Room next to the Dining Room. Handwritten ledgers recording boys'

purchases have long since given way to computerised records.

It is remarkably easy to bring the school nearly to a halt from the depths of Buzzer! Gavin Hannah managed it through a special delivery of Ghost-Shriekers during one Halloween and again with little, slimy, rubbery figures which, when thrown, clung to the ceiling only to fall at inopportune moments onto those below. The only time the authorities got their own back on the Buzzer manager was when the Chaplain banned a consignment of Vampire's Blood! Needless to say, there were hundreds of disappointed customers...

Being able to shop in Buzzer gives boys an early lesson in money management as they budget their £30 termly allowance. During the 1920s, the owner of a 'super Alpha Romeo', purchased for the then enormous sum of 24 shillings (£1.20) and about £26 in today's money, was the envy of his peers. Needless to say, his entire allowance was exhausted and extra cash had to be sent to the school by his generous father.

boarding houses, enabling them all to have a sitting room and play area. Gradually, all the boarding houses were completely refurbished – Cottage, Lower House and Newton in the summer of 2002 with Mayfield also partly re-roofed – and Upper House and Front Lodge in the summer of the following year.

A wise Headmaster once said that a school was as good as the character of the boys in the 6th XV – meaning a school should be judged not just by the best boys in every field of activity. In many ways, my aim was to ensure that all boys were given skills which would help them to thrive, to have the

confidence to be themselves, to see the best in those around them and to relate to everyone they came in contact with. Boys still played marbles, conkers and Pokemon and went to Buzzer, while showing an awareness of the outside world that belied their tender age.

As the millennium approached and passed, despite all the dire warnings the computers continued to function, and every boy produced a tile to form a ceramic tapestry of life at Summer Fields in the year 2000. A time capsule was buried outside the Headmaster's study. In addition, there was an outstanding

Trips

Outings and trips play a full part in the life of the school today. These take a variety of forms. Expedition Day is held annually in the Summer Term. Organised nowadays by Bill Bailey, it began in 1977 under the watchful eye of Nigel Chapman. On this occasion, the majority of the school departs in a series of coaches in different directions. Venues alter slightly over the years but the old favourites remain: Bath and Bowood House, Bristol, Portsmouth, Warwick Castle, the Black Country Museum and much else besides. The aim is a mixture of educational benefit and pleasure. Some 'trips' almost turn into mini-breaks. These are usually connected with the academic curriculum such as those to St Briavel's Castle (Gloucestershire) for the second-year medieval historians and to Cornwall for the Thirds or Removes, where boys pursue a carefully structured range of activities. In recent years, boys have also had the opportunity to perfect their French through short stays in Normandy.

Red Choir tour to Vienna

Millennium Concert. The chapel, for so long the centre of life at Summer Fields, saw the installation of a 'new' Henry Holiday window in the West Wall, taken from the redundant church in North Chailey (Sussex) and dedicated by the Rt Rev. David Jennings (1952–7) in May 2001.

Although the Sports Hall remains one of the most impressive facilities in the school, Macmillan now enables some memorable dramatic and musical moments to take place. It is unusual in the prep-school world for there to be a major production each term, in addition to a performance by First Year boys. Over a period of thirteen years (1997–2010) there were forty-four stage productions, including the first school performance of Disney's *Beauty and the Beast,* as well as other musical extravaganzas including *Oliver!* (with Rowan Atkinson as Fagin) and *Joseph and the Amazing Technicolour Dreamcoat.* There were classics including *A Servant of Two Masters* (the basis for the hit play *One Man, Two Guvnors*), *Twelve Angry Men, The Importance of Being Earnest* and *Billy.* The semi-professional performance of the opera *Amahl and the Night Visitors,* which raised money for charity, was a really enjoyable occasion.

The Red Choir sang in the community as well as in some illustrious locations, including Salisbury Cathedral, the Cathedral of St John the Divine in New York, Notre-Dame in Paris, Cologne Cathedral, St George's Chapel, Windsor, Christ Church and New College, Oxford.

In accordance with the school's motto, *Mens Sana in Corpore Sano*, sport continued to thrive and more and more opportunities were given for boys to represent the school. The cricket 1st XI was unbeaten in three seasons and the rugby squad toured in South Africa on four occasions.

If the new millennium is seen as a new era, so the advancement of technology must be seen to accompany it. The school was completely rewired with new fibre-optic cabling, computers were regularly updated and the whole administration of the school was transformed through a new computer package.

In many ways, an outstanding prep school results from outstanding teachers. The school was blessed with long-serving members of staff, including Nick Aldridge, Willy Pryor, David Langdon, Richard Balding, Patsy Logan, Judith Lane and Rupert and Di McNeile, all of whom retired during my tenure. Long-serving, loyal and hard-working staff remain, such as Johnny Bush (since 1980) and the indefatigable Andrew Bishop (since 1990), who will come to be seen as one of the best Deputy Headmasters in living memory. New staff were appointed to bring in fresh ideas and teaching techniques, as well as different skills.

Mention has been made already of Patrick Savage, but remembered also in a May 2004 memorial service in chapel was Ran Ogston, Headmaster of Summer Fields St Leonards and master at Summer Fields, who died in December 2003.

In addition, the three Chairmen of Governors, Sir Richard Butler (1995–2000), John Bullard (2000–7) and Edward Davidson (2007–13) helped me guide the school through the choppy waters of changing Charity and Health and Safety legislation, economic turbulence, parental boarding preferences and general educational change.

One of the major advantages of a boarding prep school compared to a day school is that boarding boys have much

Rugby tour of South
Africa, 2011

more time. They can learn how to use this time effectively and involve themselves in lots of new and interesting activities, such as camping in the new Outdoor Activity Centre in the plantation down by the river.

Camping became popular during the 1980s, when, under the guidance of Henry Riches (1979–90), boys pitched their tents on the banks of the Cherwell in a charming part of the school fields still known as 'Campers' Corner'. But things moved on. A

The Vins

The loos at Summer Fields are still known as the 'Vins'. 'Please, Sir, may I go the Vin?' remains a constantly heard request in lessons. The Vins take their name from the fact that they were originally the conversion of a real grape-growing area of a conservatory. The Vins first consisted of a number of primitive cubicles with an interesting system of flushing. At regular intervals a stream of water would sweep down the slanted sewer under the compartments, carrying all before it. This mini-tsunami was known as the 'Vinery Rush'.

It offered opportunities for high jinks, as Nick Aldridge relates:

> It was not unknown for mischievous boys to collect some paper, wait for the 'Vinery Rush', then ignite their bundle and send it floating down to fire the spirits of those in the compartments downstream!

These floating fire-ships, travelling from east to west along the common channel beneath the seats, could have some surprising results for those on the receiving end, as Thomas

Shaughnessy (1925–8) recalls:

> I remember one night becoming aware of a most pleasurable, glowing sensation, thought at first to be due to a hard game of football. This euphoria was short-lived as I realised that I was quickly becoming uncomfortably hot, and indeed, as I gained my feet, a column of flame roared out of the aperture. Someone, perhaps mindful of Cadiz, had lit a large bundle of paper and sent it downstream in a collective toast of the seats of learning.

OXFORD Mail

TEMPERS FLARE AFTER UNITED DEFEAT
SEE BACK PAGE

Wednesday, October 30, 2002   32p   www.thisisoxfordshire.co.uk

INSIDE TODAY

Shortlisted for culture

OXFORD was today named as one of the six British cities on a shortlist for the title of European Capital of Culture 2008.
● See Page 2

Celebration at new unit

FORMER patients and staff have celebrated the opening of a £8.5m Oxford Trauma Unit at the John Radcliffe Hospital.
● See page 2

Destructive events: **above**, the *Oxford Mail*'s coverage of the Red Pavilion fire 2002, and **above right**, the floods of 2005

Below: The pavilion today

FIRST GAME PAVILION,
built originally as one room in 1898,
was divided into three in the 1970s
and had the clock-tower added in 1990.
It was destroyed by fire
on 30th October 2002
and completely rebuilt
as an exact replica of the original
in 2003/4

The new Red Pavilion was opened
by Lady Caroline Faber
on Saturday 28th June 2003, in memory of
her husband, Julian Faber (1917 - 2002),
father, grandfather and Governor
for almost fifty years.
With grateful thanks for the many happy
hours spent watching members of
their family who played and are still playing,
cricket at Summer Fields.

The Plantation with its camping huts

new woodland area had been planted on the initiative of Nigel Talbot Rice. As this matured to form what is now the Plantation, boys came to enjoy the perfect place for their outdoor adventures, and for mischief! Wooden huts replaced tents and the Plantation now boasts its own permanent camp. Camping remains as popular as ever. Occasionally parents join their sons and full-scale dinner parties are sometimes held in a perfect sylvan setting on glorious summer evenings.

Boys also have the opportunity of travelling to France with *Normandie à la Carte* for between ten and fourteen days as Removes and Fifths, or participating in a varied programme of activities at school. As part of the visits to France the boys learnt that it was an OS, General Sir Alexander Stanier, Bt, DSO MC, DL, JP (1908–10), who liberated Arromanches in the British sector during the D-Day landings in 1944.

In any boarding school another strength is the nature of the school community itself, where everyone plays an important part, be it the Headmaster; Mario, the former butler; the Head Groundsman; the school caterer; or loyal gardener Roger King, who completed fifty years' service at Summer Fields in 2013.

Robin Badham-Thornhill opening the AstroTurf courts with David Faber, 2011

In addition, Maclaren Foundation awards enable talented pupils, not otherwise able to come to the school, to enjoy the benefits of a Summer Fields education.

With Savage's built and the other six boarding houses refurbished, many other improvements were implemented. Extensive construction work was completed, such as the re-roofing of much of the main school building and the refurbishment of the Lobby and of Manor.

But some will also remember other unfortunate, *destructive* events. The flooding of the Sports Hall and squash courts in 2003 sticks firmly in the mind. And none can ever forget that great conflagration which wrought the end of the Red Pavilion in 2002. Thick smoke billowed across the Near Fields and into the sky; traffic in Summertown halted as three or four fire engines arrived; a small army of fire-fighters, sustained by Jaffa Cakes from the Domestic Bursar, battled in vain to extinguish the flames. And all owing to a painter's blowtorch – flames and thatch make uneasy bedfellows!

The decision to rebuild our pavilion, since 1898 seen as the building embodying the essence of Summer Fields, was made swiftly, and a slightly bigger version of the original was opened by Lady Caroline Faber in 2003.

Further positive changes included the complete development and refurbishment of the 'Black Hole' or Staff Room. Two boys' Day Rooms were created by moving the Laundry into Kirkley House. The second and final appeal helped finance the Kitchen development and the building of the new AstroTurf and tennis courts, which I was delighted to open in 2011.

In the dining room, self-service catering (cafeteria-style) was introduced, enabling a much wider choice of dishes, reflecting the changing trends in food consumption. Key areas of the school ripe for development remain the changing rooms and Vins – vital elements of SF folklore – and these are now being addressed.

In 2010, retirement beckoned and the school baton was handed on to David Faber (1969–74) a former Vice-Chairman of the Governors. David came into education after a career in politics as Conservative MP for Westbury (1992–2001), during which time he served on numerous parliamentary select committees and as Parliamentary Private Secretary to various ministers. A successful writer and historian, his *Munich: The 1938 Appeasement Crisis* (2008), was described by one critic as 'a sparkling and perceptive account of events that resonate seventy years on'.

It was Tony Blair in the 1997 election campaign who said that his priorities for office were 'Education, Education, Education'. In the world of a boys' boarding prep school the Headmaster and his staff have more opportunity to influence the lives of their young charges and to make 'a real difference' than most people in other professions.

part two
Life at Summer Fields

chapter four

Academic Life

From the school roll of 1888 it is possible to reconstruct the academic structure of Summer Fields. In the Michaelmas Terms there was no Fifth Form. That came into being in January. The other forms were:

- Upper and Lower Remove
- Upper, Middle and Lower Fourth
- Shell
- Upper, Middle and Lower Third
- Second Form (Upper and Lower)
- Upper and Lower First Form

This shape was familiar for many years to come. Thomas Miles (1931–6), later of Magdalen College, Oxford, describes his progression through the forms, from May 1931 in First Form, as the youngest boy at Summer Fields, to his election in 1936 as a Scholar of Winchester:

In September 1931, I was promoted to the Upper Second taken by John Evans (Tarkie). John Evans was a very gentle person with the slightest of stammers. If I made a mistake in a Latin construction, he would call me a 'blue owl', or, on one occasion 'a double-barrelled blue owl'; his criticisms were totally free from malice...

In the Spring Term of 1932, I was moved up to Lower Third, taken by Mr Jeffries-Jones and in the summer of 1932 to Upper Third taken by Mr Barne. In the autumn of 1932, I was moved to Lower Fourth, taken by Mr Mullins. I spent two terms in Lower Fourth, after which I was moved up to Middle Fourth.

Previous page: The Junior Colts pavilion

Right: Expedition Day at Christ Church Cathedral, Oxford

UPPER SCHOOL.

Order of Precedence in each Subject by Examination.

FIFTH FORM.

Latin.	Greek.	Composition.	DIVISION I. English. (By term's marks).
Cheese.	Max Müller.	Hall.	Cheese.
Hall.	Cheese.	Cheese.	Max Müller.
Max Müller.	Hall.	Max Müller.	Hall.
Webber, ma.	Webber, ma.	Webber, ma.	Lewis.
			Barnett.
			Clutton-Brock.
			Empson.
			de Winton.

UPPER FOURTH FORM.

Latin.	Greek.	Composition.	
Holman-Hunt.	de Winton.	Lewis.	Buckle, ma. (with average).
de Winton.	Holman-Hunt.	Nunns.	Holman-Hunt.
Clutton-Brock.	Lewis.	Holman-Hunt.	Anderson, ma.
Lewis.	Marshall, ma.	de Winton.	Brookes.
Nunns.	Nunns.	Marshall, ma.	Thomas.
Marshall, ma.	Empson.	Clutton-Brock.	
Empson.	Clutton-Brock.	Empson.	
Barnett.		Barnett.	DIVISION II.
			Slade.

UPPER MIDDLE FOURTH FORM.

Latin.	Greek.	Composition.	
Anderson, mi.	Nash.	Robeson.	Pemberton.
Robeson.	Robeson.	Nash.	Buckle, mi.
Buckle, ma.	Barnett.	Buckle, ma.	Marshall, ma.
Nash.	Slade.	Slade.	Thrupp.
Slade.	Anderson, mi.	Bosanquet, ma.	Hutchinson.
Elsmie.	Bosanquet, ma.	Spottiswoode.	Anderson, mi.
Spottiswoode.	Spottiswoode.	Anderson, mi.	Nunns.
Buckle, mi.	Pemberton.	Elsmie.	Nash.
Pemberton.		Pemberton.	Spottiswoode.
Bosanquet, ma.		Buckle, mi.	Hemming.
			Bosanquet, ma.
			Elsmie.

LOWER MIDDLE FOURTH FORM.

Latin.	Greek.	Composition.	DIVISION III.
Thrupp.	Thrupp.	Brookes.	Jones.
Brookes.	Buckle, mi.	Jones.	Marshall, mi.
Thomas.	Brookes.	Thrupp.	Stirling.
Anderson, ma.	Jones.	Hemming.	Robeson.
Webber, mi.	Elsmie.	Webber, mi.	Arrowsmith.
Jones.	Warren.	Thomas.	Hall-Dare.
Warren.		Warren.	Warren.
		Anderson, ma.	Lockyer, ma.
			Stannus.

LOWER FOURTH FORM.

Latin.	Greek.	Composition.	
Stirling.	Talbois.	Stirling.	Talbois.
Hemming.	Hemming.	Talbois.	Webber, mi.
Talbois.	Stirling.	Hutchinson.	Gregorie.
Hall-Dare.	Lockyer, ma.	Hall-Dare.	Jackson.
Hutchinson.	Hall-Dare.	Lockyer, ma.	
Lockyer, ma.	Jackson.	Gregorie.	
Gregorie.	Gregorie.	Jackson.	
Marshall, mi.	Hutchinson.	Marshall, mi.	
Jackson.			

LOWER SCHOOL.

Order of Precedence in each Subject by Examination.

UPPER THIRD FORM.

Latin.	Greek.	Composition.	DIVISION I. English.
Arrowsmith.	Stewart.	Wood.	Stewart.
Stewart.	Kingdon.	Arrowsmith.	Strachey.
Sperling, ma.	Sperling, ma.	Stewart.	Ridpath.
Kingdon.	Arrowsmith.	Kingdon.	Biscoe.
Wood.	Wood.	Sperling, ma.	
Bosanquet, mi.	Bosanquet, mi.		Zwilchenbart.
			Bosanquet, mi.
			Wilkin.
			Courthope.

LOWER THIRD FORM.

Latin.	Greek.	Composition.	
Strachey.	Strachey.	Strachey.	Sperling, ma.
Courthope.	Courthope.	White.	Kingdon.
White.	Stannus.	Biscoe.	Wood.
Biscoe.	Biscoe.	Ridpath.	White.
Stannus.	White.	Stannus.	Miller.
Bright.	Ridpath.	Miller.	
Ridpath.	Miller.		
Miller.			DIVISION II.

SECOND FORM.

Spelling.	Greek.	Grammar.	
Wilkin.	Marshall, tert.	Sperling, mi.	Bright.
Lockyer, mi.	Higgens.	Lockyer, mi.	Maurice.
Zwilchenbart.	Marshall, quart.	Wilkin.	Elphinstone.
Marshall, tert.	Wilkin.	Maxwell.	Marshall, tert.
Maxwell.	Maxwell.	Zwilchenbart.	Higgens.
Marshall, quart.	Lockyer, mi.	Marshall, quart.	Maxwell.
Sperling, mi.	Zwilchenbart.	Higgens.	Lockyer, m.
Higgens.	Sperling, mi.	Marshall, tert.	Sperling, mi.
			Marshall, quart.
			Conolly.

FIRST FORM.

Latin.	Greek.	Composition.
Maurice.	Elphinstone.	Maurice.
Elphinstone.	Maurice.	Elphinstone.
Conolly.	Conolly.	Conolly.

School roll, showing forms and curriculum, 1880

At the end of the summer of 1933 I was approached by Mr Bolton who said to me, 'You are going to be in Upper Remove next term, young fellow-me-lad.' So there I was in the autumn term of 1933, in Upper Remove. I was the youngest boy in the form and the going was hard.

In 1934, Thomas Miles went into Fifth Form with eight other boys, remaining there for two years before successfully taking his scholarship for Winchester.

On the school roll between Upper Third and Lower Fourth was a form called the 'Modern Side', taken by the long-suffering Mr Lysaght (1915–49). The intention was to allow those boys with no bent towards the Classics to do less Latin and Greek. Modern Side consisted of only about twelve boys from the hundred or so in the school. Peter Nathan (1942–3) argues that it was a mistake to segregate these pupils, who were merely regarded as 'thwarted philistines'. Denys Moylan (1939–45) agrees. The school, he writes, was divided into three streams, Scholarship, 2nd Eleven and the Modern Side, the last 'a bit of an offence to GB's classical sensibilities'.

As today, boys could then move form. There is a tendency now to speak of moving 'sideways', which can be a euphemism for 'down', if a boy leaves the Scholarship stream. But whatever the circumstances, all moves are made with great sensitivity. Not so in the past. Denys Moylan recalled his own eviction from the Scholarship Form, 'personally by GB, in the middle of a period'. Nowadays, there i...

Fr... remains the ... ...Scholars, then follow the

Fifths, Removes, Thirds, Seconds and Firsts. The Shells have been consigned to history. These days, the forms are generally far more egalitarian with some mixed-ability teaching. Subjects like Maths are taught, in the higher years, in sets graded by ability. Potential Scholars are singled out, as in most subjects they cover slightly different material from that required for Common Entrance. They certainly take a different academic approach with a greater emphasis on analysis and original thinking. For Common Entrance pupils, outside the top sets, the aim is, where possible, to place weaker boys in smaller forms. This ensures a high level of personal attention.

New Room as a classroom with its open fireplaces and massive six-seater desks

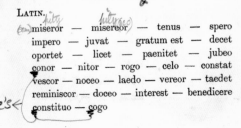

Maud 1908
PREPOSITIONS
IN
LATIN AND GREEK.
ARRANGED FOR THE USE OF
SUMMER FIELDS.
C. E. W.
SECOND EDITION.

6. Constructions.

LATIN.
miseror — misereor — tenus — spero
impero — juvat — gratum est — decet
oportet — licet — paenitet — jubeo
conor — nitor — rogo — celo — constat
vescor — noceo — laedo — vereor — taedet
reminiscor — doceo — interest — benedicere
constituo — cogo

GREEK.
χράομαι — κέχρημαι — φείδομαι — δεῖ
πείθομαι — ἕπομαι — ἀκούω — ἥδομαι
ἄχθομαι — ἄξιος — κτάομαι — φθάνω
κέκτημαι — τυγχάνω — λανθάνομαι
λανθάνω — λαμβάνομαι — ἐπίσταμαι
φαίνομαι — μέλλω — μέλει — ἡγέομαι

Above: Prepositions in Latin and Greek, by 'Doctor', 1908, with handwritten notes

Right: The Greek examination paper, summer 1924. The candidate was Adrian Enthoven (1922–7)

The Early Curriculum

Whilst always denying any notion of being an 'academic hothouse', full of 'cram', Summer Fields has maintained high standards in the classroom. In the twenty-year period 1897–1916, the school *averaged* more than eleven scholarships each year, and more than five at Eton. During this time, at Eton, 33 per cent of those in College were Summerfieldians. As Pat Savage once wrote, 'It has always been the brains rather than the brawns that have earned the extra half-holidays.'

In the early days, in fact until the last thirty years or so, the Classics dominated all. A thorough knowledge of Latin and Greek was deemed to be the optimum curriculum for a 'gentleman'. Proficiency in such studies was believed to bring with it thorough mental training, as well as access to a broad selection of literature touching the whole range of human emotions. At Summer Fields, these languages were to be studied at all times of the day, at least in Doctor's time, as recalled by Bernard Darwin (1887–9), who seemed rather to enjoy it:

> I remember in particular half-hours of Latin grammar before breakfast, at his house, Borva, sometimes in the garden, when doubtless we paid attention to the outrageously irregular behaviour of *jecur* and *supellex*. It does not sound appetising, but it was, in fact, a thrilling experience; it was romance, it was excitement, it was in short, a treat, and we got up early and went to it joyously.

Latin Grammars were also taken into breakfast. The master in charge rang the bell part way through the meal and announced, 'You may read if you have finished.' Boys were supposed to study prior to later testing. But *A Shorter Latin*

SUMMER FIELDS.

JULY, 1924.

Grammar.

Lower Remove and downwards.

1. Inflect—ἐλυσάμην, τέτυμμαι, ἐφίλεον, *audire, feror, malo.*

2. Perf. ind. act., supine in *-um*, and meaning of—*diligo, domo, emo, lego, gigno, divido, faveo, posco.*

3. Abl. sing., gen. plur., and meaning of—*socer, incus, vis, apis, virgo, nurus.*

4. Gen. sing., dat. plur., and meaning of—ναῦς, ἧπαρ, πούς, βοῦς, τριήρης, ὁδούς.

5. Latin for—13, 21, 83, 10 each, 6 times, each.

6. Greek capital letters for—x, p, r, g, u, s.

7. Form an English word from—γράφω, λόγος, ὕδωρ, φωνή, φρήν, *agger, pungo, augeo, domus, qualis.*

8. Into Latin :—(a) If I had three prizes (*praemium*) I should be happy. (b) There are some people who laugh. (c) Tell me why you went away. (d) Work must be finished before evening.

9. Gender-rule for nouns in *-os* of 3rd declension, with exceptions.

10. Give a list of verbs in *-io* which belong to the 3rd conjugation, with meanings.

11. Translate, and give syntax rule for:—(a) Sunt nobis poma. (b) Tremit artus. (c) Vos ite domum. (d) Lusum it Maecenas. (e) Bibendum est nobis.

12. Compare—κάκος, ταχέως, εὔνους, μέλας, *utilis, dubius, de, providus.*

C. A. E. W.

5 U 7

Hubert Mullins correcting
Maths papers, 1930s

Primer was too easily modified by those seeking amusement rather than knowledge and *The Shortbread Eating Primer* became a common addition to classical bibliography! In a like manner, Livy's *Hannibalian War* was soon turned into *Slimy Cannibal Swab*.

Boys were pushed in Classics, but helped when necessary. We have a charming example of what today would be called 'differentiation' – ensuring that each individual boy has his academic needs specifically addressed. All very modern, but obviously not unknown at Summer Fields in the 1930s and offering an instance of Cyril Williams' caring approach to his pupils. After such rapid promotion, Thomas Miles needed assistance with his Latin verse composition. He recounts how

Mr Williams took me to one side on my own, to show me what was needed. I had to put into a Latin hexameter, 'Here there will be peace for us while life shall remain to me.' Eventually I had it correct: *Pax erit hic nobis donec mihi vita manebit*.

Sir Roger Aubrey Baskerville Mynors (1903–89), SF 1914–16

Roger Mynors was one of the leading Classicists of the twentieth century, described by a friend and colleague as an 'extraordinary scholar, a man of broad and immense knowledge, unsullied ever by the slightest hint of intellectual vulgarity'. After Summer Fields he was educated at Eton (as a King's Scholar) and Balliol, where he became a Fellow in 1926. He took the Kennedy Professorship of Latin at Cambridge in 1944. Disappointed not to have become Master of Balliol in 1949, Mynors eventually returned to Oxford in 1953 as Corpus Christi Professor of Latin, remaining at Corpus until his retirement in 1970.

Mynors became a Fellow of the British Academy in 1944 and was knighted in 1963. Three years later he became president of the Classical Association. He is remembered today for his authoritative editions of Pliny, Virgil and Catullus, but his scrupulous erudition extended far beyond the ancient world. He worked on a new edition of Bede's *Ecclesiastical History* and was a member of the Literary Committee for the New English Bible. Mynors also nurtured a lifelong interest in the transmission of texts. After retiring from

Oxford, he catalogued the medieval library of chained books at Hereford Cathedral, having already completed similar work on the medieval collections at Durham Cathedral decades earlier. In October 1989, Sir Roger Mynors died in a road

accident outside Hereford. His name is kept alive today at Summer Fields through the termly award of the Mynors Cup for Work to the League with the most Work Reds, a small but fitting memorial to a scholar of such great repute.

A proud group of Mynors in 1960

Above: Maths set belonging to a member of the Enthoven family

Below: A sonnet by Julian Reade (1949–52)

Right: *Preparatory Greek*, by Nicholas Aldridge, 1996

The Changing Curriculum

By 1934 the nature of the work was changing. Before then the whole school had followed much the same programme, and all masters, to all intents and purposes, had taught all subjects. Now the work was divided into two blocks and masters had the opportunity to specialise in their own subject.

Latin and Greek still took pride of place, as it was for its teaching of Classics, then vital for the winning of scholarships, that Summer Fields was most celebrated. Boys were taught by rote and by the use of mnemonics. They were told to translate passages with the help of a neat system of brackets and underlining that defined the grammatical relationships of the words within each sentence. Greek was dealt with in a similar way. Boys were also introduced to Greek and Roman history as well as the major authors like Virgil, Horace, Livy, Ovid, Juvenal, Pliny, Tacitus, Homer, Aeschylus and Thucydides.

Other subjects began to creep into the curriculum, with increasing provision for Maths, English, French, History, Geography, Science, Scripture and practical elements such as carpentry.

In Mathematics, as well as the basics of arithmetic, fractions, decimals, algebra and geometry, the scholars went on to study trigonometry and the rudiments of differential calculus.

Pat Savage and Jimmy Bell both taught English. The syllabus covered etymology and the evolution of language, English composition and a rich diet of literature. Summerfieldians were generally encouraged to be self-effacing and self-critical,

THE SUMMER FIELDS MAGAZINE

SONNET: A SUMMER NIGHT

THE red sun sinks beneath the western sky,
The silver moonlight falls upon the earth.
Now sleeps the high-born noble, sleeps the serf.
There steals upon the air the soft sweet cry
Of nightingales, and owls, which nightly fly
To seek their prey, hid in protective turf,
Do roam. And vulgar jollity and mirth
Are dead, and all is peace, for cups are dry.
And in the woods strange noises of the night
Are heard, though glorious nature is asleep.
No quarrels do this blessed silence blight,
While wary foxes round dark farmyards creep.
   And the swift-fading Moon and Milky way
   Await the coming of another day.

J. E. R.

SUMMER FIELDS

PREPARATORY GREEK

A PRACTICAL & PROGRESSIVE GRAMMAR

4th Edition: Oxford : September 1996.

History was at first presented in an ingenious way through the famous *History Pictures*, canvas screens with caricatures for events in the reign of each king and queen of England, drawn by Leonard Strong in the 1920s for the Rev. Lysaght's (1914–49) lessons. They were said to combine 'amusement with instruction'. The pictures are dependent on visual mnemonics and terrible puns. Before the Norman Conquest, the information is set out century by century. From 1066 onwards, each reign has a separate picture. William the Conqueror is represented by an elephant whose feet are drawn on the map of England to indicate the scene of his exact victories. The Emperor Maximilian is shown by a horse's tail in the form of a figure one, and three dots, to represent zeros, on either side; one and six dots makes (max) a million! The Massacre of St Bartholomew's Day is depicted by an emu having a bath (work that one out...).

Generations of boys have been subjected to these, often with the effect of making even more mysterious the mysteries

Above: A Maths lesson, 1965

Right: A *History Picture* depicting William IV and Victoria, and an extract from an explanation of it

valuing quality over quantity and truth over falsehood. In their spare time they were expected to read famous novelists. Sometimes a book was good enough to be studied secretly by torchlight under the bedclothes at night.

French had less attraction than English, but masters, like dour Mr Johnstone (1946–79), managed to drill into their pupils a fair amount of the language of a people with whom, in History lessons, England seemed to be continually at war.

History Pictures: **above**, William I; **right**, aspects of the reign of Henry VIII

of the past. Richard White (1946–51) claims to have been 'intrigued, but taught no history, by Strong's daring innovation of the pictorial rolls each relating to a royal reign'. The present editor, having just joined Summer Fields as a young and pompous Head of History, on first seeing them (shown and explained to him by none other than Willy Pryor) recoiled in horror, never understood them and consigned them to the depths of the Archive Room (where, of course, he now secretly and desperately tries to unlock their secrets).

Under Harold Hartley (1947–79), history was interpreted within the context of a world that was evolving unpredictably. Boys acquired an elementary framework of knowledge concerning the political, military and social history of the British Isles and Empire from the Reformation up to the present.

Henry Gwyn Jeffreys Moseley (1887–1915), SF 1897–1901

Henry Moseley was one of the most important physicists of the twentieth century. Before his untimely death at the age of twenty-seven, he pioneered ground-breaking experimental methods and uncovered the precise mathematical relationship between an element's X-ray spectrum and its atomic number, known today as Moseley's Law.

Moseley was born into a distinguished scientific family. Both of his grandfathers – a conchologist on his mother's side and a mathematical physicist on his father's – were Fellows of the Royal Society, and his father Henry Nottidge Moseley was Professor of Anatomy and Physiology at the University of Oxford. From Summer Fields Moseley was awarded a King's Scholarship to Eton. He then proceeded to Trinity College, Oxford, where he earned a second-class degree in physics.

After graduating Moseley joined the laboratory of Ernest Rutherford at the Victoria University of Manchester, one of the scientific hothouses of the day. He taught briefly but preferred to conduct independent research, turning down a Fellowship offered by Rutherford in favour of returning to Oxford in 1913.

That year, Moseley published the results of studies allowing for a more rigorous classification scheme of atomic elements based on their X-ray spectra. His conclusions allowed for important revisions to be made to the Periodic Table of Elements published by Dmitri Mendeleev nearly fifty years earlier. Moseley's Law, as it came to be known, firmly established the relationship between atomic number and the charge of the atomic nucleus; atomic numbering had previously been considered to be a semi-arbitrary classification system vaguely aligned with, but not strictly defined by, atomic weight. The young physicist also predicted the existence of undiscovered elements and designed early X-ray spectrometry equipment.

At the outbreak of the First World War, Moseley left his Oxford research laboratory to volunteer for the Royal Engineers of the British Army. He served as a communications officer on the Gallipoli Campaign and was killed in action by a Turkish sniper on 10 August 1915. Isaac Asimov wrote: 'In view of what he might still have accomplished… his death might well have been the most costly single death of the war to mankind generally.' Rutherford speculated that Moseley could have been awarded a Nobel Prize in Physics had his life not been cut short: he accomplished in a brief but brilliant career of just forty months what few achieve in a lifetime of research.

Mr Hartley was a favourite and loved his cricket. He carried the balls in a horse's nosebag that he had carried back as booty from his soldiering days in Palestine. 'We used to carry our water in that,' he said.

Charlie Palmer (1976–80)

Geography was becoming a distinct academic subject, but merged itself in many boys' minds with other things. Julian Reade (1949–52), for instance, learnt a lot of geography from notes printed in his album of postage stamps from different countries.

Science slowly made its appearance, with an added appeal to inquisitive boys when a young woman arrived to teach Biology. She told a group of embarrassed, but attentive, twelve-year-olds, the facts of life, with diagrams. Sadly, she lasted less than a term.

There was also an unhurried trend towards observation of scientific phenomena through controlled experiments. Julian Reade describes Summer Fields' first ever scientific demonstration, given in New Room, to the whole school sitting around the walls. The visiting scientist showed that, if one placed ice in a glass of water, water in the surrounding air would condense as droplets on its exterior. The master in charge then handed the glass to the boy first in line, for him to inspect and pass on to his neighbour, and so on round the room. As each boy checked the nature of the droplets by touching the exterior of the glass, the droplets increasingly ran down the side of the glass. Thus the demonstration lost much of its point...

From the late 1960s, generations of young Summerfieldians had their first introduction to the wonders of science via the incomparable presentation of the material by Willy Pryor (1947–52; staff 1966–99). Who can possibly forget the delights of 'Baby Bio', with 'Botany, the science of plants, starting in the Boys' Gardens and ending in the Oxford Botanic Gardens', or of Zoology, beginning with fishing and bird-watching and ending in the Oxford University Museum with its marvellous collection of 'all sorts of creatures, both great and small'? In Meteorology, the star exponent, unravelling the mysteries of precipitation, was the redoubtable 'Captain Raindrop'. In Nephology, 'Cirrus the Wisp', 'Cumulus the Heap' and their friends were ever on hand to help curious boys make sense of cloud formations. This was 'Pryor Knowledge'. Willy had the knack of making the whole universe fit as snugly together as the pieces of a jigsaw puzzle. An empirical approach certainly underpinned all his teaching. His classroom – for he did not teach science in a laboratory – was equipped with all sorts of interesting pieces of kit, some of them possibly understood only by him.

Willy was always anxious lest the Inspectors disapprove. Instead they were intrigued (baffled even), but complimentary. Here, they comment on his 'Baby Bio Course':

There is specialist teaching of science throughout the school. In the lower forms, General Science is taught in a classroom

Left: Willy Pryor in a Hay Feast game

Below: Biology, Zoology and Botany from 'Pryor Knowledge'

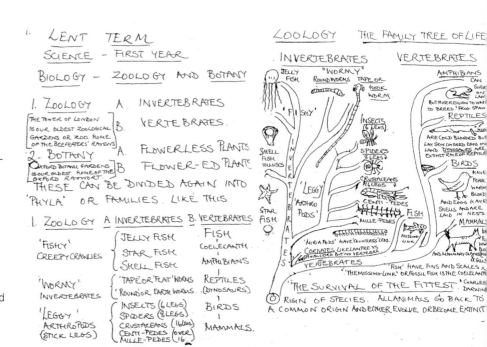

Howlers

A few genuine items from the Howlers Book.

Art:

'Look at this drawing, Miss, it's a mantelpiece!'

Teacher: 'I want you to draw pictures of cowboys and Indians.'
Boy: 'Please, Miss, can I draw General Cluster?'

Classics:

Latin for grandfather = 'grand-pater.'

'Odysseus showed himself to a maiden and his dog died of excitement.'

'Odysseus ... had been trapped in the cave of a cannibal Cyclops named Polyeatus.'

Drama:

'Sir, are you going to auction me for *Oliver*?'

English:

'For my essay, I consulted Brewer's Dictionary of Phrase and Failure.'

Definitions of a mongrel:
'Two dogs in one!'
'An animal of mixed bread!'

Master: 'Define levity'
Boy: 'Shoplifting, Sir.'

History:

'Concubines [Cluniacs] were another order of monks. They were more modern than Benedictines.'

Master: 'And how do you think Charles I could have avoided execution?'
Wag in form: 'Very easy, sir. All he had to do was to tell Cromwell that he had a music practice.'

'Cranmer was executed in Oxford in 1556, because he failed to decant.'

Letter writing:

Junior boy: 'Please, Sir, how do you spell halo?'
Master: 'H-A-L-O. Why are you asking Mummy to send you a halo? Have you been extra good?'
Junior boy: 'Oh no. It's to stick up my nose to help me breathe.'
Master: 'Ah, you mean inhaler...'

Q: Can you prove that Mr Talbot Rice exists?
A: Not provable. I saw him two minutes ago, but now he may have pespired. (sic)

Religious Studies:

'And the angel said, "Mary, you will soon bore the Son of God!"'

Sport:

'These wicket-keeping innards are really good, Sir!'

'I am absolutely neuter about the game of cricket.'

Boy about to take a conversion in rugby: 'Sir, which end of the ball should I stick in the ground?'

General:

Young Summerfieldian: 'Good evening, Mr Phillips.'
Master: 'I'm Mr Ford, actually.'
Young Summerfieldian: 'Sorry, Sir. I get confused with names that begin with the letter F.'

Boy: 'I make my pencils last longer by sharpening them at both ends.'

Boy, showing visitor around: 'On Saturdays, we have conjugational practice.'

Boy, trying to impress a housemaster after the Eton General List Tea: 'Sir, I think your tea was mouthwashingly good.'

---

which the teacher has enterprisingly equipped for his highly individual approach to the subject. Although the written Scheme is academic, the teaching is highly interactive and includes demonstration experiments, class practical work, the use of the Overhead Projector for diagrams and illustrations, plenty of discussion and a veritable bombardment of information and questions. Boys remember what they have been taught.

Scripture was also taught (now 'Religious Studies', having changed from 'Divinity'). Boys received a fair knowledge of the Bible, and usually believed everything they were told. Julian Reade relates that 'one master provided a neat answer to a question which I asked about Samson and the Philistines and somehow left me with the impression that foreskins came off the forehead'!

Practical subjects were not overlooked and could sometimes sow the seeds for a lifetime interest. Carpentry was popular and so important that it merited (and still does) its own cup. Rupert Wilcox-Baker (1964–9) maintains that 'my carpentry skills are

Design Technology in the 1980s

But 'Chippy' (Charlie Payne (1897–1931)) used to shout at the boys if too many sought his attention at once. On one occasion, opening his mouth even wider than usual, his entire set of teeth flew out and with 'astonishing dexterity, he caught them and restored them'.

The post-war curriculum continued to increase in breadth and was generally well taught. For many, academic work became more challenging as they progressed up the school. Standards were high, just as they are today, especially for the scholars. For most current boys leaving the school, GCSEs and even some Lower Sixth work hold no fears. Summer Fields has ever sought the best, just as in the 1940s, 1950s and 1960s when potential scholars coped in some subjects with material required by the O-Level examiners for pupils aged about sixteen.

However, young minds faced with strange new concepts or vocabulary can often get things wrong with an endearing earnestness leading to amusement. Laughing at pupils' errors is no longer best educational practice (was it ever?) and the Howlers Book is now a thing of the past. But that was not always the case, and the Archive Room houses a little book of delightful slips and misunderstandings.

The Modern Curriculum

Classics no longer dominates the academic curriculum, which is wide in scope and includes English, Maths, Science, French, Latin, Greek, History, Geography, Religious Studies, Music, Art, Pottery, Design and Technology and Personal and Social Education. Many others, such as Mandarin, may be learnt as 'extras'. There is also a full games programme with a wide range of sports offered to the boys, in the true spirit of *Mens Sana in Corpore Sano*.

A key element of modern teaching and learning is Computing, or ICT (Information and Communications Technology). The Computer Room, alias the ICT Suite, is perhaps the most popular place in the school after Buzzer. Boys flock there eagerly at permitted times, indeed they flock there at proscribed times and move out only reluctantly at the behest of the duty master! The modern Summerfieldian sits at his screen for hours, busily emailing, playing legal games and desperately trying to play any games banned by the authorities. Computers are now everywhere throughout the school. All classrooms and laboratories have them, there is a full set in the Design and Resources Room (the Des Res), as well as machines in Hobson's, the Kitchen Offices, the School Offices, the Bursary, the Maintenance Department and the Lodges. Even Buzzer accounts are now computerised!

still excellent thanks to my training by Chippy'. Sam Legerton (1945–50) produced a book rack for his father's birthday, besides 'making various boxes and frames for pictures or photographs'. It was the construction of 'sandwich boats and nodding parrots' that enthralled Richard White (1946–51).

> Chippy, the carpenter, taught me woodwork which was my favourite subject. I loved the smell of his glue pot always sitting on the stove. I won the carpentry prize and what he taught me helps me today, I still build and fly model aircraft as a hobby and a business.
>
> Alastair Macdonald (1951–5)

Peter Fletcher (1958–63) even built 'a substantial canoe that still graces my garden, albeit now rather the worse for wear'.

Computer competence is currently *de rigueur*. The use of ICT forms a vital and exciting element in the teaching of all subjects. On the technical side, Rupert McNeile was the pioneer and the man who led Summer Fields into the computer age.

ICT 1982–98

The first of four rooms used exclusively for computing started life in 1982. The current Archive Room housed three computers: a Dragon, a Sharp MZ80-A and a BBC Micro. Earlier the Maths Department had used a Sinclair ZX81 and a large teleprinter-like machine with a tape reader attached. This was connected to the Open University computer in Newcastle via an unreliable telephone line, courtesy of Richard Balding (1978–2001) who was studying there at the time. In fact unreliability was the hallmark of all early ventures into Summer Fields computing. Connecting wires fell out, cassette recorders failed to store data or play back properly. Something had to be done to enable the school to move forward.

A far-sighted Bursar, Bill Dixon, persuaded the Headmaster that the future lay in networked computers which could share peripherals and thus save money while giving a whole form experience of computer use. Thus, in the Easter holidays of 1984, one of the form rooms near the Headmaster's Drawing Room was converted to house eighteen BBC Micros linked by econet and sharing a disk drive and printer. Educational theorists thought that computer programming would provide rigorous mental training, perhaps the equivalent to the manipulation of all those elegiac Latin couplets by earlier generations!

After a year or two it became clear that the emphasis should change. The computer was now to be used as an important teaching aid in addition to being an essential office tool. Programming was left to the experts. During this time, Rupert McNeile wrote software to computerise the Reds and Blues system. This also meant that every member of staff had to learn how to use a machine – even the Luddites among them...

The next move coincided with a switch from BBC Micros to Research Machines computers, which came with some early programs to be used as teaching aids. This new network was installed in what is now the Junior Day Room – formerly the Pergamon Science Laboratory. This network again had its teething troubles. It was essential to log off properly if you wanted to log on again later. The Research Machines network incorporated the idea that a user could log on at any computer on the system, rather than always at the same machine, as in an office environment. All data would now be stored on a central server and individual computers would not need their own disk drives.

The final move was to the newly built Wavell building in 1991, with its dedicated ICT room. Since then the layout of the room

The computer room in the 1980s

has changed, and the equipment has been updated several times. Rupert McNeile, having overseen the development of computing to 1998 as an enthusiastic amateur, passed the ICT baton into the capable hands of Dominic Price.

ICT since 1998

With the specific task in mind of making Summer Fields 'lead the way in IT', numerous developments have been driven forward since the end of the last millennium. In September 1998 Summer Fields had thirty-nine networked computers, and expansion was about to begin. While maintaining the use of Research Machines servers and network infrastructure, the RM computers were replaced with Dell units. The first interactive whiteboard and projector were installed in the ICT Suite, along with a surround-sound system.

In the late 1990s, armed with a knowledge of intranet development, Dominic Price set about creating the first Summer Fields website.

Soon, almost every teaching room in the school had a Smart Board and projector linked to a networked computer. This enabled potentially exciting changes to teaching. To facilitate this, in 2001 all academic staff underwent thirty hours of in-house ICT training, following the *Intel Teach to the Future* course.

The year 2002 witnessed a redesign of both the ICT Suite and the Design Resources Room to improve ICT support. The

ICT Suite was reconfigured with tiered seating, in a lecture-theatre style, with wave-fronted desks and secretarial chairs. By contrast, the Design Resources Room had peripheral work surfaces installed along with twelve new computers and a Smart Board and projector. The network was also expanded to take in all three Science laboratories. The school now housed eighty computers, fifty-two being networked.

The following year saw further expansion of the network to incorporate Learning Support, the Music Department and Macmillan. In April 2003, Chris Swift arrived to provide a welcome additional pair of hands in the day-to-day running of the computer network. He continues to be invaluable in the role of Network Administrator.

By 2007, the last of the old heavyweight CRT computer monitors had been replaced by the more discreet and environmentally-friendly LCD screens. The original network cables running through the backbone of the school made way for fibre optics and all existing hubs and switches were replaced by much faster 'gigabit technology', resulting in a tenfold increase in the speed of data travelling around the school. By this stage, the number of networked computers totalled 115, with twelve stand-alone computers in Lodges.

From an administrative standpoint, the introduction of School Manager in 2009 heralded significant changes to many routine school processes. Reports, Mark Orders, Reds and Blues,

Registration and the School Diary all moved to a single platform, accessible from any computer or iPad, both on site or remotely. Data may now be shared for billing, timetabling, arranging lessons and running Hobson's, thus streamlining the overall management of the school.

The extension of the network to Lodges for staff administrative use began in 2010 and was completed two years later. Today Summer Fields has 145 networked computers and twenty-four iPads in use around the school.

The latest, cutting-edge ICT technology is, of course. on hand for the twenty-first-century Classicists. There are many programs to facilitate the mastery of Latin and Greek grammar and vocabulary. One feels that 'Mrs' would have approved!

Teaching Style: Then and Now

In the early days, outside the Classics, the teaching of some of the other subjects left much to be desired. Christopher Slade (1939–40) remembers that Mathematics was then taught 'dismally badly', while instruction in other subjects could be even worse. These recollections by James Montagu (1901–2) on

SF's early approach to history teaching are interesting in the light of his later career:

> History was primitive; unless my memory libels it, it consisted of (a) sitting in class before a blackboard ruled in squares, each square marked with the initial and date of a monarch (WI 1066), and (b) copying out from a manuscript book certain words and dates. I can remember only two: Amboyna, Massacre of, and Stampact, each with date. The book did not state where or what Amboyna was, or who massacred whom, or why, and it was many years before I discovered the Stamp Act, which I had read as one word, in equal ignorance of its meaning.

Montagu went on to be Regius Professor of History at Cambridge and the Chief Official Historian for the Second Word War!

Rote learning formed a major element of a Summerfieldian education. In History and Geography, the essential dates and facts were drummed into generations of boys. Indeed, Harold Hartley's *A Grammar and Course for History and Geography* (arid lists of facts and figures) was published as late as 1961. After 1983, it was discarded. In Divinity, Thomas Miles (1931–6) remembers drills on the names of the kings of Israel and Judah in the rhythm of Latin hexameters. In Latin, the gender rhymes

Poetry Competition

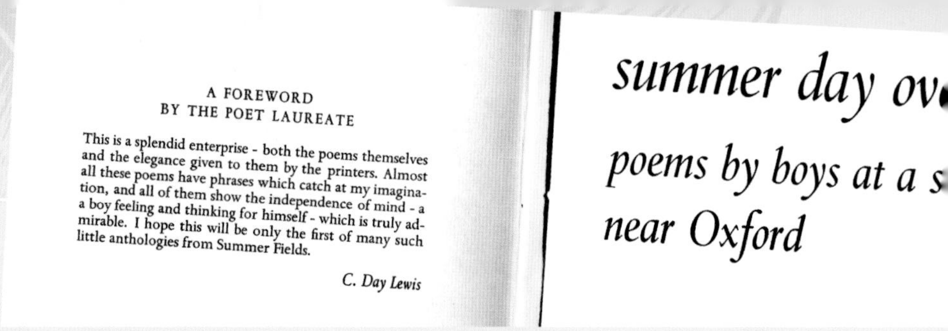
A FOREWORD
BY THE POET LAUREATE

This is a splendid enterprise - both the poems themselves and the elegance given to them by the printers. Almost all these poems have phrases which catch at my imagination, and all of them show the independence of mind - a boy feeling and thinking for himself - which is truly admirable. I hope this will be only the first of many such little anthologies from Summer Fields.

C. Day Lewis

summer day ov

poems by boys at a s

near Oxford

Summer Fields has always had a close association with poetry, and several famous poets have visited over the years. One of the great traditions of the school has been the annual Poetry Reading Competition. This began under John Evans' Headmastership and has been judged by Leonard Strong and Cecil Day-Lewis, among others. David Kidd-May (1955–2000) writes:

> Cecil Day-Lewis and his lovely wife, Jill Balcon, were very generous with the time they were prepared to give to the school and I was particularly grateful that their visits coincided with the years I was running the English Department. Each year they would come up for a couple of days, judge the Poetry Reading Competition and then the two of them would read to a select group of boys in the evening. It was a truly special experience to hear those two beautiful voices weaving magic in their intelligent and sensitive interpretation of the poems they had selected.
>
> In 1967 they came up as usual and the evening before the competition Pat Savage invited Jo and me to have dinner with them. John Masefield had recently died, and I asked Cecil if he would like to be the next Poet Laureate.
>
> 'Not really,' he replied; 'but I shall be rather hurt if I'm not asked.'

John Betjeman succeeded Cecil Day-Lewis as Poet Laureate in 1972, and a couple of years later he came to talk to the boys. At the door to New Room he paused for a moment and looked around. Then, as David remembers:

> He walked slowly up the room between the rows of boys standing in respectful silence. He began to declaim loudly in that most distinctive voice, describing everything he could see as we moved towards the front where he was going to give his talk. I am pretty sure he had never been in the room before, but everything he said was expressed in perfect iambics. It was an extraordinary experience, which made a deep impression on me, though whether all the boys were aware of the remarkable nature of the performance is not certain.

In an age when poetry reading would seem to be generally on the decline, it is perhaps more important than ever for Summer Fields to take a lead in aiding its survival and give boys the opportunity to relish such an important aspect of literature. Over the years, the 'Poetry Comp', as it is commonly referred to today, has enabled some boys to declaim their piece with the skills of Cicero. Others, it has reduced to gibbering wrecks...

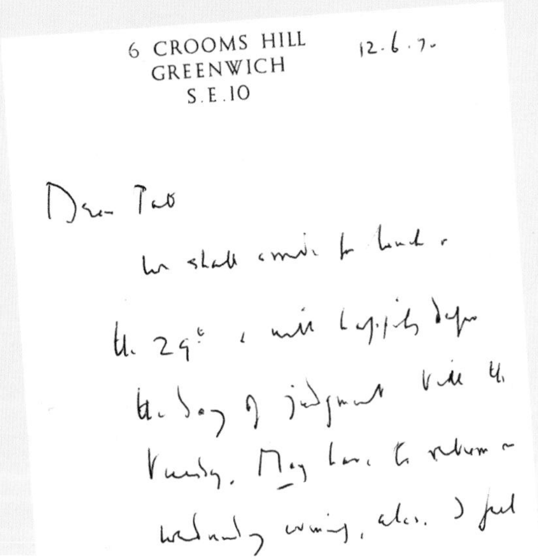
6 CROOMS HILL
GREENWICH
S.E.10

12.6.70

Dear Pat

Above: A book of poems by pupils, with a foreword by Cecil Day-Lewis

Left: Extract from a letter from Cecil Day-Lewis to Pat Savage, June 1970

of the textbooks were often supplemented by a series of jingles, rehearsed as a kind of group incantation to memorise their grammatical features. This was Gradgrind stuff, but James Richardson (1931–5) believed it effective as 'proved by the fact that, after all these years, I can actually remember it'!

Throughout the ages, lessons have been livened up through the production of various artefacts. One recent Head of History regularly brandished two bayonets from the Somme, much to the boys' delight, and there were firm precedents for such entertainment. Alan Sykes (1969–73) remembers firing Napoleon's pistol as a reward for having come top in History one term. Mr Ogston, the History Master, claimed to be descended from an officer on the *Bellerophon* who was given his pistol.

Nowadays, in all subjects, there is far more 'finding out' than 'cramming in'. Nonetheless, the boys still have to master the basics of English grammar, mathematical processes, foreign-language grammar and vocabulary, together with the material necessary to make sense of Science, History, Geography and Religious Studies, indeed every subject, but there is far more room now for a pupil's own input. Individual project work is common in many subjects. Boys are taught to think for themselves, to express their own ideas and to learn by doing and experimenting. The explosion in ICT and the use of the Internet have made the ability to handle huge amounts of data a *sine qua non* for the modern Summerfieldian. Boys are encouraged to be creative. They write prose and poetry; they paint, draw, design, model in clay, wood and metal; they argue, they debate, they act, they sing, they play sport, they play music and, above all, they still just play... The whole educational business at Summer Fields is firmly a two-way process. Yes, facts still have to be 'put in', but boys now *use* the material to develop their knowledge and understanding of the world around them. As 'Bobs' Alington (1922–37) acknowledged, little boys 'are filled with wonder and curiosity'. They are 'at a peak of

Cecil Day-Lewis

development in which they need and desire to make and do and absorb widely varying experiences'. This is exactly what Summer Fields offers them in its 150th year.

So, how well does Summer Fields do its job as a preparatory school? Is it a true 'launch-pad for life', laying down strong and sturdy foundations? Two OSS offer their thoughts:

SF laid the foundations of three subjects which stood me in good stead later on in life. The first was Latin, which was a godsend when I reached medical school. Even if you had slumbered through lectures in anatomy, if you could translate 'big toe wiggler' into Latin, that was probably the name of the muscle you were being asked about. The second was French, taught to us by Philip Johnstone. As well as the academic syllabus, at the end of the summer term he taught us cookery terms which were very useful later in life when visiting France on business. And of course classical Greek, taught by Mr Bell and GB himself. After Summer Fields I went on to Winchester where I was able to coast through Greek O-Level entirely on what I remembered from SF.

Edward Mynors (1955–60)

More than sixty years later, another pupil reflects on some of his subjects and their teachers. It should be noted that interest in many academic areas is now fostered through participation in national competitions:

Over the years that I have attended Summer Fields, our school has sent pupils to both individual and team maths challenges in the United Kingdom Mathematics Trust. Medals have been won in the Junior, Intermediate and Senior challenges. We have also qualified for the relative Olympiad papers of these

challenges. In 2013, the SF Mathematics Team (Arthur Ushenin, Dmitry Lubyako, Adrian Yam and Felix Stocker) competed in the Oxfordshire Regional Finals Competition, qualifying for the Final in London. In the end, we were placed twelfth out of 1,647 schools.

In Classics, we have the chance to learn both Latin and Ancient Greek to an extremely high level. This seems fundamental to any academic career. The Humanities remain very strong and the staff who teach us History, Geography and Religious Studies are first class.

In Science, from an early age we are encouraged to carry out experiments and find out for ourselves all about what is around us. On Thursdays, Mr Randolph, the Head of Science, holds a Science Club in which the best scientists come together and carry out experiments. Our most recent project is a homemade electric-powered car which can travel at speeds of about 20km/h.

Arthur Ushenin (2010–13)

Reports

Summer Fields prides itself on its full and efficient reporting to parents. Comments on progress are made termly. The aim is to show what a boy has achieved and to offer advice on how he might improve. Reports are produced for individual subjects, together with a tutor report,

Giles Andreae (1966–), SF 1974–9

Giles Andreae is well known today for his creation of Purple Ronnie, a cartoon character who markets a unique style of humour on a range of greetings cards and other merchandise such as T-shirts, mugs, tumblers, videos and books. Here, the essence of real-life dramas is portrayed through a world of cartoons in a plain, 'stick-men' style. The men are usually chubby; women and young girls sport huge bows in their hair. Andreae, alias Edward Monkton, has also created another series of cartoons for greetings cards, as well as writing many children's books. However, Purple Ronnie reigns supreme. The poems in his books and cards are both simple and direct. Here is a sample from *Love Poems* by Purple Ronnie:

> a poem about
> LOVE
> Sometimes it makes you feel happy
> And sometimes it makes you feel blue
> But I find it makes me feel smashingly Fab
> And that's cos I'm in it with **YOU**

Before Eton and Oxford, where he took his degree handicapped by serious illness, Andreae worked hard at Summer Fields in both Upper Remove and Fifth Form. He played football in the 3rd XI and enjoyed sailing. Other school interests included table tennis, billiards and photography. Indeed, several of his photographs feature in the *Summer Fields Magazine*.

Speaking at Summer Fields when opening the Summer 150 Art Exhibition, Andreae referred to the inspirational English teaching he had received from Nick Aldridge, who generated a love of poetry, which has since become a passion, at all times endorsing, encouraging and nurturing his first literary jottings. This led to feelings of self-belief and, later, the confidence to publish. 'This is where teachers shape the adult', said Andreae, 'and Summer Fields, through Nick Aldridge, did that for me.'

From a young age, Andreae enjoyed exploring the richness of the English language. His early poetic style is markedly different from that of Purple Ronnie, as we see from the first verse of 'A White Rose', written when he was just ten:

> The big, oval, curling petals, creamy white
> Smelling smoothly like honey
> With reddening green stalks and pale green
>   leaves
> The stalks growing from very small trees
> With small, rough speckles of moss...

A talent for prose writing is also evident from the *Magazine*, while the award of the Neville Prize for Handwriting suggests a generally legible script.

Andreae marshalled his thoughts orally as well as on paper. Skilled at debating, in a motion with the Dragon School, on the idea of modern luxury causing general moral decay, he made a 'quite outstanding, blockbuster' speech, 'ripping up his opponents' arguments and kicking the remains into the dust'. In Drama, too, there were some notable moments as he rocked through his dreams 'in the truest of Elvis styles', as Pharaoh, during a performance of *Joseph and the Amazing Technicolour Dreamcoat*.

But a love of poetry remained supreme. In a final piece before leaving Summer Fields, we are not quite with Purple Ronnie, yet there is a direct and incisive tone to the writing – the herald perhaps of things to come:

PEN POWER

> The pen, a marker of paper;
> The sword, a marker of blood.
> The pen makes a fluent hissing,
> The sword an ugly wound.
>
> One pen can kill ten thousand
> By one small scribble, in black.
> The sword no more than two,
> In less than the time of that.
>
> So now the final conclusion
> Between these two weapons, O Lord?
> And down came the answer from Heaven,
> 'Pen is mightier than Sword!'

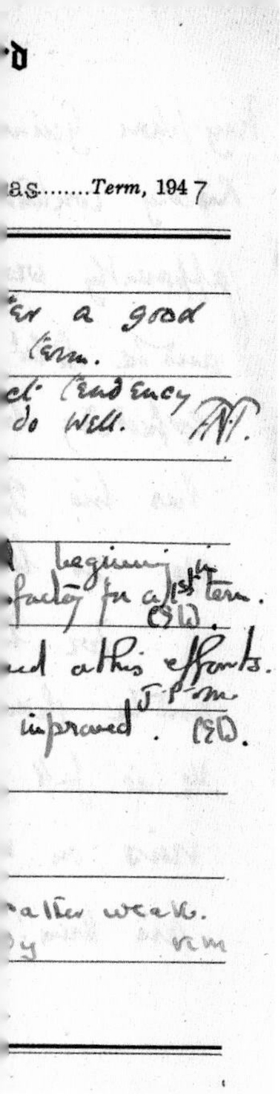

(handwritten report fragments, left margin)

...for a good
term.
...tendency
to do well. [initials]

...beginning...
...factory for a 1st term.
and all his efforts.
improved. [initials]

...rather weak.

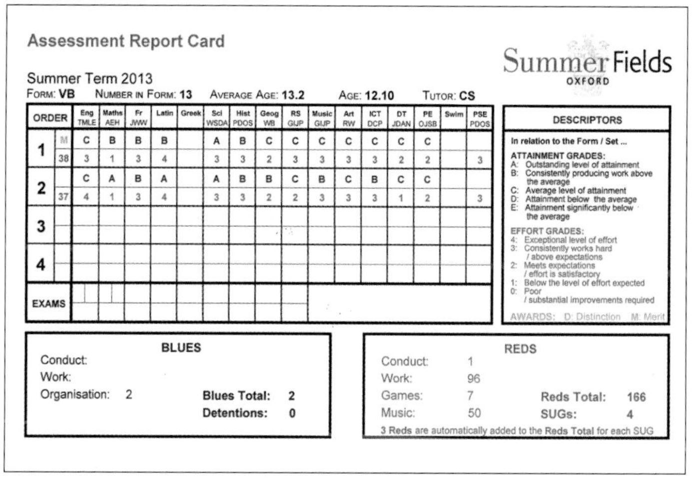

Assessment Report Card

Summer Fields OXFORD

Summer Term 2013
FORM: **VB**   NUMBER IN FORM: **13**   AVERAGE AGE: **13.2**   AGE: **12.10**   TUTOR: **CS**

ORDER	Eng TMLE	Maths AEH	Fr JIW	Latin	Greek	Sci WSDA	Hist PDOS	Geog WB	RS GIJP	Music GIJP	Art RW	ICT DCP	DT JDAN	PE OJSB	Swim	PSE PDOS
1 M 38	C 3	B 1	B 3	B 4		A 3	B 2	C 3	C 2	C 3	C 3	C 3	C 2	C 2		3
2 37	C 4	A 1	B 3	A 2		A 3	B 2	B 3	C 3	B 3	C 3	B 3	C 1	C 2		3
3																
4																
EXAMS																

DESCRIPTORS

In relation to the Form / Set ...

ATTAINMENT GRADES:
A: Outstanding level of attainment
B: Consistently producing work above the average
C: Average level of attainment
D: Attainment below the average
E: Attainment significantly below the average

EFFORT GRADES:
4: Exceptional level of effort
3: Consistently works hard / above expectations
2: Meets expectations
1: Below the level of effort expected
0: Poor / substantial improvements required

AWARDS: D: Distinction   M: Merit

BLUES		REDS	
Conduct:		Conduct:	1
Work:		Work:	96
Organisation: 2		Games:	7
Blues Total: 2		Music:	50
Detentions: 0		Reds Total: 166	SUGs: 4

3 Reds are automatically added to the Reds Total for each SUG

*Richard Guinness's report from 1947, **above**, and a modern-day assessment report card, **above right***

Below: A letter from GB to Richard Guinness's parents, 1947

Right: Richard (left) and Edward Guinness at the OS Reunion, 2013

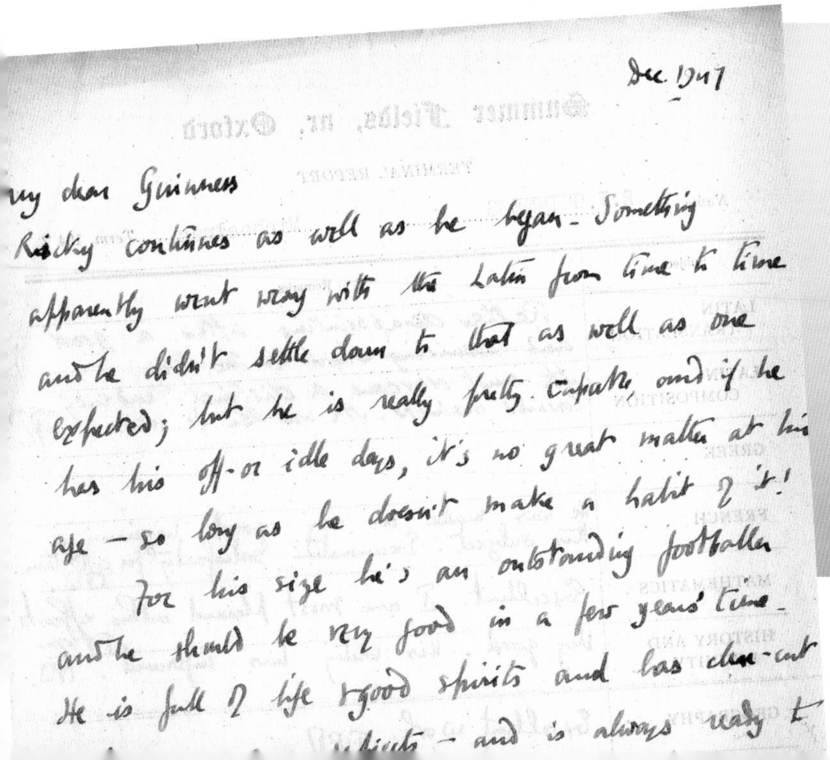

where every aspect of a boy's life is commented on. (This was discontinued in 2011.) The Headmaster then finally adds his words of wisdom. A full report is quite a work of art! These days, the report forms are generated centrally by the computer based on initial form lists. Thus if a boy leaves he may still have a report form. The eagle-eyed spot this and do not fill them in. However, it is all too easy to do so. It can even be done intentionally as a joke. Will the authorities ever notice...?

At the start of one of my earliest terms, a new boy (I'll call him Jimmy) appeared as normal on Day 1 but was gone forever by close of play on Day 2. Unfortunately, by the end of that term, the 'system' had still not caught up with Jimmy's sudden departure and a blank report form was produced for him. In those days, the report form was one sheet of paper, subdivided into boxes for each subject, Greek, Latin, English, History etc, which was then circulated to each master in turn for them to sum up the term's work with a well-crafted one-liner. There really wasn't room for much more.

First on Jimmy's circulation list was the Art teacher, Phyllis Aulden, an ethereal lady who wafted about in long black skirts like a benign witch. In her case a well-used 'two-worder' formed her standard comment. 'Good progress' was duly entered on Jimmy's report. I understand Jimmy's report then did the full round with each master in turn outdoing the last with their tributes to Jimmy's term – 'Teaching Jimmy this term has been effortless', 'I wish all the boys had given me as little trouble as Jimmy has this term' etc.

Richard Guinness (1947–52)

When reports are written about pupils who were actually present in the classroom, they provide an insightful picture of a boy's progress. Sam Legerton (1945–50) reflects on some of his reports:

At the end of my first term, I was said to have 'shown progress in Latin, worked industriously at French, always taken a high place in Maths, but spelling very poor'. The Head Master said, 'Sam is a very attractive boy – full of the right stuff.'

Term 2 and Geoffrey Bolton reports, 'He is alert and keen in all he undertakes, but must make more effort to write tidily. He looks to be a promising football player. He is too high-spirited to be able always to steer clear of mischief.'

July 1949. 'For some reason, and it is extraordinarily hard to put one's finger on the spot, Sam has not fulfilled expectations this term. He has a neat and orderly mind, but I fancy that half of it is away at Lords or Highbury when it ought to be on duty! All should be perfectly well with Sam next term if he recaptures his gay old spirit and perhaps learns something more of the virtue of humility and tolerance'.

The academic atmosphere was intense and there were many very clever boys there. I struggled to keep up in all subjects except Maths and believe that expectations of me were probably beyond my capacity to deliver.

(handwritten letter, bottom left)

Dec 1947

Summer Fields, nr. Oxford
TERMINAL REPORT

my dear Guinness

Ricky continues as well as he began. Something apparently went wrong with the Latin from time to time and he didn't settle down to that as well as one expected; but he is really pretty capable, and if he has his off-or idle days, it's no great matter at his age — so long as he doesn't make a habit of it!

For his size he's an outstanding footballer and he should be very good in a few years' time. He is full of life & good spirits and has clean-cut ... and is always ready t...

Prizes

Summer Fields today awards a wide range of prizes. Indeed, not many schools can boast three prize-givings a year – one at the end of each term. The summer ceremony is a magnificent affair. It requires hours of meticulous organisation by the Director of Studies who disappears into purdah weeks before the event, when everyone else seems to be out enjoying themselves in the sunshine. There are subject prizes, sporting prizes and cups, prizes for hobbies like carpentry and fishing; there are Headmaster's Commendations and Headmaster's Prizes for the Leavers. Great store is set by these prize-giving ceremonies, both to honour those with the laurels and to encourage the others:

> I do not remember academic life as a struggle, but in all my time at the school I only managed to win one prize (Fifth Form French) and even that was shared with someone else. Deciding which book to have as a prize was very difficult; on one side there were the books that you would like to read, and on the other the books that you knew you ought to choose. In the same prize-giving my younger brother got the prize for the most prizes, just to rub my nose in it.
>
> Edward Mynors (1955–60)

PRIZES, 1915.

CLASSICS—Fifth Form	...	Goodden.
(Supplementary Prize)	...	Shaw-Kennedy, mi.
Upper Remove	...	Runciman.
Lower Remove	...	Brinton.
Upper Fourth Form	...	Last.
Middle Fourth Form	...	Hudson.
Lower Fourth Form	...	Blech, mi.
Upper Shell	...	Watt.
Lower Shell	...	Wild.
Upper Third Form	...	Leonard.
Middle Third Form	...	Macnabb.
Lower Third Form	...	Backhouse.
Upper Second Form	...	Watson.
Lower Second Form	...	Buckland.
First Form	...	Jacques, mi.
MATHEMATICS—First	...	Finlay, mi.
Second	...	Slater.
Third	...	Deanesly.
Fourth	...	Watt.
Fifth	...	Cox.
Sixth	...	Piers.
Seventh	...	Noble.
Eighth	...	Mr. Buckley.
FRENCH—First	...	Pitman, ma.
Second	...	Mynors.
Third	...	Deanesly.
Fourth	...	Carter.
Fifth	...	Cox.
Sixth	...	Martineau.
Seventh	...	Buckland.
DIVINITY—First	...	Tuckey.
Second	...	Osler.
Third	...	Scott.
Fourth	...	Gough.
Fifth	...	Clark-Maxwell.
Sixth	...	Shaw-Kennedy, quart
Seventh	...	Wild.
GENERAL PAPER—First	...	Goodden.
(History, Geography, &c.) Second	...	Osler.
Third	...	Slessor.
Fourth	...	Tighe.
Fifth	...	Bell.
Sixth	...	Whitehead.
Seventh	...	Orr.
ESSAY	...	Cobb, ma.
DICTATION—(under eleven years of age)	...	Wild.
(under ten years of age)	...	Shaw-Kennedy, quart.
MUSIC—Choir	...	Jacques, ma.
First Piano	...	Asquith.
Second Piano	...	Slessor.
DRAWING—First	...	Tupper-Carey.
Second	...	Pitman, mi.
GYMNASIUM—Upper School (Medal)	...	Murray.
Lower School (Cup)	...	Watt.
SWIMMING—Race, 100 yards	...	Pitman, ma.
" 70 "	...	Murray.
" 40 "	...	Blech, ma.
Headers	...	Pitman, mi.
Style (for beginners)	...	Incledon-Webber.
ATHLETIC SPORTS—Cup	...	Pitman, ma.
CARPENTERING	...	Goodfellow.

Prize-giving,
July 2013

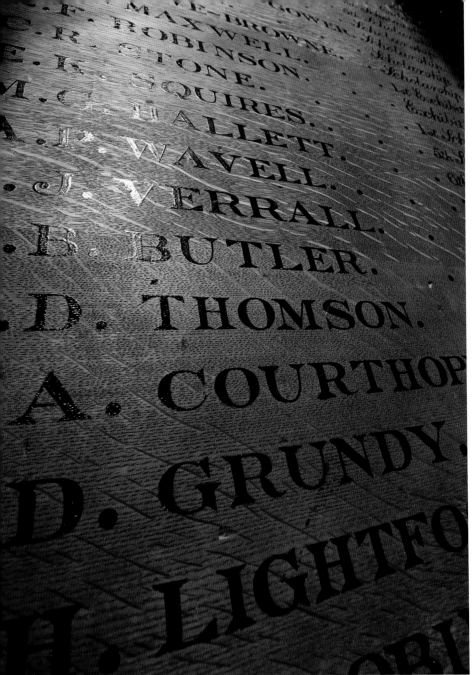

Over forty years later, Thomas Miles (1931–6) describes the rigours of the Winchester election:

During my second year in Fifth Form, GB prepared me for the Winchester scholarship. Shortly before the exam he wrote: '*Pauca sunt quae te admoneo: omnia enim satis cognita*. Still you won't forget to mark your As will you?' Yet, for all his advice when it came to the Latin translation paper in the Winchester election, I slipped up. The arrangement at Winchester was that after two days of examinations a smaller number of candidates would be told to stay on for a third day and in the course of the morning would be examined *viva voce*. The names of those required would be announced at Wells' bookshop late in the evening of the second day. My mother, who was accompanying me, suggested that I go to bed early. She would go to Wells' bookshop and would put a piece of paper under my door saying either 'wanted' or 'not wanted'. My Housemaster at Winchester used to refer to this aspect of the examination as 'the massacre of the innocents'. The news was good. We were summoned to the *viva* several at a time. I was asked to read a passage from Milton's *Lycidas*. Spenser Leeson [Headmaster of Winchester, 1935–46; Bishop of Peterborough, 1949–52] asked me if I had done any acting. When I said I had played John of Gaunt, he asked me if I could remember any of my part. Well, that was asking for it – my friends used to comment on my feats of memory, so I started. Eventually, he stopped me with the comment, 'I have no doubt you could go on for several more pages.'

I was fourteenth on the Winchester roll. I gather there was consternation at Summer Fields because I was so low down. I afterwards learnt that they had written to Winchester complaining.

Above: Academic honours board

Right: Eton Scholars, 1894

Scholarship and Common Entrance Examinations

The culmination of a boy's career at Summer Fields is usually a triumphal performance in the examination room, sitting either the Common Entrance examination (taken now in New Room) or a set of scholarship papers, often completed in the relatively strange environment of the target school. The rewards of success are huge, and winning a scholarship can be financially beneficial as well as academically satisfying:

My happiest memory of Summer Fields is of a summer afternoon when the Doctor sent for me, with a telegram in his hand and a golden sovereign in the other. He told me that I was second on the roll at Winchester.

The Rt Hon. Viscount Simonds, PC (1893–4)

Today, potential scholars for Eton are usually driven to the school from Summer Fields by the Headmaster and Andrew Bishop (since 1990), or the Master of the Scholars. Once there, they stay with various Housemasters throughout the whole time of sitting the academic papers and managing the interviews. In the past, things seemed a little more leisurely and, for years, GB ran the entire affair in his own way:

In 1952, I was a potential Eton Scholar. We were sent off for the Easter holidays with exercises that we had to complete and post back to GB. After a while I got a card saying '*Diu a te nihil habeo.*' It was the only card I have ever received that I can still remember word for word. Back at school, after weeks of terrible grammar tests, we were piled into GB's car and driven to Eton, stopping for tea at his sister's house in Henley. 'Would you care for China or Indian?' she asked. 'They don't know the difference,' growled GB. We stayed at a grand hotel in Windsor, and every morning GB escorted us to Eton for the examinations. After years of belligerent oppression, he was

suddenly fussing over us, insisting we cross the bridge in single file lest we were winged by a lorry. We all got scholarships!

Julian Reade (1949–52)

The academic *raison d'être* of Summer Fields remains the successful preparation of boys for their senior schools, be they scholarship or Common Entrance candidates. Many schools have their own papers. In particular the entrance examination for Winchester requires a careful and dedicated approach:

Summer Fields trained me for my senior school. I think that the Winchester History exam was the most challenging and difficult exam to get used to. One could not prepare for the source question and the essay was much broader than in the Common Entrance questions. Luckily I had a brilliant teacher who sympathised with my position and helped me and my fellow Wykehamists a lot during my last year at Summer Fields.

Felix Delaforce (2008–13)

chapter five

Sport

Mens Sana in Corpore Sano

As might be expected in a school founded by a woman whose husband ran a gymnasium and wrote physical training manuals for the army, health and fitness are highly valued at Summer Fields.

The school motto, *Mens Sana in Corpore Sano* (from Juvenal's tenth Satire), enshrines the notion of equal respect for brain and brawn and the idea that the two are mutually dependent, although as one would expect, sport does not hold the same appeal for all boys...

Games meant a huge amount and winter on the sports fields could be damp and gloomy. But I was good at games. An incidental bonus was the extra food, as there were fine teas after matches with other schools.

Julian Reade (1949–52)

Sport is a non-event in the Mynors family, though my younger brother let the side down by getting into the 3rd XV for rugger! My own poor sight meant that football and rugby were a mystery. There were red blobs and white blobs and a brown blob which hurt when it hit you.

Edward Mynors (1955–60)

Above: The school motto (A healthy mind in a healthy body) emblazoned on a leather-bound book of c.1896

Archibald Maclaren, the Oxford Gymnasium and Summer Fields

Archibald Maclaren was the founder of the Oxford Gymnasium and one of the first apostles of the culture of physical exercise. Born in 1819, Maclaren developed from being a simple fencing instructor to a pioneer of gymnastics, particularly as it came to be used by the army: his principles of general fitness underpin the physical training exercises of military personnel to this very day. He enshrined his ideas in a number of books and pamphlets, setting out systems of military gymnastics and fencing. Two of Maclaren's publications were reissued after his death in a compendium version under the title *Physical Education* (1895).

Maclaren believed that physical fitness was a key element in all walks of life and ought not to be restricted to the military: 'There is no profession, there is no calling or occupation', he wrote, 'in which man can be engaged … in which a fairly developed frame will not be valuable to him … to enable the mind to do its work.' Maclaren, having noted the competitive exercises of classical times with their realisation of the importance of physical well-being to overall human performance, had equal respect for the fitness of the brain and the body. He believed in the mutual dependency of physical and mental health. This is the ethos which was to be developed at Summer Fields – the notion that a mind works better in a healthy body.

Maclaren's gymnasium in Oxford, a 'very handsome and well-constructed building', erected in the 1850s by Joseph Castle to designs by William Wilkinson, was situated in Alfred Street, south of the High Street and just across the road from an ancient public house – an interesting juxtaposition! The gymnasium far exceeded 'anything of its kind in this or any other country'. An illustration of 1859 shows men training on wall-bars, ropes, beams, parallel bars and ladders. Others fence or wrestle. Such was the muscular development of the first twelve NCOs (the so-called 'Twelve Apostles') who underwent Maclaren's training programme in the 'Class of 1861', that they all outgrew their uniforms.

Maclaren further believed that gymnastic exercises were most effective at a young age when bodies and minds were growing; in other words, a gymnasium was of great benefit to a school. From the beginning, boys took regular exercise at Summer Fields, for many years under the eagle eye of Sergeant Morley (1902–37). The school gymnasium was built in 1898 and opened with a concert on 12 November of that year. It was designed by a Mr Quinton who 'produced a not undistinguished building'. Messrs Heath and George supplied the equipment: ropes, vaulting horses, wall-bars, rings, mats, ladders and beams. For the unsporty boy, it must have been a veritable torture chamber! 'The gym', in its new guise as 'Macmillan', continues to play a central role in the life of the school, as a theatre, concert hall, lecture venue and general meeting and assembly area. The original purpose of this special place is now fulfilled by the Sports Hall, where the principles of Archie Maclaren and his Oxford Gymnasium continue to flourish.

Above: Medals won by Isaac Pitman for gym in 1914

Below: Sergeant Morley in 1917 and, **right,** sketch of Sergeant Morley by Hilary Williams (1900–6)

Archibald Maclaren's gymasium today, now known as Blue Boar Court

Summer Fields is full of opportunities. It opened a new door – the door of sport. Until I came to this school I had never kicked a football, never passed a rugby ball. Five years later, I won a Sports Scholarship to Kingham Hill School. For this, Summer Fields will always remain in my heart and sport will remain my passion and pleasure for life.

Alfie Orr-Ewing (2008–13)

The *Summer Fields Magazine*, from 1897, records details of football and cricket matches and may thus reflect practice common well before that date. As soon as there were sufficient boys to form teams, formal sport could begin. Cricket and football matches probably started in the 1870s. Soon after that, the facilities for organised sport seemed well established with football and cricket pitches, as well as the fives courts on the old school playground – where Parmoor Court now stands.

Football

Football grew quickly. Skills improved and the *Magazine* notes a steady stream of matches with their attendant victories or losses. Generally, there were rather more of the former than the latter. In particular, the 1935 football XI, described as the best since before the First World War, won sixteen of its twenty-two matches. But even better things were in store for the following year with a 1st XI, captained by Brian Straton-Ferrier (1932–7). Rated as the best team to that date on account of the tremendous pace of its players and the goal-scoring power of the forwards, this side enjoyed one of the most successful seasons in the school's history. Straton-Ferrier's report of his unbeaten side's final match, against Horris Hill in December 1936, captured the nail-biting atmosphere of the occasion. The players had

A football game in the 1920s

Above: Sports Day programme, 1910

A Guide to Summer Fields Caps

Football XI

2nd XI

Cricket XI

2nd XI

1st XV

2nd XV

The School Cap

Above and right:
Football XIs, 1898 and 1935

thought of little else in the run-up to the game. Tension was high. Even GB, who coached the side, was said to be anxious. In the end, Summer Fields won, easily. GB was so delighted that he gave Straton-Ferrier a silver pencil, engraved with the single word *Invictus*.

Football flourished in the 1960s, 1970s and 1980s under Nigel Chapman (1968–88). According to Charlie Palmer (1976–80), there were 'some vintage years under his tutelage'. Charlie also notes that 'Mr Chapman caused a stir when he changed the 1st XI football colours to match his beloved Arsenal strip'. Since then, football at Summer Fields has been run successfully by a series of masters, including John Mayall, Jeremy Houghton and Johnny Bush. It is now in the safe hands of Joe Porter, assisted by Ian Barrett.

Sometimes a single goal makes all the difference, as Temi Bolodeoku (2011–13) remembers. Half time, 3rd XI, SF losing 2–1. After a stiff team talk by Mr Fradgley (2009–14), the second half went better, but still no further score. Then, with just about three minutes to go, the roar of the cheering army of parents became louder and more intense. 'This fired

Rugby

I loathed rugger, at least until I was relegated to the peaceful position of full back.

John Jolliffe (1944–7)

The Summer Fields Register suggests that there was no rugby at the school before 1921. In fact, it started in January 1920 despite the prejudices of 'Bear' Alington (1918–28), who was an Oxford football Blue. In a memorable game with the Dragon School during that first term, each XV was made up of a mixture of both Summerfieldians and Dragons in a gesture of friendliness! Two years later, after a victorious match against the Eton Junior XV, Reginald McKenna, the father of the Summer Fields captain, presented the team with a huge box of chocolates to consume on the way home. Rugby developed quickly, and by 1924 it was said that 'every boy had begun to learn the game', and that on some days, 'the whole school is hard at it'.

In spite of Summer Fields' late start to rugby, the game expanded rapidly as experience and skills increased. By 1964, it is both interesting and surprising to note that more OSS had played rugby for the Eton XV than cricket in the Eton XI.

Another surprise is that the acronym BOSFAM (Boys of Summer Fields and Masters), which most people now associate with the annual BOSFAM golf match, had its origins in rugger. It was the idea of David Kidd-May (1955–2000) to ensure that his 1st XV were a tough lot:

Top: A rugby scrummage, 1935

Above: SF badge on rugby shirt belonging to Richard Guinness (1947–52)

When I took over the rugger in the early Sixties, the custom still prevailed of selecting the 1st XV from two or three Trial Matches in which a possible 1st XV played against a side reinforced by two or three masters – an inconceivable situation nowadays. In order to try to give the final Trial an enhanced

First game of rugby at Summer Fields in 1920: an extract from GB's recollections forty years on

me up. There was a scramble for the ball in the Ludgrove penalty area and I was there and I fired the ball into the back of the net.' The final score was 2–2, the only draw, with seven other victories in the eight games played. No win, but at least this exciting moment enabled the team to remain unbeaten.

More boys than ever play in teams. During the 2013 football season, the school fielded no fewer than eight XIs, seven Colts sides, six Junior Colts teams, as well as an Under 9 six-a-side.

In the Easter term of 1920 Summer Fields for the first time played Rugger. Forty years on I recall with pride that I played in first game – it was my first game, too! I think that this was the greatest concession Uncle Hugh ever made. To him there was only one code of football and he genuinely disliked Rugger. But he was won over by his youngest son Bobs, then at Magdalen, and, vowing* he would ne'er consent, consented. For the first year it was played only on half-holidays and only in one game. We had two matches, Dragons courteously sending up a side in their soccer team and playing so skilfully that they did not score more than 50 points in either game. At the end of the term Uncle Hugh with characteristic generosity gave away completely and said that henceforth

status, I thought up the idea of giving it a special name, 'The BOSFAM Match', since it involved boys of Summer Fields and masters. Little did I think that the name to which I had given birth would still be alive today.

Winning is always satisfying, but beating the Dragon has an added piquancy and this satisfaction sticks. Julian Reade (1949–52) remembers his moment of glory when he blind-sided the scrum near the goalposts and 'hurled myself across the line with a hundred Dragons grabbing me from every angle and piling on top. The whistle blew, they let go, and there was the ball still pinned between my chest and the ground. It was just one of our three tries that day, but it seemed far and away my finest school achievement.'

Rugby continued to flourish under the dedicated coaching of Stephen Cox (1973–86) and Rupert McNeile (1972–2007). The XV of 1981 won all eight of their matches, including a tense final 4–0 victory over Lockers Park. Prior to that, some XVs had encountered sharp practice by an opposition bent on denying them the glory of an unbeaten season, as recalled by Bryan Burrough (1968–73):

My clearest sporting memory is of an unbeaten 1st XV playing away with the opposition's Headmaster refereeing. Whatever SF did that day we were never going to win that match. Near the end I remember Patrick Crawford [1966–72] running the full length of the field, only to be called back for some apparent misdemeanour. The whole 1st XV came off the field in tears.

In the experienced hands of Mark Johnson (1983–98), and now Bill Bailey (since 1988), Summer Fields rugby is perhaps at its strongest. The 2012 XV celebrated an unbeaten season, while in Lent 2013, the 1st XV were victorious in six of their seven matches. An increasing number of boys represent the school. The 2013 season saw five XVs, three Colts XIIs, four Junior Colts IXs and three Under 9 IXs. Summer Fields teams also played in the St John's Northwood Sevens Tournament, which they won in 2013, and the Moulsford Sevens Tournament. The school is also regularly represented in the Rosslyn Park National Schools Sevens Tournament. Here, over the years, Summer Fields has often shone on the pitch, reaching the semi-final in 2002, although the ultimate prize has yet to be won. Parental support and generosity are notable, as in the case of the smart scoreboard donated by the parents of Aulden (1983–88), Fergus (1990–5) and Toby Dunipace (1999–2004) and Hugo Gibbs (1992–7); a scrummaging machine from Willie Lebus (1961–6) and post protectors and flags from the Browne family, on behalf of Jonty (2003–8).

There are regular rugby tours to South Africa. Links forged with a number of schools there, along with visits to historical sites, bring a wider element to these ventures than just the sport. The boys' enthusiasm for the game is also enhanced through visits by famous players such as Jonathan Davies (Wales), Sean Fitzpatrick (captain of the All Blacks) and Dewi Morris (England).

Cricket

In summer, the early mornings were often bright, and I would watch out of the classroom window, hoping that the sun would last till afternoon. Vampire jets practised overhead. I vividly remember particular moments in cricket – a late cut through the slips for four; an off-drive skied and nearly caught; a leg-sweep copied from Denis Compton; a successful cow-shot; the ignominy of being clean-bowled by a Yorker.

Julian Reade (1949–52)

That 'Cricket', along with 'Classics' and 'Chapel', has been considered one of the three great pillars of the school, says something of its importance at Summer Fields. GB and many of his peers were passionate about the game. Many still are, and several talented players on the current staff are well able to pass on their skills to the boys. From 1897, through careful analysis of the *Summer Fields Magazine*, it is possible to relive the excitement, and occasional disappointment, of all major school matches. Detailed reports abound, as do precise comments on the key players in the various XIs. There is a mass of statistical data and the performances of individual OSS may be reconstructed by the patient scholar.

The setting for 1st XI matches has largely remained unchanged, with a well-drained pitch, embellished by a thatched pavilion in the school colours, standing for all that is valued at Summer Fields. Rebuilt after a disastrous fire, the pavilion testifies in its own quiet way to the enduring excellence of the school. Change is in evidence all around. Even the cars that park close by it on match days are not the same as they were, but the pavilion, like a sentinel, patiently stands guard, conserving the *genius loci*. It is even said that some fathers have sent their sons to Summer Fields owing to the appeal of this iconic building.

Cricket has been played here since the 1870s. It remains today an important element of the games programme. By 1890, there were fixtures against Cothill, the Dragon School, Cordwallis (later, St Piran's), while the 1st XI also played junior sides from Eton, Winchester, Pangbourne and Radley. There have been some notable seasons like that of 1901, which saw a triumphant XI savour an easy victory over the Dragon. In 1958, the XI contained Rupert Daniels (1953–8), who, as a devastatingly effective bowler, took sixty-four wickets in just sixteen games. While also in the side, David Calvert-Smith (1953–8), later Director of Public Prosecutions, made two 50s in the same week that he took the fifth King's Scholarship at Eton, thus epitomising the school's ethos of *Mens Sana in Corpore Sano*.

Top: Cricket in 1929

Above: Cricket cap belonging to Brian Straton-Ferrier (1932–7)

Left: A letter home from Michael Pemberton (1887–90)

Below: Cricket XI, 1887

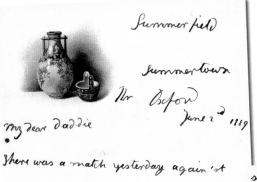

Summer field

Summertown

Nr Oxford

June 2nd 1889

My dear daddie

There was a match yesterday again'st Radley (under 15) but I think that they brought two chaps who were about 16. We were beaten by about 20 runs. Next Saturday we play again'st a team called "The Dagons" who are very bad

so I think that we shall win. Last year when we played them we got them all out for 2. The eleven Gerard and I are in play fourth eleven to morrow and I think that we shall win. I expect that we shall begin bathing either next week or the week after. There was a very heavy thunderstorm this morning and it woke me up

Cricket XI,
1962

Nurtured by a series of skilful coaches – Charles Churchill, Nigel Chapman, John Mayall, Rob Lagden and currently Ollie Bishop – the game continues in good heart. Facilities are excellent. There are several pavilions, many good pitches, plentiful nets (both indoors and out), as well as a bowling machine to enable batsmen to hone their shots and deal with specialist deliveries.

Along with inter-school games, League matches remain important, and the annual Broomstick Match is still a prominent feature at the end of the Summer Term. Furthermore, a range of staff fixtures ensures that cricket coaches are able to practise what they preach, showcasing their skills under the critical eye of their pupils.

Cricket remained strong throughout the 1960s with Mark Faber (1958–63) and John Barclay (1962–7), both of whom became Sussex county players. Indeed, Barclay went on to captain Sussex and to become President of the MCC. The 1962 XI contained the record-breaking bowler Dennis Tabor (1957–62) with his tally of eighty-two wickets in a mere fifteen matches. Since then, many other boys have continued to play serious cricket. Tom Cox (1994–2000) captained the Shrewsbury Saracens XI to win the Cricketer Cup and has represented Shropshire in the final of the Minor Counties One-day Competition. Tom's Club, Shrewsbury, also triumphed in the National Club Knockout Competition in 2011, as well as winning the Birmingham Premier League twice.

Sir George (Gubby) Oswald Browning Allen, KBE (1902–89), SF 1912–15

Gubby Allen, Test cricketer, England captain and cricket administrator, was born on 31 July 1902 in Sydney, Australia. He was a natural sportsman, spending three years in the Eton XI (1919–21) before winning a Blue at Cambridge in 1922 and 1923. He then moved on to play for Middlesex and England, gaining a reputation as a genuinely fast bowler and no mean batsman. Of no more than medium build, Allen achieved his pace through timing, thrust, and a fine follow through. Between the late 1920s and the mid-1930s, there was no English fast bowler, apart from Harold Larwood, capable of more dangerous spells.

His sporting prowess was nurtured at Summer Fields, where he showed early all-round promise, playing both 1st XI football and captaining the cricket XI. In the 1915 season, 'where disappointment was the key as the result of measles, lack of match practice and nerves', Allen played some 'excellent cricket, showing a great variety of shots'. He averaged 22 runs with a personal best of 78 not out in an abandoned match

Gubby Allen with his brother Geoff at nets, 1911

against Horris Hill on 24 July. Overall, Gubby Allen was rated as 'promising with bat and ball'.

'Promising' indeed! He went on to enjoy a world-class career, playing for England against Australia in 1930 and 1934, against New Zealand in 1931 and against the West Indies in 1933. He captained England against India in 1936 and against the West Indies in 1948. In all, he won

twenty-five England caps. Passionate about cricket, Gubby Allen was elected to the MCC committee in 1935 and for half a century there was scarcely an issue connected with the game in which he was not closely involved. Allen chaired the England selectors (1955–61), was President of the MCC (1963–4) and Treasurer (1964–76). He was a member of the Cricket Council from its formation in 1968 until 1982, being a prime mover in founding the national coaching scheme. With H. S. Altham, he wrote the *MCC Cricket Coaching Book* (1952), which remains a standard work.

Charlie Palmer (1976–80) remembers Gubby Allen visiting the school and signing cricket bats in the pavilion. Indeed, there have been several visits by famous names. In recent years, Shane Warne signed bats for a queue of excited boys and, on a wet day, when a match against the University in the Parks had been abandoned, the entire Australian side – yes, the whole team – practised in the Sports Hall nets to the sheer delight of what seemed like the whole school.

Over the years, there have been many specific cricketing episodes which have stuck in the memory of several OSS. Bishop David Jennings (1952–7) recalls

> the absolute beauty of the Cricket teas, which, as I was absolutely useless at cricket, I was allowed to enjoy as scorer of the 1st XI. These teas were served in the gym and were bacon and eggs – a fascinating thing to have at about 5pm on a hot summer's afternoon.

Thomas Miles (1931–6) remembers an Under 10 victory over Abingdon against all the odds. All out for 40, 'with only four of us avoiding ducks', things were not looking too good when the Cothill team batted. However, a sensational catch by Russell started a collapse and 'we just got home. In fact we got them out for 32. I remember that catch of Russell's, a Cothill master compared it to plucking an apple from a tree.' [John Russell (1932–6) was killed in action in 1943.]

Masters, of course, always give the 'correct' decisions when umpiring, and their word is law. No lesser person than GB himself adhered strictly to this precept, sometimes to the dismay of others:

> While umpiring at square-leg (aged about twelve), and having to adjudicate on an appeal for run-out, I remember being furious at my 'decision' being over-ruled by GB who was standing at *extra cover*!
>
> Professor D. R. Myddleton (1948–53)

Even the Second World War was not allowed to get in the way of cricket, as Peter Fullerton recalls:

Throughout the war, despite petrol rationing, we continued to play our rivals the Dragons, Cothill and Swanbourne, home and away, at cricket, football and rugger.

In cricket, any number of things can happen. Richard Guinness (1947–52) recollects an unusual hat-trick in a school match of 1950:

Sammy Legerton (1945–50) took two wickets with consecutive balls, so polishing off our opponent's innings. With his first ball in the next match, bowling from the Pavilion End, he took another wicket, so achieving a remarkable and unusual hat-trick.

In modern times, Harry Christopherson (2008–13) enjoyed beating Cheam in the final over of his final game for the 3rd XI:

We got their number eleven out. Our parents on the side line jumped up at this unexpected victory and we couldn't believe our eyes. This is why I loved the cricket at Summer Fields, it always kept you motivated to keep at it and not give up even if a defeat looked near.

Edward Doughty (2008–13) enjoyed a highly successful final season with the 1st XI and remembers a memorable match against Aysgarth in June 2013. Summer Fields had suffered a crushing defeat in 2012 and needed to put the record straight. Put in to bat, Edward, as opener, went on to score his fifth fifty of the season, being out finally for 61, with the score on 103 for 4. Summer Fields declared at 131 for 7. Edward takes up the story of what happened next:

> After tea I opened the bowling for the first time for the 1st XI. Their opening batsman, after a play and miss to my first ball, was given out lbw to my second. The next batsman was clean bowled for a golden duck and the No. 4, having narrowly survived a confident appeal and a potential hat-trick, fell lbw to my fifth. A triple wicket maiden was a promising start! In the final over of the match, with Aysgarth on 75, I took the last wicket, securing a memorable victory and finishing with my best bowling figures of 6 for 15, which included my fiftieth wicket for Summer Fields.

The scorecard of a match against Horris Hill on 20 June 1914 makes interesting reading when a certain Summerfieldian, G. O. Allen, was dismissed, lbw, b. Jardine for 2. As many readers will know, both Allen and Jardine were later to captain England.

The 1st XI of 2013 enjoyed an excellent season, with only one loss in thirteen matches. As in the other major sports, a large number of boys now represent the school. Apart from the 1st XI, sixteen other cricket teams took to the field, resulting in some memorable Under 9 victories against Cothill, St John's Beaumont and the Dragon School. At the other end of the scale, as part of the school's 150th anniversary celebrations, a special match was arranged between the MCC and a Headmaster's XI, in which the latter enjoyed a victory by seven wickets.

Hockey

The combination of the arrival of Ollie Bishop in 2009, a skilled hockey player from Marlborough, and new all-weather pitches have enabled hockey to be played seriously within the last couple of years. It is now a growing game, allowing boys to try something different and thus extending their overall sporting opportunities. A recent leaver describes his new-found experience and looks forward to developing his skills:

> I have never been that good at the main sports, but when the school got an AstroTurf, I found out in the Removes that Hockey was a game that I could actually play well. I played hockey for two years in the 1st VII. Summer Fields has set me up for the next years at my senior school.
>
> James Tollemache (2008–13)

Fred Corbett (2008–13), as befits the Head of School, had the honour of playing in the first ever hockey match, at home. The opponents were the Dragon. At half time, the score was 0–0. Then, 1–0 to them, then 2–0, then 2–1, then, with virtually the whole school chanting 'RED ARMY' and 'SUMMER FIELDS':

Ajay Gupta (2009–12) passed me the ball. I managed to dance my way around all six outfield members of the Dragon's team, moving and stopping; reverse-stick, flat-stick; deceiving both the crowd and the opposition. With only the goalkeeper to beat, I ran straight at him and put the ball between his legs and into the goal. There was a sudden silence as the ball hit the back of the goal. All eyes looked to the referee. His arm slowly pointed at the centre circle, and the goal was awarded; I was overjoyed, and the school went wild.

The final score was a draw 2–2, honours even. But for Fred, even more joy was to come. With due humility, he records that 'some Fifth Years were saying: "Have you seen Corbett play? He's just amazing!"'

Golf

Golf is popular at Summer Fields and has long been so:

I enjoyed all games and athletics, but the golf course around the outside of the playing fields probably gave me more pleasure than captaining the 2nd XI cricket team in my later years.

Alastair Macdonald (1951–5)

The school is fortunate to have a splendid nine-hole course, sited in the Far Fields with some neatly kept greens and many strategically placed bunkers. This new course was the brainchild of Charles Churchill (1964–96), who ran golf here for many years. Keen golfing parents were each encouraged to sponsor the landscaping of a 'hole' and thus the new course was created. In the early 1980s, golf was still played, partly, in the Near Fields, which was never quite appropriate in terms of personal safety…

Competitions now include those for the Marston Cup, the Dudley Medal and the Paget-Cooke Cup. There is an annual

Bernard Darwin, later golf correspondent for both *The Times* and *Country Life* and prolific author of golfing books, enjoyed playing at Summer Fields on the first proper course created in about 1889. Forty years on, Thomas Miles (1931–6) offers a detailed description of its layout:

> The school possessed its own golf course, five holes being within the playing fields and four in the rougher fields adjoining the farm which lay just outside the grounds. The playing fields were divided by a road. The first hole started at the north end and one had to drive over the road to the far south corner of the ground. Pat Marston, who had been a golfing Blue at Oxford, could just about drive this green. The second hole involved travelling back to the north end. The third hole ran alongside the boundary to the playing fields on the east.
> Thereafter one went out of the grounds over a stile and remained in rougher territory for holes four, five, six and seven. I remember taking nineteen strokes at hole number seven, which for this particular round, played havoc with my card. Holes eight and nine were back in the playing fields, hole nine being a short one from the road to the corner of the fields.

Darwin had some interesting points to make when he returned to Summer Fields for a golf match against the masters. He wrote that the greens outside the area of the playing fields were hard to approach because, 'If we pitched short, we stopped short and if we pitched on, we went over. Yet the shot was clearly playable.' He added that his opponents regularly landed on the green without going over it.

There are many first-class golfers on the current staff and the popularity of the sport is as high as ever. Boys return to school with increasingly sophisticated golfing kit and one feels that it will not be too long before buggies become the order of the day!

Above: Edward Guinness (1933–8) in 1934

Parents and Sons Golf Day and, of course, the famous BOSFAM Competition held at the end of each Lent Term, where the best boy golfers partner non-golfing staff and vice versa. Such matches were well established by the 1920s. Pat Marston (1918–22; staff 1931–70) notes what he calls 'the annual Masters and Boys Foursomes', with the 'current Boy Champion trying to carry the worst of the Masters to victory' – *plus ça change…* Your editor was victorious in 1988, partnering the best boy player, and has an engraved tankard to prove it! BOSFAM golf is always a most entertaining and enjoyable day. Indeed, it allows many who have never swung a club before to try their hand at a new game.

Golf has a long history here and, according to Bernard Darwin (1887–9), it was played originally with hockey sticks and fives balls. Sir Earnest Holderness, CBE (1900–3) writes that during the winter terms, boys were allowed to hit and chase golf balls 'on the playing fields and adjoining meadows, where some rough nine holes were laid out'. Dr Williams would appear on his lawn, clad in a red coat, with his clubs and tee off. For the boys, the red coat signified that golf was allowed that day.

Tennis

In 2011, tennis received a considerable fillip with the opening of a splendid new facility catering for multiple sporting needs. Two tarmac competition courts finished in striking electric US Open Blue, with extended run-offs behind the baselines (great for coaching observation), and four cushion (dry) based AstroTurf courts (converting to a superb hockey/football area during the winter months) ushered in a new era for the game.

There had been no tennis during the 1930s, but, fifty years later, it was flourishing under the direction of Anthony Browne (1974–87) and coach Tony Beale. Today the game is popular among the boys and competition is keen for the Singles and Doubles Cups, as well as the Beale Improvement Trophy. Pandy Stoop (since 2003) runs a series of fixtures against opponents such as Elstree, Cothill and the Dragon and boys play regularly in the Radley Tournament at 1st VI and Colts IV levels. BOSFAM tennis, in which the more athletic staff partner boys, remains popular, under arrangements similar to those for the BOSFAM golf. However, the Mothers and Sons Tennis Competition is an occasion without equal, for its range of elegant fashion and balletic beauty, which, in a few cases, more than compensates for any lack of skill with the racket!

Fives

There are several references to fives in the first fifty years of Summer Fields' history, both in school magazines and in letters in the school's archives. However, at that stage, it should have been more correctly called 'racquet-fives', as it was actually the game we know now as squash. 'Hand-fives' was not played at Summer Fields until 1922, when the first fives courts were completed in the school playground, where Parmoor Court now stands.

In 1919, the school determined to honour the memory of all those OSS who gave their lives in the First World War, and funds were raised for this. There was some debate about how to use the money. Apart from the chapel memorials, a decision was taken to spend approximately £900 building three open fives courts, one of each type – Eton, Winchester and Rugby Fives. A stone tablet was to be attached, indicating their role as a war memorial. Thomas Miles (1931–6) remembers these courts and how they affected the different variations of the game:

> There were three fives courts. Rugby Fives involved simply a rectangular court. In the Winchester version of the game, there was a small buttress about two-thirds of the way up the court and if one could hit it, the ball went forwards at an angle. Finally, there was the Eton court which contained a massive buttress and whenever this was hit, the play was in the front of the court.

Sadly, the courts were demolished when the playground was sold in the 1970s. Later, when the Sports Hall was planned, Nigel Talbot Rice chose to include two fives courts alongside three squash courts. Early designs were for Rugby Fives, but the Headmaster fortunately heeded advice, so that from 1995, Summer Fields was able to join the distinguished ranks of prep schools playing Eton Fives. The memorial tablet from the original courts was duly installed in the gallery and on each Armistice Day a poppy wreath is laid there. Another custom is an annual fives match, on Remembrance Sunday, between the Jesters and Oxbridge Past and Present; in 2012 this fixture fittingly became Jesters vs. Old Summerfieldians.

Above: The fives courts today, and **left,** the original fives courts in the playground

The first SF fives match on the new courts took place on 4 February 1996, against Belmont School. The school's First Pair featured Guy Negretti (1991–6) and Euan Davidson (1990–6). Bashir Moukarzel (1991–6) was Captain of Fives in the inaugural season, and his family kindly presented a cup, awarded annually to the outstanding SF player. Since that first fixture, over 220 Summerfieldians have represented the school at fives.

Twice we have been runners-up in the National Schools Under 12 Championships, no mean achievement when the four semi-final berths are often occupied by Highgate School, which has dominated the game at this level for many years. Thomas Cox (1994–2000) and Jamie Bingham (1994–2000) achieved it in 1999, followed by Freddie Fairhead (2003–8) and Max Koe (2003–8) in 2007. With his partner at Shrewsbury, Cox went on to win the Open in 2004 – a feat matched only once before or since by an OS, when Richard Westmacott (1926–30), then at Eton, took the championship in 1935. Since 2000, a further twelve SF pairs have won through to the semi-finals of the Under 12s. At the annual Prep Schools Tournament, six pairs have reached the semi-finals in recent years, but the school still awaits its first appearance in the final to win that laurel crown.

Squash

Squash now flourishes in the excellent Sports Hall courts – yet another sporting opportunity for the boys before they pass on to their senior schools. The 2012–13 season was particularly successful, with the 1st V and Colts teams achieving a clean sweep against all opposition. But the annual Fathers vs. Common Room match was a different story. An evening of games played in a 'fabulous spirit' resulted in a convincing win for the visitors, despite loss of the score sheet! Matters were later resolved in a local restaurant, and the Common Room determined 'to do better next time'.

Constantine Louloudis (1991–), SF 2000–5

Constantine Louloudis first came to Summer Fields in 2000. He excelled in the classroom, always in the top forms, and won a string of prizes throughout the course of his career. He capped his academic achievement by taking the second King's Scholarship at Eton. He also gained awards for art and music certificates for his piano playing. He acted in school plays and handled responsibility and power both as a prefect and Head Boy. He gained his colours for swimming – perhaps a useful attribute for a future oarsman – but rugger was his principal sport. Beginning in the Colts B, he graduated to the 1st XV where he was always effective as part of 'a solid scrum'.

At Eton, Louloudis had taken up rowing, so as the boats lined up at Eton Dorney Lake for the start of the Men's Eight Final on Day Five of the 2012 Olympics, he was very much on home territory. Having been troubled with a back injury that had threatened to end his London 2012 dreams, he was thrilled to receive the last-minute call-up to take his place as stroke for Team GB's Men's Eight.

Constantine Louloudis, front row right, at the 2012 Olympics

Naturally the opposition was fiercely strong: Germany was unbeaten since 2009 and Canada were the defending Olympic Champions. The race began. Having been neck and neck with the Germans for the first 1,000m, Team GB moved ahead to take a shock lead. The Germans responded, regained the lead inside the final 250m and took gold. Canada finished strongly overhauling Team GB to take silver on the line.

There were hints that the bronze medal was a disappointment for such a determined crew, yet Summer Fields cannot have been more proud of Constantine Louloudis – the only one of her Old Boys (so far) ever to have won an Olympic medal.

Prior to the Olympics, he had won the Men's Pairs with George Nash at the FISA World Rowing Under-23 Championships on the Bosbaan on 24 July 2011, in Amsterdam. Having taken a year out of his studies for Olympic training, Louloudis is now back at Trinity College, Oxford, to complete his degree. In 2011, he won his first Blue in the six seat of the triumphant Boat Race crew. He again rowed in the victorious Oxford Eight of 2013, before stroking the university to what has been described as 'its most comprehensive victory … for more than a century' in the Boat Race of 2014. What a way to mark his prep school's 150th anniversary, not to mention his third Rowing Blue!

Swimming

Until the opening of the outdoor pool in 1964 (since surpassed by the lovely, warm indoor pool of 1985), boys bathed at Deep End in the cold, reed-filled Cherwell, 'a muddy old river then', according to Alastair Macdonald (1951–5). The boys wore 'bum bags' and, in the 1920s, an enormous man called Webb taught the breast stroke and made a huge splash when he dived in. The last vestiges of the diving boards remain visible on the river bank. Swimming was a popular pastime, and many Old Boys comment on it. During the summer months, GB took senior boys for an early-morning dip, as did Leonard Strong, until one boy 'accidentally' threw one of his shoes into the water.

A swimming test was imposed in the interest of boys' safety, but there were some clever ruses to get through this if swimming was not one's forte:

> My swimming career was not impressive. We walked to the bank of the River Cherwell, where we were each issued with trunks of the right size. They felt, even when clean and dry, somehow slimy on the skin. With our modesty safe, we waded into the murky river. The swimming test entailed crossing to the far bank and returning, under a master's critical eye. Although quite short, I myself passed the test, since the water happened to be low, by walking steadily there and back with my feet on the mud while making vigorous breast-stroke motions with my arms.
>
> Julian Reade (1949–52)

Above: A swimming race in the Cherwell in 1931

Right and below left: swimming in 1935

Below: The outdoor pool in summer use today

Sport today

For the boys, sport continues to provide an opportunity to develop and improve their health whatever their standard. There is no doubt that the twenty-first-century Summerfieldian is kept fit and well exercised through the immense range of sports on offer at the school.

Off site, he may ride or play polo. Indeed, equestrian activities seem to be flourishing. In 2013, a grant from the Schools and University Polo Association enabled SF to acquire some new, lightweight polo mallets, which have proved to be invaluable, especially to smaller boys. History was made as the polo team played its first match, against Bruern Abbey, and Summerfieldians are now participating in an increasing range of tournaments. Showjumping, too, is developing, and in recent years the Ljungstrom brothers (Ludvig, 2006–10; Lukas, 2006–11; Leo, 2007–13) have taken their fences in fine style, placing the name of Summer Fields firmly on the equestrian circuit.

Away from school, too, but on the water, sailing and sculling are on offer. Sailing began life in 1971, when David Langdon (1965–2003) invited the Fifth Year non-cricketers to join him on Farmoor Reservoir, to the west of Oxford. Two boats were employed, occasionally increased by parents bringing a third. A few years later, after joining the Oxford and District Schools Sailing Association, the school was able to use their fleet of boats. In 1990, SF took part in the first Prep Schools Sailing Regatta (in the Oxford area), competing for the Radley Bowl. Later, in 2002, the school managed to beat the Dragon School. Sculling is relatively new to Summer Fields, but one day it may produce SF's second Olympic oarsman.

Back at Summer Fields, a boy may break clays with a shotgun. In summer, he may wish to draw a bow. The pools offer swimming and water polo, not to mention an introduction to scuba-diving. New Room now resounds to the thump of bodies on rubber mats as the boys enjoy their judo. However the cheers, bells and grunts which accompanied fights in the gym (now Macmillan) have long been silenced, as boxing ceased in 1964.

SF's two Olympians in athletics, Wilfrid Tatham (1908–12) and Lawrence Clarke (1998–2003), testify to the school's excellence in this respect. Indeed, there is such a range of track and field events that boys are spoilt for choice. Activities include cross-country running, various distance

Summerfieldians enjoy an immense range of sporting opportunities

races, discus, javelin, long jump, high jump, putting the shot and throwing the cricket ball, this last being one of the oldest of the school's events.

In terms of the sporting achievements (Olympians aside) enjoyed by Summer Fields in recent times, success on the athletics track stands out. In this area the school has performed superbly on the national stage.

Tade Ojora (2008–13) was victorious in the 70m–75m three years in a row. In addition to this, he also won the 200m three times and the 100m once. Gus Skinner (2010–13) won the 1,500m three years in a row. Sile Ogundeyin (2007–12) came first in the 75m twice and last year, Bofe Moses-Taiga (since 2011) triumphed in both the 100m and 200m. However, the most impressive result on the track came from last year's Under 14 4×100m relay team, who took the victory laurels for the event in a time of 48.486 sec. They set a new national record, shattering what had stood for over twenty-five years! At the Prep School Athletics Meeting held at Radley College in June 2013, the Summer Fields squad took thirty-two individual medals, including twenty-one of the possible thirty-eight golds, and snapped up four of the five team trophies into the bargain.

Athletic skills are fully showcased on Sports Day, held at the mid-June Leave-Out. This is the culmination of a long series of preparatory heats. There are numerous track and field events, with the Parents' Race being ever popular. Indeed, there is now a special cup awarded for this. Thomas Miles (1931–6) recalls a parents' obstacle race where, 'mothers had to run balancing an egg on a spoon and fathers had to jump with their feet tied together'. Over the years, such events have died out – perhaps there is a case for resurrecting them?

After all the competitive exercise of the morning, followed by sports prize-giving with its cups, medals and the announcement of the *Victor Ludorum*, boys are free to join their parents for a scrumptious picnic before heading home for a well-earned break.

Wilfrid George Tatham OBE, MC (1898–1978), SF 1908–12

Wilfrid Tatham was born on 12 December 1898. He came to Summer Fields in 1908, took a King's Scholarship to Eton in 1912, followed by an exhibition to King's College, Cambridge, in 1917. His studies were then interrupted by the First World War, where he served on the Western Front with the Coldstream Guards and gained an MC.

Returning to King's after the war, Tatham was active in many fields. A fine violinist, he ran the Music Society. He captained the Tennis Club and played rugby. He also embarked on a busy athletic career, winning his Half-Blue for the Open Mile. In March 1920 he ran for Oxford and Cambridge in the USA, in the Two-Mile College Championship Relay Race, at Pennsylvania University. His team not only won, but broke the world record.

As a member of the Oxford and Cambridge Athletic Team touring Central Europe in 1922, he won the 1,500m and Mile at Prague, and the 1,500m at Budapest, beating the Czech record holder. Coming back to England, he took his

degree, then a teaching job at Eton, becoming a Housemaster and, later, Master-in-College. However, his work was interspersed with sporting commitments, representing Great Britain on the athletics track.

In 1924, having won the Great Britain 440 Yards Hurdle Open Championship, he travelled to Paris to compete in the 1924 Olympics. He finished sixteenth from twenty-four competitors in the 440 Yards Hurdle. At the 1928 Olympics in Amsterdam, Tatham again represented Great Britain, this time in the 800m event, where he was placed twentieth from forty-nine contestants.

On the outbreak of the Second World War, Tatham returned to the Coldstream Guards, serving as a major. Captured by the Germans in 1943, he escaped but was caught in Italy. A second escape also brought only short-lived freedom. In March 1944 German radio reported that 'Major W. G. Tatham, the Olympic Games athlete, who escaped from an Italian camp last autumn, is now a prisoner again in Germany'.

After the war, Tatham returned to Eton before working as the British Council Representative in Greece. For this he received an OBE. He was then briefly Bursar of the Royal College of Art, before retiring to St Helena where he died in 1978.

So, how did Summer Fields shape this exciting life? Tatham's musical talent was nurtured by the school. He studied the violin, giving solo performances at concerts in 1908 and 1910. He sang treble in the choir and performed solos at various school concerts. His undoubted athletic prowess was also developed. His results demonstrate gradual improvement. In 1910, he finished second both in the Under-12 Hurdles and the Under-12 Mile; in the following year, second in Upper School Hurdles and fourth in the Senior Half-Mile. When he left Summer Fields, Tatham had won the Upper School Hurdles, the Upper School Half-Mile and the Upper School Quarter-Mile. He came second in the High Jump just for good measure. At Summer Fields, the seeds of future international athletic success were firmly planted.

Lawrence Clarke (1990–) SF 1998–2003

Lawrence Clarke arrived at Summer Fields in 1998 before moving on to Eton. He was sound in the classroom, winning prizes for Latin. He enjoyed a promising football career both with the Colts and the 3rd XI, where his turn of speed could be used to advantage. Promoted to the 1st XI, for football, he was, surprisingly, placed in goal. Here, he was rated 'an excellent shot-stopper from close range'. He won his colours for swimming. But even from his first days, athletic talent was evident. As Junior *Victor Ludorum* in 1999, it was noted that he 'runs and hurdles with great freedom'. He went on to represent the school in various athletic competitions, such as the West Surrey Area Athletics Championships in 2003. However, at Summer Fields, Clarke, although a useful athlete, was not the best. Nonetheless, he persevered.

Early in 2012, he ran a new personal best of 13.33 seconds in the 110m hurdles, taking him to the top of the UK rankings, as five Britons achieved Olympic A qualification standards at the EAP and Swiss Meeting in Geneva.

Thus it was that, in a packed Olympic Stadium in August 2012, Clarke set a personal best of 13.31 seconds to reach the final as the eighth-fastest qualifier. Two hours later, he returned to the track to finish just outside the medals. Aries Merritt led an American one-two, ahead of team-mate Jason Richardson. Merritt's time of 12.92 seconds was just 0.01s outside the Olympic record set by Liu Xiang in Athens in 2004, with Richardson clocking 13.04 and Jamaica's Hansle Parchment claiming a surprise bronze in a national record of 13.12 seconds. Clarke was fourth in 13.39 seconds.

Clarke remains enthusiastic about his athletics and encourages others at all levels to participate. He was kind enough to hand out the medals on Sports Day in 2010 and 2013, much to the delight of the boys. On the latter occasion, he presented top athlete, Tade Ojora (2008–13), with a pair of Team GB running spikes. Ojora wore these at the prep schools Athletics National Championships, when winning the gold medal in the 75m hurdles and setting a new national prep-school record.

Lawrence Clarke at Summer Fields, **above**, and at the 2012 Olympics, **below**

High jump: **left**, today, and **below**, in 1924

The Ski Trip

The annual ski trip is a chance for pure enjoyment. Strictly speaking it is not a school trip as such, but more of a communal venture by Summerfieldians. The ethos is that of a family holiday under the banner of Summer Fields, with parents having the overall responsibility for their own children.

Organisers have included David Langdon (1965–2003) and Charles Churchill (1964–96) in the early days. Recently Rob Lagden (since 1996) has taken over the reins. The ski trip remains very popular with boys, staff and parents alike, and 2014 sees its fiftieth anniversary, with a group of over one hundred skiers.

Ski trips were held in Val d'Isère at the Hôtel les Crêtes-Blanches from 1992 to 2002 and for one year in the Hôtel Val d'Isère, an expedition attended by David Faber, our current Headmaster, as a parent. Charles Churchill recalls how it all began:

> In 1968 Ian Dunbar (1966–71) (whose idea it was), David Langdon and I took a small group of Summerfieldians to Sauze d'Oulx in Italy, including Toby Jenkins (1963–9) in very old ski kit. The next year we took about twenty boys, including Toby in brand new ski clothes! He went out on skis, contrary to instructions, immediately we arrived and within ten minutes he had broken a leg! Bad luck, but the others all borrowed his kit for the rest of the holiday!
>
> Then some parents expressed regret that they were not able to come with us to ski. So, the three of us thought, 'Why not?' From then on we took boys' parents and sisters as well.

The annual venue moved to Klosters in 2003 owing to the influence of the Countesse von der Schulenburg. Ten happy trips followed with the general enjoyment much enhanced by the excellent service provided by the hotel, especially from the owner Christian Erpenbeck.

Ski trips: **above**, in 1968, and **left**: to Val d'Isère in 1995

One sport not available at school is Alpine skiing. Nonetheless, that small fact does not prevent SF from celebrating the achievements of yet another OS Olympian, as Guy Sucharitakul (2001–5) competed for Thailand in the Winter Olympics at Sochi in February 2014.

There are some excellent sportsmen on the staff – including several members of the MCC, and one colleague with a collection of England caps. However, it is principally from the training and maintaining of their teams that staff draw immense pride and satisfaction. It would amaze people to know just how much time is spent discussing the various highs and lows of the respective sides. Post-match drinks are far from mere social

occasions! Virtually every game is analysed, looking at what went well and what did not. Some top games are even videoed to focus future coaching.

Games these days is split, with the First, Second and Third Years playing in the early part of the afternoon, while Removes and Fifth Years come out later, after lessons. This allows maximum use of the facilities, especially in the summer when the weather can often be temperamental. 'Minor sports' continue to be held on Thursdays, and the choice of optional extras available to the boys is astounding.

In terms of fixtures, SF still takes on a number of historic rivals, such as Horris Hill. The Headmaster (1969–74), as a keen,

Guy (Kanes) Sucharitakul (1992–), SF 2001–5

It is only fitting that Summer Fields should field an Olympian during its 150th anniversary. An academic at Summer Fields – prizes in both Upper Remove and Fifth Form – Guy did all that was asked of him. His sporting career – he played rugby for Colts B, fenced with sabre and foil, won his swimming colours and enjoyed tennis – cannot have directly prepared him for Olympic Alpine Skiing events. Nonetheless, Summer Fields at least inculcated an early love of sport and a desire for physical fitness without which no skier is able to succeed. These elements were developed at Eton and Cambridge, where he won a boxing Blue. At Sochi, Guy finished sixty-fifth in the Alpine Ski Giant Slalom on his second run, but failed to complete the Slalom course on Day 15 of the Games. Thus, no medals, but a great achievement to be one of only two athletes representing Thailand (the other being the skiing violinist, Vanessa Mae) and a greater honour still, perhaps, to be the bearer of the Thai flag at the Opening Ceremony.

sporty OS, is always particularly happy after a victory over them! However, more recently, the school has branched out and now travels to London in order to provide the boys with the opportunities for even more matches. In its 150th year, there are around 440 fixtures in football, rugby, hockey and cricket for Summer Fields. This is a huge undertaking and the whole community plays its part with immense pride.

One of the most satisfying aspects of the job of Director of Sport is when the school has a big, block fixture against opponents like Cothill or Ludgrove and three-quarters of the school turn out for Summer Fields. At all skill levels, never in the school's history have so many boys had the opportunity of match experience. Elite teams there are (as there should and must be), but many with less talent now have the chance for their moment of sporting glory. Inclusion is the name of the game.

Thus, sport at Summer Fields is in extremely good health. On the match circuit, the school appears to have an excellent reputation, both for producing first-class sportsmen and, perhaps more importantly, for having boys who enjoy their sport and play it in the correct manner.

chapter six

The Creative Arts

Art

Early Times to 1968

For well over a century, Art has been a powerful vehicle for the development of creativity in the Summerfieldian mind, although is it not easy to say exactly when Art lessons began. From 1912 until 1930, James Allen Shuffrey, a local watercolourist, arrived weekly on his tricycle to teach Art in New Room. Boys were sometimes set to copy Victorian country scenes 'with pencil and sepia brush', many wishing they could be drawing racing cars like Shuffrey's son, Alan, who illustrated the *Boy's Own Book of Motor Cars*. Nonetheless, it was said that those fortunate enough to attend Mr Shuffrey's classes were inspired. Two boys, in particular, with special talent, were carefully nurtured. The first was John Merton, MBE (1922–6). Merton enjoyed fives, was a strong swimmer and an 'especially good performer on the parallel bars', winning the Gym Competition in 1926. He also acted in *Henry VI – Part II*, in 1925, as Prince Humphrey of Gloucester, 'with a pleasing stage manner and a good voice'. But it was in Art that he excelled.

On his arrival at Balliol from Eton in 1930, Merton's talent for Art was immediately recognised and he was allowed to study at the Ruskin School of Drawing instead of reading for a degree. Noted for his meticulous brushwork, he later became a regular exhibitor at the Royal Academy. Three of his pictures achieved

Art class,
1960s

particular fame. The first was a triple portrait of Mrs Daphne Wall (1948), second, a triple portrait of Jane Dalkeith (later the Dowager Duchess of Buccleuch), which won an immediate vote of acceptance from the Academy Committee, and finally, another triple portrait, this time of Diana, Princess of Wales, wearing a figure-hugging yellow dress. Merton also painted a portrait of Her Majesty the Queen which is currently in the Royal Collection. John Merton died in 2011 at the age of ninety-seven, having enjoyed fame and success within his chosen field.

The second of Shuffrey's protégés was Victor Pasmore (1918–23). Like Merton, he learnt his careful drawing skills at Summer Fields as we see from his charming sketch of a dog, completed while at school.

Victor Pasmore, CH, CBE (1908–98), SF 1918–23

Victor Pasmore was one of the leading abstract artists of the twentieth century. After Harrow, while working as a clerk for London County Council in the 1930s, he studied part-time at the Central School of Art. He began to develop various styles, moving from landscapes and tranquil images of the Thames with hints at Impressionism, to still-life compositions and later to abstract paintings and collages. After 1947, Pasmore became a pioneering figure in Constructivism, championing the synthesis of art and architecture. He contributed a large mural to the Festival of Britain (1951).

In addition to showing in both solo and group exhibitions, Pasmore had a distinguished teaching career, both in independent art schools and in universities. He notably headed the Painting Department of Durham University from 1954.

Pasmore was made CBE in 1959 and Companion of Honour in 1981. He died in Gudja, Malta, in 1998 at the age of eighty-nine. His work can be found in public collections around the world, including Tate Britain, the Royal Academy of Arts (London), the Museum of Modern Art (New York), the Yale Centre for British Art and numerous regional British galleries.

Victor Pasmore, right, in 1923

A sketch by Victor Pasmore drawn during his time at Summer Fields

Burne-Jones at Summer Fields

In 1853, twenty-year-old Edward Burne-Jones went to Oxford to study Theology at Exeter College. A sickly youth, he enrolled in Archibald Maclaren's gymnasium to improve his strength and resilience. 'I continue my fencing lessons &c and feel almost unutterable benefit from them,' Burne-Jones wrote to his father. 'My strength grows perceptibly, and Maclaren promises to send me forth a very different object to what I was when I entered.' A lasting bond developed between the two men despite their age difference of twelve years, and soon Burne-Jones and his college friend William Morris were regular guests at the Maclarens' home. 'Maclaren interested us greatly', Burne-Jones wrote, 'and we him, I suppose, for he did an almost unheard-of thing, inviting us to his home at Summertown, where we went three or four times in the term to dine with him... I think our enthusiasm was always a pleasure to him, and he aided and abetted us in all the inclinations of our heart.' Soon Summerfields became a veritable sanctuary for the young artists of Oxford: in June 1857 a party including William Holman Hunt arrived at the house to find 'Morris painting a tree in Maclaren's beautiful garden with such energy that it was long before the grass grew again on the spot where his chair had stood'. Hunt was so impressed by the Maclarens that he entrusted his son, Cyril, to them two decades later, when they had established their school. Cyril Holman Hunt (1877–81) left a bequest to the school to fund an annual Science prize, still awarded each summer.

In 1854 Maclaren, having already noticed the talent of his young friend, gave Burne-Jones his first artistic commission: illustrating *The Fairy Family*, a collection of fairy-tale poems and ballads. There were to be more than eighty monochrome pen-and-ink designs: title pages, full-page illustrations, vignettes, borders and decorative capitals.

The drawings for *The Fairy Family* were never finished. Burne-Jones worked on them until 1856, the year that proved to be the decisive turning point of his artistic career. In January he met Dante Gabriel Rossetti, who completely revolutionised his sense of style. Embarrassed by his early trials, he ultimately decided they were not fit for publication. When *The Fairy Family* was published in 1857, only three designs were included, none of which was credited. Maclaren kept all the unused drawings, but Burne-Jones never reclaimed them.

Despite the failed commission, Maclaren remained close to his artistic protégé for many years. Georgiana Burne-Jones in the *Memorials* of her husband published after his death described Maclaren as 'one of the truest friends [Edward] ever had, and one whose eyes discerned his pupil's genius from the first... The unfailing belief and encouragement that he gave in these early days were never forgotten.'

A series of teachers followed James Shuffrey: Mrs 'Bobs' Alington, Miss Tremlett, Phyllis Alden (by now, Art was taught in Mayfield), Mr Wardle, Jackie Black and, in 1968, Judith Lane, who was to set the department firmly on its path to modernity. Here, she recalls her appointment and some aspects of her career.

Art 1968–2004

In 1968 Pat Savage telephoned Bear Lane Art Gallery in Oxford to ask 'if they knew someone who would care to do a spot of art with small boys in a school in Summertown'.

I can't recall any sort of formal interview, but I was shown a charming room in Mayfield where the art took place. It contained a few tables, a handsome fireplace, a small sink in the corner and had a lovely view across the tennis courts to the playing fields. I was instantly charmed by the sight of small boys in tweed jackets, ties and grey flannel shorts running across from the main school for their weekly Art class.

In those days Charles Churchill (1964–96) and Jimmy Bell (1927–32, staff 1938–78) ran Mayfield; the latter was known for his lavish dinner parties. It was not unusual for my lessons to be interrupted by Jimmy in order to have a tasting of that evening's forthcoming repast. Another memorable moment was being offered snuff by Richard Porthouse (1950–78) on my first day!

There was only one other female member of staff, Patsy Logan (1966–98), who taught the very junior boys. We took our morning coffee upstairs with Nancy Lovatt (1953–75), the Matron, and not with the men in the Drawing Room. We sat alone at a table for lunch in the dining room with Matron and Cynthia Hartwell, the visiting piano teacher.

In 1973 I left to have my family and was succeeded by 'Tinker' Stoddart (1973–80) and Ann Boning (1980–3). However, in 1982, with Nigel Talbot Rice as Headmaster, I was delighted to be invited back. By this time Art had found a home within the main school in what is now the Drama Room, and a small kiln had arrived. Art was now timetabled throughout the school, and boys came to enjoy a widening range of artistic pursuits, as well as a flourishing Art Club at weekends and on half days.

The building of the Wavell Centre in 1991 vastly enlarged the scope of the Art Department thanks to the splendid facilities. Available now were a separate Art studio and designated pottery area, a special kiln room and a spacious exhibition area. The new department had the capacity for large-scale projects such as the creation of the metre-square ceramic murals to celebrate the millennium. Each boy made his unique contribution, which may be enjoyed today in the Junior Day Room and in Upper Bolton. Visiting artists were invited to hold one-day workshops with the boys. These became very popular.

An important annual event came to be the Royal Academy Outreach Programme, when a whole day at school was devoted to figure drawing. The results were then exhibited for all to see, to the delight of those who found their work on show.

The *Summer Fields Magazine* sprang into colour during this period, and generous space was given to photographs of boys' work displayed in the Sports Day exhibition. Visits to London galleries became regular events, notably to the Royal Academy and the National Portrait Gallery, the latter in conjunction with the History Department, creating valuable cross-curricular links. Summer Fields also took part in prep-school art exhibitions such as that held annually at Stowe.

I established a Scholarship class for talented pupils, many of whom went on to win awards, including top scholarships to Radley and Harrow. Relationships were formed with public-school Art Departments, so we could fully understand the recipe for success.

Retirement in 2004 marked the end of a happy and rewarding teaching career. I had the satisfaction of being at the heart of the development of Art at Summer Fields and of taking it from modest beginnings to the vibrant department that it is now.

Under the guidance of Claire Tottem (2004–8) Art developed. Boys drew, painted, modelled, printed; in fact they worked in an increasing variety of media. Detailed landscapes were carefully executed, as were life-sized sculptured figures and animals, along with a range of colourful pottery. On Claire's departure, the department came under the leadership of Rachel Williamson, whose account follows.

Above: 'The Swan' mosaic from the 'Carnival of the Animals'

Below: Summer Art Exhibition, 2013

Art from 2008

My first encounter with Summer Fields was via a postcard inviting me to the preview of the Summer Art exhibition; both Claire Tottem's name and the name of the school were new to me, but the cover image was so arresting – an upright piano painted in a multitude of colours – that my curiosity was piqued and I emailed asking if I could come to see the show, that year held in Kirkley House.

Claire graciously gave me a private tour of the exhibition, which was filled with enormous sculptures of magical creatures hanging from the ceiling and all sorts of dazzling artworks, including a painting incorporating its own sound installation. There were also numerous examples of boys' pottery, reflecting partly, no doubt, Claire's interests as a ceramicist.

The circumstances of my appointment were somewhat unusual. I was on jury service at the time of the interviews, so I was invited to attend an evening Art Club after my day in court. I had no idea what was expected of me as I smiled a little nervously at the boys, all buzzing about in the Art and Pottery Rooms.

Quite quickly a scenario emerged where I was asked by the boys to throw a pot on the wheel, a skill in which my grasp was fragile, to say the least. I wondered if my appointment hung in the balance over the success of this pot! The Director of Studies had been lurking in the room to 'monitor' my progress, hopefully with the boys rather than the clay. To my intense

relief, I was soon whisked off to the Headmaster's study for the interview.

I have always thanked my lucky stars that Robin Badham-Thornhill ultimately decided to take a punt on an Art teacher

Above: Reviewing the Summer exhibition

Below: Rachel Ducker, Artist-in-Residence

Above: The etching press; **above right,** drypoint prints from the press

who had never led a department before, never worked in a boarding school before and who had spent the previous ten years teaching girls. I hope he feels that the gamble paid off...

The Art Department has grown enormously in the last six years, both in the scope of activities that take place, the trips that boys undertake and the professional artists they are fortunate enough to encounter. The teaching of ceramics has been developed under the expert guidance of Maryon Phelps (since 2011), as we are well equipped with a fantastic kiln and a separate Pottery Room.

The use of personal sketchbooks has been championed as a tool for recording ideas, drawing plans, developing observational skills and experimenting with various media. My personal passion for printmaking has led to some excellent screen-printing, mono-printing, collographs, lino cuts and drypoint prints, the last being made possible by an etching press, donated by a generous parent in 2013. The day the press was delivered (it was handmade in the Black Country by a man who previously worked for the Royal Mint) was (literally) a turning-point in the life of the department. Many exciting prints have since emerged, as its roller has turned and turned to generate a host of individual creations by the boys.

A highlight of our Art year is now the week spent hosting an Artist-in-Residence. A series of professional practising artists has introduced the boys not only to new materials and processes (recycled art, mosaics, drawings of skeletons, wire sculpture) but also to the reality of a career in art – something to which our especially talented Art Scholarship boys may wish to aspire.

Art at Summer Fields seeks to offer a breadth of opportunity, igniting that spark of inventive potential within each boy and kindling the sheer pleasure of the creative process. Judging by what the boys are turning out, it seems to be succeeding.

Above and left: Self-portrait canvases

Drama

Summer Fields has long been well known for mounting ambitious and challenging productions and this tradition continues unabated. Drama is taught to boys in the First and Second Years as part of their timetable and thereafter they have opportunities to audition for each term's major play or to help out backstage or in the sound/lighting box. Many of them surprise themselves – and their teachers! – by hitherto undiscovered skills.

At first, plays were staged each December, in the gym. The earliest productions were pantomimes with songs and general direction by 'Ping-Pong' Penny (1893–1927). Shows such as *Ali Baba, The Tinder Box* and *Rumpelstilzkin* covered the years 1901–5. In the last of these appeared a certain Harold Macmillan as the Prime Minister. It was observed that he 'was very obsequious and did his part excellently'. From 1915, Geoffrey Alington (1909–12) wrote plays such as *Queen Bridget and the Dragon* and *Alexander the Great*, especially for the school. A number of musicals were staged under William Sterndale Case (1910–22), a fine musician trained in the UK and Germany. These home-made shows like *Ever Afterwards* (1917), *Emerald* (1919) and *Moonshine* (1921) were very much in the Gilbert and

Left: *Peter Pan*, 2011

Above right: *A Regular Fix*, 1899. Henry Moseley is back row, third from the left

Right: Programme for *Blood, Bluff and Bravado*, 1913

Sullivan tradition. Case's death in 1922 marked the demise of these musicals and heralded the beginning of a long succession of Shakespeare productions much encouraged by Hermione Williams and Gill Alington. Of note among these were the staging of *Henry V* (1934) and *Richard II* (1935) enhanced by the fine performances of Patrick Macnee (1930–6), Robin Sinclair (1932–6), Christopher Lee (1931–5) and Brian Straton-Ferrier (1932–7).

The flavour of these times is captured well by Thomas Miles (1931–6), who recounts how Summer Fields nurtured the careers of future professional actors, and how the original texts were censored to make them suitable for use by small boys:

> In 1931 the school did *The Taming of the Shrew*. Although at the age of eight, I did not understand the plot, it was clear that people were having a hilarious time throwing the meat about! In 1932, they did three one-act plays: one by A. A. Milne called *Wirzel Flummery*. I have forgotten the second, but the third was a rather gruesome play by Lord Dunsany called *Night at an Inn*. Here, most of the characters came to a sticky end. Antony Lyttelton (1930–4) was The Toff and Patrick Macnee, who was only ten at the time, had the part of Sniggers.

> My first personal involvement was in 1933 in *Julius Caesar*. I was one of the crowd. Patrick Macnee was Brutus, Antony Lyttelton, Mark Antony, and Peter Solomon (1930–5), Caesar. Incidentally, it was an interesting decision by the producers that, because the line, 'Friends, Romans, countrymen, lend me your ears', was so well known, we in the crowd were told to drown out Antony as he said the words and thus prevent the audience from hearing them.

> In 1934, we again did a Shakespeare – this time *Henry V*. Patrick Macnee was the King, Henry Thorold (1930–5), the Bishop of Ely and Christopher Lee, the Dauphin. I myself was Fluellen. I claimed to be able to speak with a Welsh accent on the grounds that my grandmother was Welsh. For both *Julius Caesar* and *Henry V*, we used what was called the 'Plain Text' Shakespeare. This meant that in our version of the text various obscenities had been removed.

Sir Christopher Lee, CBE, CStJ (1922–), SF 1931–5

Christopher Lee, 1935

Christopher Lee has become a famous actor, making his mark in particular in 'ghoulish' parts. One of my memories when I shared a dormitory with him was that he would cover his head with his dressing gown and flap the sleeves, saying, 'Ghostly, ghostly!' In retrospect, I regard this as a foretaste of the kind of part he preferred as an actor.

Thomas Miles (1931–6)

Lee began his acting career at Summer Fields. Indeed, he claimed that school plays were 'directly responsible for my career as an actor'. In two of the best Shakespeare productions, he appeared as the Dauphin in *Henry V* (1934) and as the Duke of Norfolk in the 1935 presentation of *Richard II* alongside his contemporary, Patrick Macnee. Here, he relished his costume: chain mail, magnificent surcoat and an impressive shield. In a lighter vein, Lee again took to the stage in his final term as Valère in Molière's *Le Médecin Malgré Lui*. This was a Fifth Form play put on as relaxation after the strain of their various scholarship exams. The review was positive.

In sport, Lee inevitably ended up in goal owing to his long reach and great kicking powers. As the result of an accidental trip, considered by others to have been a spectacular tackle, he was promoted to the 1st XV. He also enjoyed cricket as a member of the 3rd XI, batting usually at No. 3. His final season (1935) was perhaps not his best. In May, he made 10 in a match against Cothill in which his side 'should have done better'. He was bowled for 3 and 1 respectively in the following fixtures against the Dragon.

The distinguished actor holds more screen credits that any other international star, having appeared in over 250 productions. Although best known for playing Dracula in a string of popular Hammer Horror films from the 1950s to the 1970s, his memorable performances also include Lord Summerisle in the cult classic *The Wicker Man* (1973), Francisco Scaramanga in the James Bond film *The Man with the Golden Gun* (1974) and Pakistan's founder Muhammad Ali Jinnah in the biopic *Jinnah* (1998).

In his eighties he played Count Dooku in two of the *Star Wars* trilogies (2002 and 2005) and Saruman in the first two films of *The Lord of the Rings* trilogy (2001–3). In his nineties he appeared in *The Hobbit* film trilogy (2012–14) and on his ninety-second birthday he released a heavy-metal album, *Metal Knight*, inspired by the life of Don Quixote.

In 2013 Lee remarked: 'I always ask myself "well, what else could I do?" Making films has never just been a job to me, it is my life. I have some interests outside of acting – I sing and I've written books, for instance – but acting is what keeps me going, it's what I do, it gives life purpose.'

Patrick Macnee (1922–), SF 1930–6

Patrick Macnee was born in London to a wealthy and eccentric family. His father was a racehorse trainer in Lambourn who gambled away much of the family money. After his parents' divorce Patrick was brought up mainly by his mother. He arrived at Summer Fields in 1930, moving on to Eton in 1936.

After war service in the Royal Navy and several jobs in the United States, Macnee returned to England in 1959 to take the part which made him famous with the British public. In the television series *The Avengers,* Macnee played the role of secret agent John Steed, a suave bowler-hatted character whose chief weapon was a lethal umbrella-sword. Reviving the part in *The New Avengers* (1976) did not win such popular appeal. Throughout the 1980s, Macnee worked on American television, before retiring to live in Palm Springs.

Interested in acting and the stage from an early age, Macnee was already a promising Shakespearian actor at Summer Fields. His notable roles in various school productions included Brutus in *Julius Caesar* (1933), the King in *Henry V* (1934) and Bolingbroke in *Richard II* (1935). Praise from the reviewers was fulsome: 'Brutus (Macnee) was excellent, every word being

Patrick Macnee, *c*.1934

clear and firm in the longest and most difficult of parts.' Of his performance in *Henry V*, GB said:

> I find it difficult to write of Macnee's Henry. I don't want to use the language of exaggeration or to suggest that Macnee is a

second Irving; but when I consider that in less than a month he had to learn some seven or eight hundred lines and that he was to all intents and purposes word-perfect in them, I find it hard to restrain my admiration.

No less a person than the famous Oxford English scholar Nevill Coghill reviewed *Richard II*, writing of Macnee that 'throughout the play he moved with fine grace and a real sense of the stage – he shows exceptional promise'.

At Summer Fields, Macnee was also a talented sportsman. In 1934, he skilfully captained the 2nd XI at football, playing at half-back. After Cothill lost 5–1 in November, the match report stated that 'Macnee is to be congratulated on such an encouraging display by his team'. In the following year, he played 1st XV rugby, being described as 'a good, steady worker in the scrum'. In football, now promoted to the 1st XI, as a right half, he was rated 'as a most determined tackler and kicker, always at his best in a crisis'.

Programme for *Richard II*, 1935

In 1935, we did *Richard II*. Robin Sinclair (1932–6) was given the part of the King. Brian Straton-Ferrier (1932–7) was the Queen. There was an unfortunate event during the dress rehearsal with some not very sensitive spectators from North Oxford. There is a scene where the King and Queen have to part and kiss each other – a difficult enough assignment for twelve-year-old boys. As Brian and Robin did their final kissing, some of these spectators were tactless enough to laugh. Nothing of the kind happened during the main performances, but afterwards my mother admitted that although no one would be so insensitive as to laugh, 'it did look like two little boys tumbling into each other's arms'.

Thomas Miles (1931–6)

KING RICHARD II.

By WILLIAM SHAKESPEARE.

CHARACTERS
(in order of appearance).

John of Gaunt	
The Lord Marshal	T. R. MILES.
King Richard II	C. E. McGRIGOR.
Bushy	R. M. SINCLAIR.
Green	E. DE L. CAZENOVE.
Bagot	S. GURTEEN.
The Duke of York	J. LYTTELTON.
The Duke of Aumerle, son of the Duke of York	D. W. LANE.
The Earl of Northumberland	P. S. LOVEBAND.
Thomas Mowbray, Duke of Norfolk	I. J. H. LEWISOHN.
Henry Bolingbroke, son of John of Gaunt, afterwards Henry IV	C. F. C. LEE.
The Queen	D. P. MACNEE.
Lady attending on the Queen	B. I. STRATON-FERRIER.
Bolingbroke's Ho...	

However, there was certainly nothing 'sissy' or effeminate about playing women's parts, as Brian Straton-Ferrier himself comments:

> I was small and fair, so I played the queen opposite Robin Sinclair in *Richard II* and the French princess in *Henry V* opposite Patrick Macnee. I had spent two years in France, so could do the French princess ('ze 'and, ze fingres, ze bilbow')! Not quite what you'd expect from some one who later became captain of rugger and football and Head Boy!

At this time, there were also a series of Lodge Plays put on by Cottage and Mayfield and renowned generally for being 'acted with more zest than polish'.

Jimmy Bell (1927–32; staff 1938–78), was famous for his excellent school productions. Between 1945 and 1960 *Androcles and the Lion*, *The Critic*, *Tobias and the Angel*, *The Boy with a Cart*, *A Midsummer Night's Dream*, *Julius Caesar*, *Ajax* and *Lady Precious Stream* were staged. Bell also put on *Macbeth*, in which Richard Guinness (1947–52) recalls his performance as the Porter, together with its interesting vocabulary:

> I don't suppose I was very clear what it all meant – I mean, carousing, equivocator and Beelzebub are not words I use much, even now – but again I did it in Lancashire and it seemed to go down quite well. And what's more, no one ever asked me how it was that a Lancastrian came to be keeping the gate at the eleventh-century Glamis Castle!

> *My drama career at Summer Fields was short and inglorious. I never strutted upon the stage, but I was in charge of the lighting for* A Midsummer Night's Dream. *There came a point when the lights needed to be gradually dimmed, to denote the passing of day into night. Unfortunately my hand slipped, so that the lights denoted an abrupt change from day to night, without any intermediate phase of twilight.*
>
> Professor D. R. Myddleton (1948–53)

In 1965, staff plays were revived after a twenty-year lapse. A freely adapted version of *The Ghost of Thark* (1966) was followed over the years by *See How They Run* and *Pools Paradise*. These were staged for the boys' entertainment and were somehow kept secret from them until the masters were able to revel in their various stage antics.

The late 1970s saw the revival of large musicals, with performances of *Noyes Fludde* (1977) with half the school as animals, followed by *Joseph and the Amazing Technicolour Dreamcoat* (1979 and 1997), with Summer Fields' own five-piece band under the direction of Richard Balding (1978–2001). These presentations ushered in a period of experimental and home-grown drama, with plays written by numerous members of staff. There were many performances of 'straight' plays as well, notably *Doctor Faustus* (1980) and *Julius Caesar* (1984). These often alternated with musicals like *Oliver!* (1981) and *The Pirates of Penzance* (1985). By the 1980s, there was a play of some sort during most terms, with the occasional notable exception to the routine, such as the staff revue staged in February 1983.

Over the following decades, Drama has moved from strength to strength, with a huge range of plays and musicals, well supported by increasingly sophisticated music and special effects. More recent productions have included *Rosencrantz and Guildenstern are Dead* (1995), *A Servant of Two Masters* (1998), *Musical Magic* (2001), *The Government Inspector* (2004), *Amahl and the Night Visitors* (2005), a memorable performance of *Oliver!* with a combined cast of staff, boys and, as a special treat, Rowan Atkinson as Fagin.

A number of OSS are currently making a name for themselves in the world of film and theatre: Sebastian Armesto (1990–5), Harry Lloyd (1992–7) and Tim Webber (1973–8). Armesto acts on both screen and stage. He took the part of Edward Sparkler in the BBC's adaptation of Dickens' *Little Dorrit*. He also played the Holy Roman Emperor Charles V (1519–56) in the TV series *The Tudors*, and King Ferdinand VI of Spain (1746–59) in *Pirates of the Caribbean: On Stranger Tides*. Armesto has also appeared at the National Theatre, as well as writing and directing drama with his critically acclaimed theatre company, simple8. Among his productions and adaptations

Sebastian Fernández-Armesto, early 1990s

Films

Films have always been popular at Summer Fields. First, they are a good way to educate the boys. Second, in free time, they are an efficient way to keep them out of mischief. Today, films are usually shown (often a choice of two) on Sunday afternoons, just when the duty masters are at their wits' end and some boys are beginning to feel the weight of a long weekend. The penultimate day of term is often the occasion of a compulsory film for the whole school. The Deputy Headmaster has found this to be a convenient way of knowing where to find a boy as the gappers and gapper-matrons trawl the school for stray possessions which need packing to go home.

During the 1920s, the so-called 'Kinema' show was started by Bryan Buckley on Thursday afternoons, showing serious presentations. One early film, if not the first, in 1925, entitled *The League of Nations Building at Geneva*, was devoid of all movement save for a man who bicycled past the camera, drawing wild cheers from the audience.

More popular with the boys were the comedies hand-projected by Roger Jacques (1924–39) and later by Geoffrey Frodsham on Sunday afternoons between tea and chapel. Throughout the 1930s, Eric Bowtell (1931–61), through his family connection with the Scala cinema in Oxford, was able to procure the latest full-length films for Sunday afternoons to keep the school entertained, with a cheerful selection of 'shorts' for Saturday evenings. Sound arrived in 1939, colour from about 1957, by which time New Room was properly wired along the rafters.

Eric Bowtell in 1966

In the Lent Term of 1942, Bowtell screened his first film showing scenes from school life, which was the start of a succession of such shows which ran on to the 1960s. First appearing in monochrome, these were later presented in colour. The films were shown in New Room, set up as a cinema with benches. Early-Bedders saw about half the Saturday evening show. During the war, Eric chose some of his titles to reflect current events:

> Eric Bowtell, the school secretary, operated the 16mm projector and I was his assistant. We had a lot of *Popeye the Sailor Man*, Charlie Chaplin and *Mickey Mouse*. But we also had *Gaumont British News* films about the war. We saw *Chamberlain the Peace Maker*, the *Sinking of the Graf Spee*, RAF Air Sea rescue work, and *Careless Talk Costs Lives*. Bowtell also made films of the school which caused much cheering (or hissing) when popular (or unpopular) boys or masters appeared on the screen.
>
> Peter Fullerton (1938–43)

Richard White lived only for these film shows. They dominated work, games, and chapel, indeed everything. Eventually, sparked by his early years at Summer Fields, Richard took to films professionally:

> My main secret was the film shows. Life delivered me slowly to films – my father despised the cinema and I first tried other professions which did nothing for me until I fell into the film business through lying to hide my inexperience. I soon found myself among manifest liars, all sharing my opportunism and determination, skills Summer Fields had little prepared me for. But I carried a library in my head of fables and moral tales, warnings and insights, myths and legends. I drew upon countless Sunday memories which still entertain and enlighten me now. There was *Henry V* for heroism, *The Overlanders* for dogged determination, *The Treasure of Sierra Madre* for the lure of obsession, and *Oliver Twist* for injustice. I read the novels much later and might never have done so without the influence of Eric Bowtell.
>
> Richard White (1946–51)

Eric Bowtell calculated that about 544 miles of film were shown in New Room between September 1939 and March 1964.

feature *Les Enfants du Paradis* and a play based on Hogarth's *The Four Stages of Cruelty*.

Harry Lloyd, like Armesto, first trod the boards at Summer Fields and is now successful both as actor and producer. He has appeared as Will Scarlett in the BBC's drama *Robin Hood* and took a part in the film version of *Jane Eyre* in 2011. In the same year, he played the young Denis Thatcher in *The Iron Lady*, starring Meryl Streep.

Tim Webber (1973–8), a special-effects pioneer, was awarded an Oscar and a Bafta for his innovative visual effects for the film *Gravity* (2013). Tim has worked on many other films such as *The Dark Knight* (2008) and *Avatar* (2009). Asked

Hamlet, 2013

recently what he liked best about his career, he replied: 'Collaboration. It is very satisfying to work with talented people. I love being creative, I love exploring the links between artistic and scientific creativity. I love storytelling and innovation.'

More recently an ambitious staging took place of *Jesus Christ Superstar* with a cast of over ninety boys and many more playing important supporting roles behind the scenes. It would be no exaggeration to say that these days the various shows staged in Macmillan resemble those of many West End productions in terms of their professionalism and vitality.

Right: *We Will Rock You*, 2012

Below: *Jesus Christ Superstar*, summer 2014

Music

Music is a prominent feature of life at Summer Fields, and a glance at the current *Calendar* reveals the impressive range of specialist teaching on offer. Tuition is available for piano, violin, viola, cello, double bass, trumpet, French horn, saxophone, flute, oboe, clarinet, classical guitar, electric guitar, drums, percussion, bagpipes, harp and singing. This is not even an exhaustive list – recently, a number of boys have been marimba virtuosi! There is virtually no limit to what may be played, and a variety of ensembles – orchestra, string quartet, wind group, brass group, recorder consort, jazz group, to name but a few – give the boys that wonderful experience of making music together and of playing in public at concerts, in chapel and at assemblies. Over 80 per cent of the school are learning at least one instrument. But when did it all begin?

The Early Years

During the 1890s, a Miss Wheeler taught music, imposing a strict initial assessment of talent. New boys had to parade before her and then, following her instructions, place one finger on the piano keys and try to play the National Anthem. 'You will not learn music!' was her stern command to those who failed.

R. Douglas Slater directed the musical side of the school from 1902 to 1909 and Nick Aldridge suggests that he may be the first Music Master as such. Then came B. M. Barker, who left rather suddenly in 1915. By then William Sterndale Case (1910–22), a fine musician and composer, was on the staff and became the natural successor. After Case died, H. R. Annis took on the role of both choirmaster and organist until the war. Miss Violet Harris taught piano from 1934 to 1957 and the choir was developed notably by Albert ('Stodgy') Thomson (1939–46), followed briefly by Thomas Tunnard (1947–50).

Some OSS remember embarrassing moments in concerts. Denys Moylan (1939–45) put 'an extra Hallelujah in Handel's anthem, well at least a half Hallelujah', after everyone else had stopped. Many others recall, with evident pleasure, the communal singing sessions in the gym, especially during the war:

> My favourite class was the choral singing class led by Mr O'Connor (1942–6), who played the piano. We sang things like 'Waltzing Matilda' and I enjoyed this very much. Mr O'Connor measured time in shakes of a bee's knee, so for

example he would say, 'I have to leave now but will be back in three shakes of a bee's knee.' I mention this because I have myself been using this expression all my life!

Reggie Norton (1943–5)

Julian Reade (1949–52) remembers that in these once- or twice-weekly singing sessions, the boys were issued with books of traditional national melodies:

Someone played a piano on the stage, and the rafters reverberated to our manly treble voices: 'Men of Harlech', 'Loch Lomond', 'Cockles and Mussels', 'Clementine', 'Drunken Sailor'.

After some short-lived appointments, the post of Director of Music was put on a much more secure footing with the arrival of David Langdon in 1965, who inaugurated a period of exciting expansion and innovation.

Music 1965–2001

In 1965 there was a small but thriving Music Department of four teachers. Class music lessons were held in New Room and the only resources were the Bluthner grand piano, a recently donated record-player and a few community song books. The few individual music lessons, mainly piano, violin and recorder, took place in Lodges, classrooms, or in a small cupboard-like room (currently the Bursary Archive) off what is now the Junior Day Room. Small group lessons took place in the 'Tool Shed', on the site of the present Music Room. The annual Music Competition was already a regular feature, and soon the school orchestra was formed and quickly flourished. Later, class

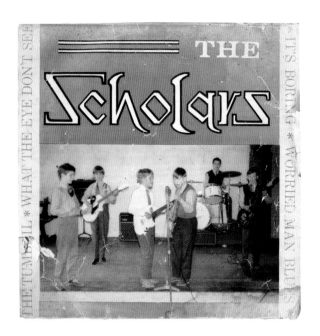

lessons moved into the space between New Room and the chapel, which had been converted into a Music Room.

The first biennial, Lent Term Choral Concert, a performance of Fauré's *Requiem*, was held in 1969. This inaugurated many memorable musical occasions, the Blue and Red Choirs comprising core singers, with staff and parents providing the lower parts. Regular Summer Concerts started in 1969, and the Music Society also began life.

Occasionally, famous musicians visited Summer Fields. In 1967, Sir Charles Groves came and took choir practice, conducting 'And the glory of the Lord', from Handel's *Messiah*. Leo Dobbs (1967–71) recalls meeting Groves, then conductor of the Royal Liverpool Philharmonic, a 'distinguished-looking gentleman with grey hair and a beard', who also conducted the last night of the Proms. As a friend of Dobbs's form master, Wilfrid Williams (1949–75), Groves invited Leo's form to watch the Philharmonic rehearse in the Sheldonian: a big mistake! 'Sir Charles became angrier and angrier as a dozen restless boys scampered over the building, including the roof, and generally caused a racket. The conductor had to ask us to keep quiet several times.' Did that friendship survive?

Julian Slot and Simon Wade won Summer Fields' first Music Scholarships to Eton in 1973, thus beginning a long line of such achievements. From 1974, boys attended the IAPS Orchestral, Concert Band and Choral Courses, held in Suffolk and Derbyshire.

Above: Sleeve of a recording of Fauré's *Requiem* by Summer Fields in 1970

Left: The Scholars, a group started by Nick Aldridge, 1964

Opposite page: Composing using *Sibelius* software

Perhaps one of the greatest musical performances at Summer Fields was Benjamin Britten's *Noyes Fludde* (1977) in St Michael's Church, Summertown – this involved almost the entire school. The renowned pianist and Summer Fields parent John Ogdon wrote: 'It was a memorable musical experience.' The following year he gave a brilliant piano recital at Oxford Town Hall in aid of the School Appeal.

Subscription Concerts at St Edward's School and Radley, from 1977 and 1987 respectively, provided outstanding opportunities to hear great performers such as James Blades ('The World of Percussion'), Philip Jones Brass Ensemble, the Scholars, Christopher Hogwood, Julian Lloyd-Webber, the Academy of Ancient Music, Humphrey Lyttelton, Kenny Ball and His Jazzmen and the Swingle Singers.

Harold Macmillan, OS, opened Macmillan Hall (now known simply as Macmillan) in 1979 which dramatically transformed the department, offering a music room with teaching and practice rooms, instrument storage, and space for small ensembles. Later, electronic keyboards were added to the list of resources, allowing keyboard classes into the Third Form curriculum. Composition was introduced to Removes and Fifths and, in 2000, senior boys began to tackle the mysteries of sound engineering – recording, editing and mastering a CD.

A new Bechstein grand was acquired in 1995 – a worthy addition to the department. With the new 'theatre' space came the staging of more adventurous musical productions. Termly formal and informal concerts began, and the Associated Board of the Royal School of Music exams could now be held at school. In these, by early 1980, boys were achieving passes and merits at Grades 6 and 7, while in 1990, Julian Perkins (1985–90) became Summer Fields' first Grade-8 pupil, gaining a Distinction on the treble recorder.

An Inter-League Music Competition was first held in 1980. At the same time Summer Fields became involved in the SATIPS Orchestral Festivals, at Radley or St Edward's, giving boys the chance to play in an orchestra of around two hundred instrumentalists.

By the summer of 1983, weekly assemblies in Macmillan always started with the orchestra playing the hymn, often followed by solos from other musicians. In the following years, each form performed as an instrumental ensemble, with every boy playing something. Inclusion and opportunity were paramount in the Music Department's philosophy.

Anthony Grunwell arrived in 1983 to become the first Assistant Director of Music, succeeded by Martyn Ford (1986) and Tim Bennett (1990). Further new elements of these years

included boy trumpeters playing the 'Last Post' at the Remembrance Day service, the Blue Choir singing Christmas carols to pensioners at the Ferry Centre, recorder players taking part in the Oxford Music Festival (1986) and, from 1988, Summer Fields hosting the regional auditions for IAPS Orchestral and Choral Courses.

The year 1990 was special: Benedict Ausden (1984–9) played the piano in the Inspector Morse film *Infernal Serpent* for ITV. Then, with the department in full swing, David Langdon broke his leg, on Christmas Day, leaving Tim Bennett bearing the full brunt of all the work during much of 1991.

Growth continued apace nonetheless, with many new features: Junior Concert (1991), Second Orchestra (1992), Concerto Concert (1993), 'Coffee' Concerts (1998), given by year group. Inevitably, the year 2000 provided the opportunity for a Millennium Concert – a 'Last Night of the Proms' in St Michael's, Summertown, with over two hundred performers, including boys, staff and parents.

Very few prep schools can boast *three* organists on the staff at the same time, but 1998 saw an organ recital in chapel by David Langdon, Paul Cheater (1994–2012) and Bruce McCrae (1994–2005) to celebrate the centenary of our Father Willis instrument. Finally, in the same year Tim Bennett was appointed Director of Choral Music. When David Langdon became Senior Master, Tim took over the reins of a breathtakingly busy department to be succeeded, in 2001, by Gareth Price.

The Rt Hon. Harold Macmillan, OM, PC, FRS, 1st Earl of Stockton (1894–1986), SF 1903–6

Macmillan is famous for winning the 1959 Election with the slogan, 'You've never had it so good'. Nicknamed 'Supermac', he was known for his wit, pragmatism and unflappability. A private Member of Parliament (1924–9 and 1931–40), Macmillan went on to hold a string of high offices: Secretary for Air (1945), Housing Minister (1951–4), Defence Minister (1954–5), Foreign Secretary (1955), Chancellor of the Exchequer (1955–7) and Chancellor of Oxford University (1960–86).

After leaving Eton early, owing to ill health, Macmillan was privately coached by Ronald Knox (1896–1900) for the Oxford Scholarship examinations. He obtained an exhibition and matriculated from Balliol in October 1912. He took a First in Classical Mods in 1914, but the outbreak of the First World War prevented him from sitting Greats.

Macmillan served with the 2nd battalion Grenadier Guards, first tasting action at the Battle of Loos in September 1915. He was wounded lightly in the head and seriously in the right hand. Such was his bravery that, as a contemporary later recalled, 'During the next two years or so, anything brave was described by the Guardsmen as "nearly as brave as Mr Macmillan".' After convalescence, he returned in April 1916 to the 2nd battalion, then at the Ypres salient, and was lightly wounded again on 19 July.

During the battle of the Somme in mid-September 1916, Macmillan was seriously wounded in the pelvis and left thigh. He lay for a day in a shell hole in no-man's-land. 'I had in my pocket Aeschylus's *Prometheus,* in Greek. It was a play I knew very well, and seemed not inappropriate to my position... I read it intermittently.' He also feigned death to deceive a German patrol. Later, after dark, he was rescued. He was returned to London and spent the rest of the war in and out of hospital, and unable to return to France. The war left him with 'a limp handshake, a dragging gait, and sporadic pain'.

Harold Macmillan was born on 10 February 1894 at 52 Cadogan Place, London, the youngest of the three children of Maurice Macmillan, publisher, and his wife, Helen (Nellie). He attended Mr Gladstone's day school near Sloane Square from the age of about six. At the beginning of the Lent Term, 1903, when he was almost nine, Macmillan was taken to Paddington by his nanny and put on the train for Oxford. He then travelled by horse-tram to Summertown, in those days an isolated village 'near' Oxford, and so to Summer Fields. There, on his first night, he cried himself to sleep after a sparse meal of bread and milk and was comforted by Evelyn Baring (1903–7), an older boy, with the famous words, 'Don't cry – your situation is bad, but not desperate.' Harold Macmillan left Summer Fields in 1906 having won third King's Scholarship to Eton. The evidence of his success may be read on an honours board in New Room.

At Summer Fields, Macmillan was grounded in Latin and Greek prose and verse. He read widely, as he continued to do throughout his life. An erudite boy, his reading list included St

Macmillan aged twelve

Mark's Gospel, the Acts of the Apostles, three books of the *Odyssey,* two of the *Aeneid,* to which were added works by Herodotus, Horace, Ovid, Xenophon, Dickens, Walter Scott and Conan Doyle. It is perhaps no surprise that Macmillan should have been carrying a copy of a Greek play in his tunic pocket on the Somme. Richard Thorpe writes that at Summer Fields, Macmillan 'thrived on the scholarly work, though he was not keen on gymnastics and climbing ropes'.

On Saturday 16 November 1905, Macmillan took the part of the Prime Minister in a school production of *Rumpelstiltzkin.* He wore a long cloak, crimson cape, buckled shoes, silk stockings, knee breeches, a long waistcoat and a curly judge's wig which, he later commented, 'looks more like the Lord Chancellor's'. He trod the boards again as a member of the crowd in a scene from *Coriolanus.* It was from Summer Fields that Macmillan discovered Oxford. During the termly visits from his parents, there was little to do, 'so we visited Oxford', he wrote.

Macmillan retained great affection for his old prep school or 'private' school, as he would term it. He made regular visits. In June 1958 he planted a tulip tree on the Masters' Lawn in the afternoon,

having received an honorary degree at Encaenia that morning. In 1979, he opened the Macmillan Hall. He occasionally presented the prizes and served Summer Fields as a governor from 1955.

Harold Macmillan died on 29 December 1986, after a brief illness. In February 1987, his memorial service took place in a packed Westminster Abbey. It was a majestic occasion. But after the solemn 'Grenadiers Return' played by the band of the Grenadier Guards, the entire congregation, led by the Grenadiers, burst forth into the joyous and exhilarating 'Battle Hymn of the Republic'. In the words of Alistair Horne, 'The juxtaposition of the two pieces of music somehow seemed to epitomise most perfectly that gentle distinction between the serious and the less serious that had so characterised Harold Macmillan's whole attitude to life.' For Richard Thorpe, 'Supermac' 'had style, vision, breadth of view and compassion'.

The tulip tree today, **above**, planted by Harold Macmillan in 1958, **left**

Concert in Macmillan

Music from 2001

The Music Department continues to flourish in the twenty-first century, accumulating seventeen awards to public schools between 2001 and 2013. The majority are to Eton, although St Edward's, Radley and Harrow also feature on the honours boards. Regular concerts take place in Macmillan, the annual programme usually comprising five Coffee Concerts, String, Wind, Brass and Piano Concerts, an Informal (or as some boys call it, 'Infernal') Concert in the winter months and a large Summer Concert.

Music plays its part in the school's outreach to the local community – particularly the elderly. 'Christmas Cheer' remains a favourite for local friends and a Tea Concert was added to the schedule in 2013, with performances accompanied by the clink of fine china and the polite passing of cakes and sandwiches. Organ recitals and concerts, by parents, friends, or

professionals, supplement the regular fare. Highlights have included a performance of the original version of *Carnival of the Animals,* marking the arrival of some stunning mosaics for the department, created by Artist-in-Residence Clare Goodall, ably assisted by every boy in the school.

The League Music Competition restarted in 2010, and the Associated Board of the Royal School of Music exams continue to be the main method of assessing boys' progress. Summer Fields still boasts an almost perfect pass rate, with many candidates gaining Distinctions or Merits. A point of pride in recent years is the number of Grade 7 and 8 successes achieved by the boys.

Large-scale musicals have become regular entertainment for boys and parents alike, with shows such as *Billy.* This trend is likely to continue, strengthening musical links with Drama. However, the most recent excitement centres on our newest instrument in the department – not physically in the

department, but housed in chapel! This is our fine three-manual, bespoke organ which was installed in December 2013 to replace the old Father Willis, which had reached the end of its working life after faithfully serving Summer Fields for about 110 years.

Summerfieldians are certainly embracing Addison's observation that music 'is the greatest good that mortals know'.

chapter seven

Chapel and Choir

The Chapel and Worship

The Christian ethos has been at the heart of Summer Fields since its beginning. In the early days, spiritual life was usually well cared for, as many of the first masters were clergymen. However, in 1896, Doctor decided to build a chapel. He designed it himself and dedicated it to his mother-in-law, Mrs Maclaren. It was completed by 1903. The essential shell of the building remains much the same today, but there have been major changes. The organ, a Father Willis, installed in 1900, in a specially constructed vestry to the north of the chancel, was moved to the south side in 1984, as part of a plan to improve the changing rooms. It was replaced by a fine new instrument in December 2013, the result of a generous donation to Summer Fields by the Columbia Foundation Fund of the London Community Fund. The old instrument will undergo a thorough restoration before installation in St Laurence's Church, Warborough, south Oxfordshire. The intimate side-chapel to the south was developed for private prayer and is still used regularly by the parents' Prayer Group. Another important alteration was made in 1979 when the west end was opened up, initially to fill the double function of an extension for chapel seating and a Day Room for the Removes. An upstairs gallery was added at the same time.

The original plain brick walls were whitewashed. Oak choir stalls were in place by 1917, funded in part from a successful appeal by Doctor. In 1974, new pews were installed in the nave,

replacing chairs, first introduced in 1932. In April 1919, memorial brasses, listing the 139 names of OSS killed during the First World War, were put up along the west wall of the chapel. They were dedicated by the Head Master of Eton, Dr Alington, in the Easter term of 1920. These brasses were moved to their present position, on the exterior south-west wall of the chapel, during the extension of the west end and the construction of the

The chapel showing the chairs in the nave

The Rt Rev. Monsignor Ronald Knox (1888–1957), SF 1896–1900

In 1957 Ronald Knox was found to be suffering from cancer. He went to stay with Harold Macmillan (1903–6), an old friend and pupil, at 10 Downing Street, where Sir Horace Evans confirmed the diagnosis of a terminal illness. On his departure, Macmillan accompanied Knox to Paddington in his official car and wished him a good journey. Knox replied that it would be a long one... He died on 24 August at the Manor House, Mells, Somerset. His body was taken to Westminster Cathedral, where a Requiem Mass was celebrated on 29 August. On 30 August he was buried at Mells.

So passed away one of Summer Fields' most celebrated sons. Flourishing under the strict classical ethos of Doctor, Knox won first King's Scholarship to Eton in 1900. Thereafter top honours fell to him rapidly. He was elected to Pop (the popular name for the elite Eton Society – members of Pop may choose to wear highly coloured waistcoats) and became Captain of the School, delegating his responsibility for corporal punishment to another boy. He won the first Balliol Scholarship and Davies Scholarship from Eton to Oxford. He took the expected First in Greats in 1910. As President of the Union during Hilary term, 1909, Knox was reputed to be one of the finest speakers of his generation.

Knox's interest in Anglo-Catholicism, begun at Eton, led him to accept a Fellowship at Trinity College, Oxford, with a view to ordination to the college chaplaincy. In 1910 he was private tutor to the young Harold Macmillan, but lost the post when he refused the Nonconformist Mrs

Macmillan's request not to discuss religion with her son. Macmillan recalled that Knox was 'the only man I have ever known who really was a saint... and if you live with a saint, it's quite an experience, especially a humorous saint'. Knox was ordained as an Anglican priest on 22 September 1912.

Scholars, 1900, with Knox in centre

There followed a period of writing and reflection, leading to conversion to Roman Catholicism on 22 September 1917. He was ordained priest on 5 October 1919. Knox then devoted the remainder of his life to preaching, teaching, study and writing. He served as Catholic Chaplain to Oxford University from 1926–39. One of his most notable achievements was his translation of the Vulgate Bible, the New Testament of which was published in 1945. The Old Testament received the Westminster archdiocesan *imprimatur* in 1948, being printed 'for private use' in 1949. In a lighter vein, Knox, throughout his life, wrote satirical and humorous pieces, as well as a series of detective stories with titles such as *The Viaduct Murder* (1926), *The Three Taps* (1927), *The Body in the Silo* (1933), *Still Dead* (1934) and *Double Cross Purposes* (1937).

Ronald Knox was born on 17 February 1888 at Kibworth rectory, Leicestershire. He was famously precocious, declaring at the age of four that 'at night I think about the past'. He read Virgil at six, and contributed a Latin serial, *Publius et Amilla*, to the family magazine. At Summer Fields, Knox composed numerous Latin verses, famously

rendering Kipling's *Absent-Minded Beggar* into Latin Elegiacs – no mean feat for a twelve-year-old!

Some extracts from his letters home illustrate his scholastic progress:

30 January 1897 [aged eight]. I have done another scene of my Latin play, Dactylic with 18 lines.

24 May 1897 [aged nine]. I have finished Caesar and am going to do Livy. Last week, I was top in Latin and Greek. We had a cinematograph show on Saturday.

28 November [aged ten]. I am getting on finely with my play. It is all in Latin. I was top in Greek and English.

4 February 1900 [aged eleven]. Tomorrow we are going to do some Lyric (Sapphic or Alcaic) verses! Of course I have never done any yet, except on my own book, besides Elegiacs.

Knox was no good at cricket or football, but much happier in the water. However, he spent a large part of his free time writing poetry in a variety of metres and languages. His only major complaint at Summer Fields seems to have been the daily distribution by Matron of three sheets of lavatory paper which he found both niggardly and indelicate. Overall, Knox's time at SF was happy and uneventful. He was a reflective boy with the sparks of true scholarship, sparks which were gently fanned into vigorous flames during his early Oxford days in Summertown.

Above: The new organ

Below: A Eucharist in chapel during the 1960s

gallery. Lent Term 1923 saw the installation of two panels (now removed), copied from Perugino's famous altar-piece triptych. These were hung opposite one another on the north and south walls, 'in affectionate remembrance of those masters and boys who served and laid down their lives in the First World War'. In Michaelmas Term 1962, two statues, of the Virgin (left of the altar) and St Nicholas (right) were erected soon after the chapel had been dedicated to St Nicholas by the Bishop of Oxford. The wooden panel memorial to those who died in the Second World War was put up on the north wall in 1951 and dedicated by the Bishop of Coventry, the Rt Rev. Cuthbert Bardsley (1916–19). On

the south wall may be seen the Roll of Honour to those from Summer Fields St Leonards who fell in both World Wars. This memorial was rededicated in 2006, after transfer from St Peter's Church, St Leonards, where those boys and masters worshipped. It records twenty-one names from the First World War and forty-five who sacrificed their lives in the conflict of 1939–45.

The stained-glass windows constitute one of the chief glories of the chapel. Admired and enjoyed for well over a century, they replaced original panes of plain glass. The new windows are by Henry Holiday and were installed in stages between 1900 and 1915. The second window on the north side (from the choir) commemorates Tom Coventon, who died when he developed pneumonia on top of measles in the Lent Term of 1913. 'He was only nine and had not been here very long, but quite long enough to have endeared himself to everyone, masters and boys alike.' Perhaps the most appreciated is the great east window, dedicated to the memory of Mrs Maclaren. The main characters from left to right are: William of Wykeham, founder of Winchester and New College, Oxford; St Monica, mother of St Augustine who brought Christianity to southern Britain in 597; St Catherine, shown with her spiked wheel on which she was tortured before her beheading; and Erasmus, the great Classics scholar and theologian. Known collectively as 'The Four Scholars' owing to their strong connections with education, they are appropriate figures to grace our school chapel.

The subtle west window, often unnoticed, is seen to best effect with the late-afternoon sunbeams streaming through it. One of Holiday's earlier works, when he was designing for J. Powell & Sons, it was rescued from the redundant church of St Mary at North Chailey, Sussex, to be reunited with some of its brothers. The window depicts Mary, Jesus as a young man and Joseph. After negotiating the legal and practical difficulties involved in moving ecclesiastical glass, the new window eventually arrived at SF, to be blessed on Sunday 20 May 2001, by the Rt Rev. David Jennings (1952–7).

These days, there are short (ten-minute) weekday morning services together with a weekly 'congo' (congregational practice) to enable the boys to blast out the hymns on Sundays. Such enthusiasm often spills over into public school and not without notice:

> It is not considered 'cool' to sing loudly in chapel at senior school [Eton]. Often boys actually turn round and stare at those singing with some gusto and, invariably, these are old Summerfieldians. The chapel singing at Summer Fields was second to none and I often complain with fellow OSS at how poor it can be at senior school – a testament to SF!
>
> Barnaby Harrison (2008–11)

Henry Holiday and the Chapel

The Chapel of St Nicholas at Summer Fields was built in 1896. Dr Charles Williams (Doctor) commissioned Henry Holiday, one of the most successful window designers of the day, to complete its stained-glass lancets. Holiday was a disciple of Edward Burne-Jones, who had been the protégé of Archibald Maclaren. Considering that the chapel was built in the memory of Gertrude, Archibald's wife, the choice of artists was particularly fitting. Holiday had replaced Burne-Jones as a stained-glass window designer at Powell's Glass Works when the older artist had left the firm to work for his friend William Morris at Morris & Co.

The east window (1896) is the earliest in the chapel. It was presented by pupils and parents 'in pious memory of Gertrude Isabel Frances Maclaren, founder of this school...' Its four main lights depict (from left to right) William of Wykeham, St Monica, St Catherine and Erasmus. Collectively known as 'The Four Scholars', they all have some connection with education. The five windows on the north side of the nave portray scenes from the early life of Christ. Those on the south wall illustrate Christian VIrtues such as Faith, Charity and Fortitude.

The east window, *The Four Scholars*, 1896

North windows: *illustrating scenes from the early life of Jesus*

South windows: *illustrating the Virtues of Charity and Fortitude*

Windows depicting Hope and Love on the east wall of the side chapel

At the centenary year of the chapel's foundation, the windows were inspected with a view to eventual restoration. One of the restorers, impressed by the quality of Holiday's workmanship, remarked that he had recently seen windows by the same artist in a redundant Sussex church. After years of negotiation, and thanks to the generous sponsorship of current and past Summerfieldians, a three-light window representing the Holy Family was transferred from the disused church to the west wall of the chapel.

In addition to illuminating the Summer Fields chapel, Holiday's stained-glass work can be found in some of the finest ecclesiastical buildings in England, including Westminster Abbey, Worcester College, Oxford and the chapel of Trinity College, Cambridge.

Sunday services now mainly take the form of Mattins or Evensong. Selected preachers are sometimes invited to address the school, a tradition first started by Bear Alington in the early 1920s. Anthony Trollope in *Barchester Towers* wrote that 'there is, perhaps, no greater hardship at present inflicted on mankind, than the necessity of listening to sermons', and it is maybe for this reason that Summer Fields preachers have ever tried to lighten their addresses (or even to press home their point) through the deployment of a few gimmicks. Chapel in recent times has seen cricket, casting a trout rod down the length of the nave, a helium balloon floating to the ceiling (and remaining there for some days), as well as various pyrotechnics. Leo Dobbs (1967–71) remembers some 'very strange' sermons, with one guest preacher bringing 'a working model plane to illustrate his sermon'.

About once a term a morning Sung Eucharist is held, an idea first introduced by Cyril Williams (HM 1928–39) as an alternative to Sunday Mattins. The academic year remains punctuated by annual services such as Harvest Festival, Remembrance Sunday, Carols by Candlelight and Confirmation.

> *I remember nothing of what the Bishop said at my Confirmation in the chapel in November 1956, but I do remember the smell of the chrysanthemums!*
>
> The Rt Rev. David Jennings (1952–7), current governor

The principal Christmas Carol Service, based on the pattern of that at King's College, Cambridge, takes place at St Michael's, Summertown, as the SF chapel is too small to accommodate the whole school and parents.

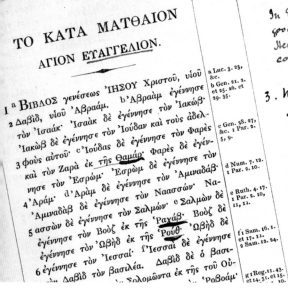

MORNING AND
EVENING DEVOTIONS

FOR THE USE OF

Preparatory Schools

COMPILED AND COMPOSED

BY THE

REV. C. E. WILLIAMS, D.D.
(BRASENOSE COLLEGE, OXFORD).

✠

"I say unto you, that in heaven their angels do always
behold the face of My Father, which is in heaven"

✠

NINTH EDITION — 1959

Above: Dr Williams's annotated Greek Testament, 1872

Above right: The ninth edition, dated 1959, of *The Morning and Evening Devotions*

Below: The 'Thin Red Service Book', 1980

Opposite page: 'Congo' – congregational practice

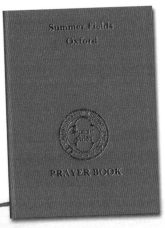

There were prayers each morning in chapel lasting about five minutes. On weekdays, there was a twenty-minute evening service and on Sundays there were both morning and evening services. They lasted for about fifty minutes. All this gave me the opportunity to learn the Collects from the Prayer Book, the Psalms and many new hymns. I do not remember being particularly devout, but the chapel services were a part of life, like everything else. From the very start we had to learn the catechism from the Book of Common Prayer. *My recollection is that I could say the Ten Commandments off by heart, including the seventh, but I do not think I had the least idea what 'Thou shalt not commit adultery' meant.*

Thomas Miles (1931–6)

Weekday evening prayers were abolished in 1975, and in 1980 the new SF Prayer Book offered a selection of worship for Mattins, Evensong and Holy Communion. Boys now play a full part in services which, although retaining a due sense of dignity, are far removed from the rigours of the 1662 Prayer Book.

In times past, hymns could be gloomy, as Thomas Miles recalls:

A few more years shall roll,
A few more seasons come,
And we shall be at Rest,
Asleep within the tomb.

This is not the most cheerful material for small boys during long services, also faced with:

Days and moments quickly flying,
Blend the living with the dead,
Soon will you and I be lying,
Each within our narrow bed.

Some hymns, however, were more joyful, and known to cause amusement as contemporary in-jokes were enjoyed. When singing, 'A noble army, men and boys / The matron and the maid,' Thomas remembers, 'We immediately thought of the Matron at Summer Fields and the maids who waited on us in the dining room!'

Some boys were overcome by the formality of the services. Alastair Macdonald (1951–5) remembers being 'overawed by chapel and its most structured and correct liturgy with beautiful singing and the old organ'.

From 1987, the Authorized Version of the Bible ceased to hold sway, and Summerfieldians are no longer as familiar with this text as they were when Bible reading was a daily occurrence. Thomas Miles (1931–6) describes the whole school assembled in New Room after breakfast, when 'each boy in turn read a verse from the Bible. I think we were restricted to the four Gospels and the Acts of the Apostles, which meant that all five books were read more than once during my five years at Summer Fields'. For juniors, the Authorized Version had its traps, as Nick Aldridge noted on hearing, 'Woe unto you, scribes, Pharisees, hypricots' – as Nick commented, 'what a delightful cross-bred fruit that must have been!'

This daily Bible reading was abolished by GB, who amalgamated it with morning prayers in chapel. This can have

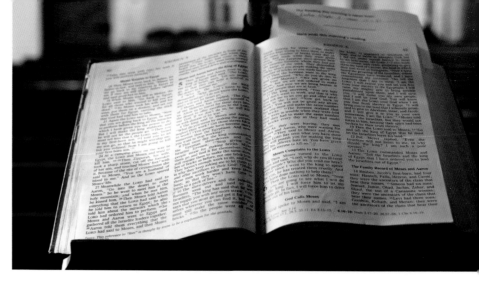

done nothing but good, as breakfast had previously been sandwiched between two forms of Divine Service.

Every opportunity to strengthen classical knowledge was seized; even chapel time could be used for academic as well as spiritual purposes. Thomas Miles was given access to a copy of the New Testament in Greek: 'Since New Testament Greek is not difficult, I was easily able to follow the lessons in chapel as they were read.' In his later years, Nick Aldridge could also be observed quietly doing just that, in his pew at the back of chapel, on the north side.

Nothing was allowed to interfere with religious worship even during the power cuts and the economic crisis of the early 1970s. The situation may have been depressing for adults but…

for a ten- to twelve-year-old it was very exciting. The school coped with the crisis with amazing efficiency. Within minutes of the lights going out, teachers and other staff would be going around with hurricane lamps and torches. I think it was during a Carol Service that the lights went out once. There were a lot of candles already in place, so the chapel wasn't plunged into total darkness. But the organ, in the middle of playing, slowly died out with a plaintive groan, before air was restored to it by one of the choir quickly rushing round and using the old manual pump that was still in working order.

Alan Sykes (1969–73)

On the other hand, human weakness could sometimes wreak havoc during a chapel service, as recalled by Dr John Spalding, now aged ninety-seven:

My principal memory of the chapel choir is that I was chosen to be a member of it. They soon realised their mistake for I cannot sing and I was demoted to pump the organ. This was before the organ was provided with air under pressure electrically. I never failed to provide the necessary air, but I remember that another boy failed to do so, perhaps having fallen asleep during Headmaster [Cyril] Williams' sermon.

Dr John Spalding (1928–30)

Guy Rendel (1934–9) 'failed' when 'for no apparent reason' he relaxed when pumping the organ. The air supply dwindled, a

Te Deum followed, 'on low power' and Guy was fired by the Headmaster immediately after the service!

Chapel had a profound long-term effect on many boys, often influencing their religious practices in later life. Sam Legerton (1945–50), confirmed by the Bishop of Oxford on 24 November 1949, 'embraced the Church and became very serious and pious'. He continued in this vein for a long time, much to the chagrin of his father who feared he was destined for ordination. Edward Mynors (1955–60), in the choir from beginning to end of his time at the school, 'carried on singing in chapel at public school and joined a choir at university'. Chapel made a deep impression on most of his family. Edward is now a Lay Reader, and his younger brother a canon of Peterborough Cathedral. His youngest brother is Chancellor of the diocese of Worcester.

Above left: The Register of Services for 1965

Above: The 'Good News' Bible presented by the Amies family, 1986

The Choir

In chapel, the Red Choir plays a prominent role in worship. Excellence in this respect sticks in the mind of many OSS. James Fairhurst (1972–7) remembers 'the choir and the wonderful old organ, with David Langdon's fingers and feet flying across the keys and pedals playing Bach's *Toccata and Fugue in D Minor* at the end of the Sunday service. Zane Dalal (1972–7) and I would rush to watch, with fascination.'

But as well as serving the chapel, the choir often moves further afield. Choral highlights include trips to sing in many beautiful and well-known buildings: the cathedrals of Salisbury, Gloucester, Lichfield, Winchester and Strasbourg. Leo Dobbs (1967–71) recalls singing at Salisbury Cathedral with the Dragon School, 'who seemed very scruffy next to us choristers in our cassocks and ruffs'. Other venues include some fine chapels such as St George's, Windsor, New College and Christ Church, Oxford, Eton and Radley Colleges, as well as parish churches like St Michael's, Chester Square and St Mary Redcliffe. Country houses – Ditchley Park and Aynhoe – have also reverberated to the dulcet tones of young Summerfieldians.

The Red Choir has spread its wings, as foreign tours constitute a regular feature of choral life. Destinations include New York, Florence, Rome, Belgium, Germany and Paris (which

Father and son: the Rt Rev. David Jennings, **left**, and Michael Jennings, Assistant Director of Music, **above**

The choir in 1906, **above**, and 1943, **right**

included a concert in Notre-Dame). A recent trip to Vienna was a great success.

In the 1930s, Choir Feasts usually involved punts, often moving quite a distance upstream for a picnic on the river bank, the Headmaster and his wife travelling sedately behind in a rowing boat. The return journey often became a punt race, with crews paddling furiously while bombarding each other with cherry stones and other picnic remains. Today, Choir Picnics are quieter and often supplemented by suppers in restaurants after singing Evensong. Such treats have always been much appreciated. Christopher Cockburn (1940–1) recollects that he 'enjoyed being in the choir, not least as we were given an extra "feast" at Christmas'. In 1977, the Choir Outing was to the Royal Albert Hall for the Golden Jubilee Celebrations of the Royal School of Church Music.

However, for most of the time choral life consists of sheer hard work in a variety of contexts. Choristers have taken part in many special musical events. They sang the *ripieno* part in Bach's *St Matthew Passion* in Oxford Town Hall (1976 and 1987). Dominic Parr (1981–6) and James Spilling (1982–7) sang solo treble in Britten's *A Ceremony of Carols,* for Summertown Choral Society's Christmas Concert. 1991 saw the Red Choir in Brasenose College Chapel singing for a Granada film entitled *Dinosaur,* while in 1995 Patrick Massey's (1991–6) carol *Shepherds in the Felds* was played on Classic FM during SF's Patronal Festival (St Nicholas' Day).

Other compositions by boys include Edward Morton Jack's (1983–8) school carol, 'Ring out the bells', and Julian Perkins' (1985–90) 'To us is born a Holy Child', which delighted the congregations at the 1987 and 1989 Carol Services.

In 2014, choirs continue to flourish. The Red Choir comprises about twenty-four treble choristers, with never fewer than eight lower-part singers. The size of the choir has remained fairly

constant over the years. Peter Fullerton (1938–43), who joined in 1940, recalls twenty-seven choristers, well drilled by choirmaster 'Stodgy' Thomson (1939–46):

> He got this nickname from a rehearsal one day when he stopped us in mid verse and barked, 'No, No No! That's too *STODGY*.' He was known as Stodgy from then on. He taught us a repertoire of anthems such as 'How Lovely are Thy Dwellings Fair' and 'Let the Bright Seraphim', which we sang every Sunday.

The repertoire has since grown and now covers the whole gamut of sacred choral music, ranging from Tallis through Bach, Handel, Mendelssohn, all the great Victorians to more modern composers such as Howells, Rutter, Poulenc and Duruflé. Two works have been specially commissioned for the school's 150th anniversary, the first by Paul Mealor (best known for a commission for the last royal wedding) and the second by John Tavener, who passed away a short time after its completion. However, John's widow was in the audience at the Sheldonian Theatre to enjoy the world première of *A New Commandment,* on Saturday 1 February 2014, as part of the school's Anniversary Concert.

The Red Choir continues to be an ambassador for Summer Fields with its Christmas visits to Sir Michael Sobell House (since 1983), while the Blue Choir plays its part at the Ferry Centre and Parmoor Court.

A chorister has status, privilege, extra treats, but also opportunities to show that boys will be boys, or that a knotty problem might generate ingenuity in its solution:

> One day we were cleaning the chapel silver and got our hands on the holy wine and wafers, which we proceeded to drink and eat. But we left traces of our crime on the floor, drops of wine and wafer crumbs. Henry Thorold [1930–5; Chaplain 1968–75],

the Chaplain, started by interrogating me and I soon crumbled under the pressure and grassed on my felons in arms. I rushed to tell them and, fearing he would inform Patrick Savage [HM 1960–75], we came up with a cunning ploy. We decided to go to formal Confession, which meant going to the early morning service the next day, but also ensured that the Chaplain could tell nobody of our behaviour!

Leo Dobbs (1967–71)

As the school enters the fifty-year run-up to its bicentenary, let all Summerfieldian choristers note that important line in 'The Holly and the Ivy' and ensure that, at all times, there is indeed 'sweet singing in the choir'.

Avete atque Valete
Last Impressions

My happiest memory of Summer Fields is the day that I left it. My unhappiest, the four terms I had to spend there. This may seem exaggerated, or it may leave the impression that I was a horrid little worm. I wasn't really. I was simply a very stupid boy, whom the authorities rightly guessed could not be educated up to Scholarship standard. They therefore took little interest in me, except they beat me as they did everyone else.

VINCENT BALFOUR-BROWN (1892–3)

Valete

It seems my youth to dotage yields
For I must go from Summer Fields.
I do lament it, and I grieve
That now it's time for me to leave.
I hate a long drawn-out goodbye
Which lengthens grief and damps my eye.
And would it not disturb and trouble you
To leave behind C.A.E.W.?
Nor will it please me when I say
'Farewell, adieu to A.F.A.
And most unpleasant it will be
To bid farewell to J.F.E.
My tears will flow like iron, molten,
When I depart from Mr Bolton.
And it is not a very nice art
To say goodbye to Mr Lysaght.
Many will be my sighs and sobbin's on
When I have gone from Mr Robinson.
My tears will come like snow in flakes,
When I depart from Mr Jacques.
And I will not refrain from them
When I have gone from H.M.M.
I'm very sorry now my time's passed on,
For I must go from Mr Marston.
I'll feel as though condemned to gallows
When I depart from Mr Fallows.

And why should I endure such ills
As going from the two Miss Hills?
Goodbye, goodbye to all my friends!
And thus this awful poem ends.
All my goodbyes are now complete –
Agri aestivi, valete!

THOMAS MILES (1931–6)

My memories of SF are golden – good days, always busy, full of fun and competition in form and sport, friendships, and masters who were good to us or eccentric or both. So Summer Fields for me gets an Alpha as my *Alma Mater*.

PETER FULLERTON (1938–43)

I loved Art, became a reasonable long-distance runner, remain bored by cricket, nearly drowned at a swimming contest in the now out-of-bounds Cherwell. If Harold Macmillan learnt to act at Summer Fields, I emerged with other accomplishments. I hypnotised the Dean of Westminster by speaking Latin with the old pronunciation. I am skilled with the handsaw and the plane since learning them from Mr Allsop, and Mr Bowtell struck a spark in me for the cinema which still glows today.

RICHARD WHITE (1946–51)

Summer Fields, when I arrived there in 1948 as a nine-year-old, was a pleasant-looking house with various extensions and two enormous playing-fields ringed by high trees. It owed its success partly to the number of scholarships which its boys had won to public schools. That was why I was sent there. Money was short, so I had to be a Scholar. The idea of sending me to a free state-school near my home was never for a moment considered. Yet stories of my schooldays cause incredulous laughter among European friends. Apparently I resemble a nineteenth-century anthropologist describing life in some obscure tropical island.

I emerged from the system with a healthy body, and with an agile mind, full of useful knowledge. I am unsure how far Summer Fields influenced my character, but I had been sent there to get a scholarship, and I got one.

JULIAN READE (1949–52)

Summer Fields was genuinely interested in educating boys and promoting values (albeit perhaps with an excessive emphasis on the innate sinfulness of man) that may now seem just a little old-fashioned, but in reality form the basis of any civilised society.
HENRY POOLE (1957–62)

I hated the place and ran away three times!
   Sorry!!
THE EARL OF SHREWSBURY AND WATERFORD, HENRY J. B. C. C. CHETWYND-TALBOT, VISCOUNT INGESTRE (1960–6)

In the summer of 1964, we celebrated the centenary of the school, which included a service at St Michael and All Angels, Sports Day and a lot of strawberries. My grandfather came along and was much pleased that he was the oldest Old Boy. By the

time I left, the school had embraced the swinging sixties by having its own band, The Scholars, and cutting a record under 'management' of Nicholas Aldridge. I enthusiastically played their EP to my older brother who was a record producer at Abbey Road; to my disappointment he declined to sign them up!
NICHOLAS SANSOM (1963–8)

I loved the whole experience of Summer Fields: swimming lessons in the Cherwell before the pool was built, brrrr!; finding a spider in the gravy at lunch – with only seven legs!; early dances with the girls' school; the Hay Feasts – what fun they were. I loved my sport, studied both the violin and piano and sang in the choir. I was also the proud owner of Boogle, the largest teddy-bear in the school.
MALCOLM YOUNG (1965–70)

When I started at Summer Fields in the autumn of 1985, it was still just about recognizable as its much older self. The cane was held over our heads as a sanction (I'm not sure it was ever actually used), bins were called 'wagger-paggers', access to the newly built indoor pool involved a counter-intuitive naked, outdoor dash, Cecil ruled over the Vins, and end-of-term films were projected onto a big screen in Macmillan. Unless you were a day boy, parental contact beyond exeats was limited to (censored) weekly letters, and less attention was paid to health and safety than I imagine is the case now. Log-fighting was an officially sanctioned pastime, access to chemicals – including the vicious stop-bath – was no problem providing you joined the photography club! When Port Meadow froze we were taken there to caper about on the ice. Pandemonium broke out one afternoon when it was established that the *Kool Mintz* we'd been given as sweet rations were in fact potent laxatives!

Inevitably, most of my memories involve bad behaviour (at which I excelled). I wish I remembered more about the Battle of Blenheim, or the formation of oxbow lakes. However, I vividly recall Justin Gayner (1985–90) making a clay phallus in Art (and subsequently protesting to Mr Talbot Rice, the Headmaster, that it was a lighthouse), and my own *pièce de résistance* – the Gay Club, inspired by our favourite book of the time, *The Growing Pains of Adrian Mole*. We put our notice up in the lobby one evening, announcing that the Gay Club, 'for pupils who want to be frisky, frolicsome, lively, playful, sportive, vivacious or gamesome during break', would have its inaugural meeting in the gym, after Second Prep. To our consternation, half the school turned up! The summons to the Headmaster's study came at breakfast!

It was only after leaving SF that I realised how unusual it was for young boys to use obscure words in normal speech, to be taught Plautus and Orwell, to play croquet like it really mattered, to have a Dendrology Club and do cryptic crosswords for fun. The Summer Fields I attended was an eccentric and hermetic world, then – but rarely an unhappy one.
RICHARD MORTON JACK (1985–90)

I don't believe I could have received a more fulfilled education at any other school in the country.
FRANKIE PARHAM (1997–2002)

Summer Fields has been my home for so long that I can hardly remember my first years here. Nonetheless I can clearly bring to mind my first memory, shaking Mrs Badham-Thornhill's hand. She was always warm and kind to everyone; she gave me my first Red. She used to read stories to the First Years on a Sunday and give sweets to people on their birthday. As I went up through the school, teachers became more like friends, outside lessons. Summer Fields now seems more like a mother to me than a school.
PETER YUNGHANNS (2008–13)

Two words from Mr Faber's sermon at the Leavers' Service stick out in my mind: *friendship* and *independence*. Those words, for me, sum up Summer Fields.
MATTHEW TAKAVARASHA (2011–13)

It was Leavers' Day, Sunday 30 June, 2013. Waking up early, I realized that in less than a week I would be an Old Summerfieldian. I was just so helpless – it struck me so suddenly that all the pleasant memories I had, all the friendships I had shared, all the music and shows I had played and put on, would vanish into nothing. Only then, in the last week of term, did I begin to appreciate everything we did every day.
MAX SALATA (2011–13)

After two and a half years at Summer Fields, I came to know it as well as home, which it became for many people. I still regard it as a home that took me in and looked after me.
BORIS KHALIMOVSKIY (2011–2013)

Hay Feast

There is absolutely no doubt that there is one special tradition of Summer Fields which sticks in the minds of virtually all OSS – the annual Hay Feast. 'Hay Feasts – what fun they were!'

The Hay Feast was known in the early days as the 'Hay Picnic', a sort of *fête champêtre* as C. Day-Lewis put it. This takes place at the end of the Summer Term in one of the fields by the Cherwell. Details of the occasion have altered over the decades, but in essence the event has not changed since its origins. The beginnings of the Hay Feast are lost in the mists of time. No one really knows how, or when, it began. Did it evolve, suggested Nick Aldridge, from an informal picnic in July to watch or help the haymakers on the farm? However it started, it remains popular today, and in the occasional year when inclement weather prevents the production of the requisite amount of hay, the boys are inconsolable. A classic description of the event is provided by Leonard Strong in the mid-1930s in his novel *The Last Enemy*:

> The annual Hay Rag was the year's one great period of licence. Everyone, boys and masters, trooped down to the large hayfield in which the hay had already been cut. There they divided into forms and each, with the help of its form master, built itself a fort out of the hay. Half an hour was allowed for this, and then the whistle blew for tea. The whole assembly lined up and received each a paper bag containing food and a mug. The boys carried theirs off to the fort, where they sat peacefully and consumed it.
>
> After tea, the assembly paraded again for grace and then rushed off for the real purpose of the day: the Hay Rag. This was a fight on the good old principle of all against all. It began as form against form, one defending its fort against another, a regular alternation of sorties in which the masters joined; but in a very few minutes all trace of order was lost.
>
> The rag lasted till everyone was tired out. After that came the races; and, last of all a period of quiet when everyone lay in the hay and held a kind of informal sing-song, before linking arms and going off in one huge line across the field and back to the school. Once

in the large school playing field, they all made one enormous line, and, at a signal, advanced towards the school singing, *One man went to mow, went to mow a meadow*.

From a similar time comes another account of the Hay Feast, this time factual:

> In the summer, after the hay had been cut, we celebrated the Hay Feast. The hay lay around in a field beyond the farm. Members of the school went there to have tea and to build nests in the hay. I remember on one occasion, we were allowed to pelt hay at Mr Alington, until, becoming rather breathless, he asked the boys who were doing it to stop, which they did.
>
> Thomas Miles (1931–6)

Hay Feast evenings were sometimes enlivened by wonderful Zulu war-dances performed by Mr Mullins (1928–39), who was South African. These days much remains the same, but there are differences, including the absence of the war-dance... The feast now takes place either in the afternoon or evening. The boys still build their hay-castles in the meadow and are firmly enjoined by the Deputy Headmaster to include no stinging nettles or barbed wire in the parapets. Plastic water bottles have replaced mugs; cherries have vanished from the meal; Grace is no longer said before and after the picnic; it is inappropriate now for teachers to join in the ragging or for boys to pelt them with hay; a swim in the outdoor pool on the way back to school – like sheep through a dip – has replaced the Dettol baths remembered by many OSS. A selection of post-rag games remains, although the once-traditional egg-throwing has ceased. Finally, arriving back at the main school buildings, each boy receives an iced lolly and then moves on to Lodge if it is an evening feast. Teachers tend to repair to another venue...

Envoi: The Boys Today

So far, most observations in this book have been from OSS, but what about the boys today? What do the members of the school in its 150th year think about the place? How do they see their school? Is it worth negotiating that deep slough of homesickness and despair finally to reach the broad plateau of happiness and self-fulfilment? Do preconceptions match subsequent reality? What are the opportunities for sport, hobbies and activities? Do the boys take them? What are the teachers and lessons like? What is life like in general? What impact does Summer Fields have on its modern pupil? Here follow some reflections on some of these questions from boys who were asked to write candidly about 'My Summer Fields', treating the subject in any way they wished. The commentators are arranged by year group, as in 2014.

Second Year

When I came to SF I didn't know if I would have many friends, but it turned out that I found one of my best friends on the first day! It's not toys that give you internal happiness, it's friendship that counts.

ERIC HUANG

What SF means to me is happiness and joy.

ALBERT SITWELL

Third Year

SF is an inspiring place. All the teachers are fun to be with, yet great about work as well.

PATRICK MURRAY

It is not only the boys who are nice, the teachers are also very nice. They love teaching and they want to make the boys the smartest they can be. I also love the sport. At Summer Fields, almost everybody is good at sport. This school also gives us healthy food and we do lots of fitness.

TJ AMUSAN

Removes

To me, SF is not just a school. It is a family in which everyone has different qualities, and everyone has their needs catered for.
BEN PORTER

SF doesn't just teach lessons, it teaches you how to behave and be a leader. It teaches you LIFE.
RONNIE ORR-EWING

During my years here so far, not only have I learnt a lot in the classroom, but I have developed and overcome many of my faults and difficulties. I struggled through my first year and was about to leave, because of homesickness, but I pushed through and I feel I have a much stronger character now.
BILL CHALMERS

You can say what you want to say even if you are wrong and you will not get laughed at or embarrassed. Summer Fields is a place where you can learn from your mistakes.
ALAN WHEATCRAFT

The school has given me chances to do things I have never done before such as playing the saxophone and golf. It has let me excel at my own pace.
HIPOLIT HODGES

As soon as I heard memories of SF from my dad I decided that I wanted to come here.
WILLIAM SCOTT

To me SF means perseverance and achievement.
JACK COHANE

SF means to me somewhere I can always feel free to express my thoughts to my friends and all the teachers.
A. J. OKOCHA

Fifth Year

The school is where I live, where I work, where I play, and where I enjoy my life.
JUSTIN WONG

SF is the birthplace of opportunity.
EDWARD BARLOW

SF is my second home. I have felt welcome every minute I have been here.
EDGAR STRUGAR

SF is where I discovered my inner self. SF has created me. The teachers and pupils have an unspoken relationship which is very special.
MARCUS STUART-BOURNE

I will be sad to leave this year, especially with the renovations and changes taking place, but I hope to come back to visit and see the new buildings.
GREGORY TAYLOR

Without SF I don't know where I would be. It has given me a huge chance to express what is inside me and fulfil my potential.
TRAJAN HALVORSEN

Summer Fields: It is not just a prep school. It is a safe place to learn at your own pace, with excellent teaching.
FLYNN STUDHOLME

I like knowing that what I do matters to people.
LOUIS MANSON

When I first arrived I did not understand the importance of respecting other people's religion and now, as a fifth year, I am a lot more tolerant.
HARRY GUJADHUR

Our family has been coming here for fifteen years. The school has brought us together. It has made me into a sportsman, a diligent worker, taught me how to interact with adults and, most of all, I have strong bonds with my friends.
HUGO ROLLS

Summer Fields is a place I can be proud to be part of.
HARRY ARKWRIGHT

The School
2014

Appendix

Chairmen of Governors

1955–76	The Rt Rev. R. C. Mortimer, MA, DD, Bishop of Exeter
1976–8	C. H. Christie, MA
1978–87	The Rt Hon. Sir Christopher Slade, PC, MA (OS)
1987–95	M. M. Jones, MA, FRSA, ARICS
1995–2000	Sir Richard Butler, Bt
2000–7	J. G. Bullard, TD (OS)
2007–13	E. A. Davidson, QC, MA, LLB
2013–	A. E. Reekes, MA, FRSA

Headmasters

1864–96	Gertrude Isabel Frances Maclaren
1896–1918	The Rev. Dr Charles Eccles Wiliams, MA, DD
1918–28	The Rev. Edward Hugh Alington, MA
1928–39	The Rev. Cyril Archibald Eccles Williams, MA (OS)
1939–56	John Fitzgerald Evans, MA
1956–60	Geoffrey Bolton, MA
1960–75	Patrick Morris Boscawen Savage, MA
1975–97	Nigel Talbot Rice, MA
1997–2010	Robin Francis Badham-Thornhill, BA
2010–	David James Christian Faber, MA (OS)

Sources and Further Reading

Primary Sources

Nearly four hundred pieces of evidence were received by the editor. Some consisted of a few sentences; others ran to several thousand words. All were read, analysed and arranged. Regrettably, lack of space prevented the inclusion of everything. However, all material, whether included or not, has been placed in the school archives.

Manuscript Sources

A selection of typescripts, emails and hand-written reminiscences
Unpublished Recollections of Summer Fields by Geoffrey Bolton
Unpublished Recollections of Summer Fields by Patrick Savage
School Reports
Boys' letters

Printed Primary Sources

The Summer Fields Magazine, 1897–2013
The Summer Fields Register 1864–1960 (Oxford, 1960)
OSS Database from 1960
A Selection of Archival Photographs
A Selection of Modern Photographs

Secondary Works

Aldridge, Nicholas. E., *Time to Spare? A History of Summer Fields* (David Tallboys Publications, Oxford, 1989)

——, *In Search of Cyril* (Joshua Horgon, Oxford, nd)

——, *GB: Master, Monster or Myth?* (A. H. Stockwell, Devon, 2008)

——, *The Stained Glass Windows of Summer Fields Chapel* (Joshua Horgan, Oxford, 2009)

Amery, Julian, *Approach March: A Venture in Autobiography* (London, 1973)

Connell, John, *Wavell: Scholar and Soldier* (London, 1964)

——, *Wavell: Supreme Commander 1941–43* (London, 1969)

Corbishley, T., *Ronald Knox the Priest* (New York, 1964)

Danchev, Alex, and Todman, Daniel (eds), *War Diaries 1939–1945 Field Marshal Lord Alanbrooke* (Phoenix Press, 2003)

Fasnacht, Ruth, *Summertown since 1820* (St Michael's Publications, 1977)

Fitzgerald, Penelope, *The Knox Brothers* (London, 1977)

Fort, Adrian, *Archibald Wavell, The Life and Times of an Imperial Servant* (London, 2009)

Horne, Alistair, *Macmillan 1894–1956: Volume I of the Official Biography* (London, 1988)

——, *Macmillan 1894–1956: Volume II of the Official Biography* (London, 1989)

Knox, R. A., *A Spiritual Aeneid* (London, 1918)

——, *The Viaduct Murder* (London, 1925)

Larsen, E., *A Flame in Barbed Wire* (2001)

Macmillan, Harold, *Riding the Storm* (London, 1956)

Sparrow, Christopher, *No Time to Spare?* (Gresham Books, Oxford, 2006)

Strong, L. A. G., *The Last Enemy* (London, 1936)

—, *Green Memory* (London, 1961)

Thorpe, D. Richard, *Supermac, The Life of Harold Macmillan* (London, 2010)

Usborne, Richard, *A Century of Summer Fields* (Methuen, 1964)

Waugh, Evelyn, *Ronald Knox* (London, 1959)

Wavell, A. P., *Other Men's Flowers* (London, 1944)

Subscribers

Jay Adams 2003–8
Ayomide O. Ajibola 2014–
James Allen 2013–
Will Allen 2006–11
Ebube Amadi 2011–14
Kwame Amaning 2008–11
Nana Amaning 2010–
TJ Amusan 2012–
Giles Andreae 1974–9
Frederick Anton-Smith 2012–
Benjamin Atkinson 2002–6
Sam W. J. Bailey 2002–7
William H. J. Bailey 2006–11
Bill Bailey .... 1988– (Staff)
Temi Balogun 2013–
James Bannister-Parker 2012–14
Geoff Bantock 1959–64
T. P. E. Barclay 1959–63
Christopher Barker 1939–41
Julian R. P. Barker 1945–50
Edward Barlow 2009–14
Mr and Mrs D. P. Barrie
Joss Barrie 2012–
Tom Barrow 1974–9
Helen Leigh Barstow .... 2012– (Staff)
Roger A. Bates 1951–7
Adrien Thomas Baudon 2010–
Zac Baylis 2009–
The Bell Family
Christine Berry .... 2000– (Staff)
Caroline Bewes (née Talbot Rice) 1971–97
Anthony Biggins 1943–8
William Birkbeck 1947–52
Andrew and Jane Bishop .... 1990– (Staff)
Toby Blanchard 2011–
The Bossom Family 1997–2009
Jack Boteler 1995–2000
Harry Boyd-Carpenter 1980–6
Nicholas Bradshaw 1949–54
Ian Breminer 1960–6
Henry Brigstock 1989–95
Mervyn Brigstock 1924–7
Nicholas Brigstock 1950–6

Jonathan Broke 1988–93
Robert Broke 1922–6
Robert Broke 1990–5
Simon Broke 1953–7
Api Brown
Hector Brown 2013–
Nicholas Brown 1963–8
William Brudenell 2008–13
George Buchanan 1983–8
John G. Bullard 1960–5
Eddie Burnaby-Atkins 2013–
Bryan Burrough 1968–73
Mary Bushell
Sir David Calvert-Smith 1953–8
Neill Campbell 1956–61
Jake Carr 2013–14
Jamie Carr 1975–80
Henry Carson 2009–14
Andrew Cartwright 1956–62
William Cayzer 1999–2004
Gilbert Chalk 1955–61
Anthony Chamier 1944–9
Daniel C. Chaplin 2001–6
Sir Malcolm Chaplin CBE 1943–7
Nigel Chapman .... 1964–7, 1970–88 (Staff)
Harry Chatfeild-Roberts 2003–8
John Chatfeild-Roberts 1970–5
Tom Chatfeild-Roberts 2001–6
Paul and Diana Cheater .... 1994–2012 (Staff)
Alistair Cheng 2005–2010
Anthony Chisenhale-Marsh 1949–53
Charles Churchill .... 1964–96 (Staff)
Lord John Gillford 2006–11
Lord Clanwilliam
Oliver C. D. Clarke 2002
Willoughby A. C. Clarke 2010–
Richard L. de S. Clauson 1964–9
Mervyn Coller 1938–43
Robin Collins 1995–2000
Rory Collins 1999–2004
His Honour Judge Christopher Compston
    and Caroline Compston
Rupert Cook 1977–82

The Corbett/Heron-Watson Family
Oliver Corso 2013–
Stephen Cox .... 1973–86 (Staff)
Tom Cox 1994–2000
Mark Crawshay-Williams 1963–8
Jack Cross 2011–
Hormazd Dalal 1970–5
Zane Dalal 1972–7
Chris Darlington 1951–3
Edward Davidson QC .... 1998– (Governor),
    .... 2007–13 (Chairman)
Alexander de Broë-Ferguson 2009–14
Alfred de Franssu 2001–4
Louis-Victor de Franssu 2001–3
Augusto Monteiro de Sá Subiotto 2011–
Max de Trense 1952–8
Paul Dean .... 2008– (Staff)
Felix Delaforce 2008–13
Aliotto della Gherardesca 2012–13
Sam Deutsch 2005–10
Leo R. S. Dobbs 1967–71
David C. A. Doughty 2011–
Edward G. A. Doughty 2008–13
Maxi Ducam-Davies 1999–2004
William Dunhill-Turner 2009–14
George Dunn 2007–12
Thomas Dunn 2010–
Jamie Dykes 1979–84
Spencer Eade 1958–63
George Eaton 2006–12
Peter Eaton 2004–9
S. G. P. Eccles-Williams 1962–6
Matthew Egorov 2012–14
Tristan Elbrick 1978–83
David Elliot 1938–9
John Elliot 1935–9
John Alun Emlyn-Jones OBE JP 1933–6
Alexander Ershov 2010–
Valentin Ershov 2010–
Graham Penrose Evans 1956–60
David Faber .... 1969–74 (OS), 2010– (HM)
Henry Faber 2000–5
Memorable Factor 2014–

James Fairhurst 1972–7
Fred Fernández-Armesto 1993–8
Sebastian Fernández-Armesto 1990–5
Peter Flach 1961–6
Peter C. Fletcher 1958–63
Harry Flynn 2009–13
Vernon Flynn QC
Nicholas J. H. Ford 1991–6
Rory D. G. Ford 1997–2002
Roddy Forman* .... 2000–13 (Staff)
William H. Fowler II 1964–9
James Fox 1946–51
Francis Frankopan 2011–
Mr and Mrs Aidan Freyne
Hector Freyne 2000–5
Theo Freyne 1998–2003
Peter Fullerton 1938–43
Jonathan Gaisman 1964–9
Nicholas Gaisman 1997–2002
J. E. J. N. Giles (Magoo) 1973–7
Eric Gleason and Pippa Robinson
Oscar Gleason 2013–
John Gledhill 1955–60
Jamie Glover 1999–2004
Pitt Griffin 1967–72
C. E. Guinness CVO 1933–8
Richard Guinness 1947–52
Christopher Gujadhur 2012–
Harry Gujadhur 2009–
Zhengyuan Guo (Benson) 2012–
Mr Jingwen Guo and Mrs Lujia Wang
Rupert Hall 1999–2004
G. P. A. Halstead 2009–14
H. M. C. Halstead 2012–
J. F. G. Halstead 2005–8
Richard Hamilton 1974–8
Ann Hannah .... 1989– (Staff)
Giles Hannah 1991–6
Marcus Hannah 1987–92
David Harden 1962–7
Barnaby Harrison 2008–11
Mr and Mrs C. S. Heinrich ...... 1985–2001 (Staff)
Will Heseltine 2011–
Andrew H. C. Heywood 2011–
Christopher J. Heywood 1939–41
Harry Hill 2002–7
Oliver Hill 2003–8
James A. C. Hills 2010–
Oscar James Hilton 2011–
George Hopkinson-Woolley 2011–
Christopher Howe 2012–14
Augustus Howland 2012–

Sebastian Howland 2012–
Tomotaka Iba 2002–7
Romarho Ibru 2011–
Osita O. O. Ighodaro 2006–11
Martin and Deborah Ives ...... 2011– (Staff)
The Right Reverend David Jennings 1952–7
James Jillings 2010–13
Mark and Jane Johnson .... 1983–98 (Staff)
Saam Jourabchi 2013–
HRH Dushan Karageorgevitch Prince of
   Yugoslavia 1986–91
Rahul K. P. Kaushal-Bolland 2009–14
Nicky Keattch 2012–14
David Keddie 1940–3
Augustus Kelly 2003–8
Barnaby Kelly 2001–6
Henry Kendall 2013–
Boris Khalimovskiy 2010–13
David Kidd-May .... 1955–2000 (Staff)
The Earl of Kinnoull 1971–5
Usman D. Ladan 2008–14
Charlie Lagden 1996–
Georgina Lagden 2002–
Robert Lagden .... 1996– (Staff)
Sophie Lagden 2002–
Alexander Laing 1995–2000
George Laing 2013–
Jamie Laing 1997–2002
Adrian and Hazel Lane ...... 1986–2009 (Staff)
Jeremy Lane 1988–1993
Judith Lane .. 1968–73, 1982–2004 (Head of Art)
David Langdon .... 1965–2003 (Staff)
S .G. Laoye (Debo) 2013–
Timothy Lebus 1959–63
Max Lee 2014–
The Leeming Family 1998–2006
Sam Legerton 1945–50
The Duchess of Leinster .... 1998– (Staff)
James Blount Lewis 1962–7
William W. Lewis 1967–71
Mrs P. Logan .... 1966–98 (Staff)
Rupert Longsdon 1981–6
Thomas Longstaff 2011–14
Harry Luard 2003–8
Cornelius Lysaght 1973–7
Alastair Macdonald-Buchanan 1969–74
Edward Macdonald-Buchanan 2005–10
James Macdonald-Buchanan 2005–9
Inigo Mace 2012–
Orlando Mace 2011–14
Samuel Mackie 2012–
Scott MacNaughton 2009–

Roderick Manley 1983–8
Louis Manson 2011–14
Charles Marnham 1959–64
Jonathan Mason 1972–7
Oliver Matusch 1990–5
Ian Maxwell 1964–9
Cassian McDonald 2010–14
Rory McNair 2013–
Rupert McNeile .... 1972–2007 (Staff)
Hugo Meakin 2001–5
Luke Measelle 2010–11
Rory Measelle 2011–14
Theo Mellor 2012–
Jack Metcalfe 2010–
Mr and Mrs J. Metcalfe
Mark J. H. Meynell 1979–84
David Millar OBE 1939
Ivar Milligan 1992–7
Henry Minter 2013–
Alex Monro 1944–6
William Morgan 1975–80
Afure Moses-Taiga 2011–
Bofe Moses-Taiga 2011–
Gigi Moses-Taiga 2011–
Carel Mosselmans 1938–43
Christopher Mouravieff-Apostol 1970–1
Mahir Raja Mujtaba 2010–
Patrick Murray 2012–
James Peter Charles Musgrave 1998–2003
David Myddelton 1948–53
Edward Mynors 1955–60
Rebecca Nash (née Talbot Rice) 1973–97
P. G. Nathan 1942–3
Sir Philip Naylor-Leyland 1961–6
Henry Nell 2014–
Rory Nell 2012–
Alexander Nevill 1974–8
Giles Nevill 1972–7
Richard Nevill 1946–50
The Nicholl Family .... 1991– (Staff)
Guy Nicholson 2009–12
Yoshi Nishio 1975–9
Sir Timothy Noble 1952–6
Philip Noel-Baker 1968–72
Harry Norris 2008–11
Christian Oberschneider 2011–
Jeremy Ogbonna 2013–
Olisa Ogbue 2013–
Richard Ogdon 1973–8
Brian Ogilvie .... 1984–9 (Staff)
Marc Ortiz-Patiño 2011–13
Andrew Ovey 1979–84

Marcus Ovey	2012-
Sebastian Ovey	2012-
George A. Palin	2012-
Charlie Llewellen Palmer	1976-80
Dominic Parr	1981-6
Edward Pascall	2008-14
James Pascall	2004-9
Thomas Pascall	2008-13
Sebastian Peacock	2011-13
Alexander Peake	2001-6
Freddie Peake	2007-12
George Peake	2005-10
Toby Pemberton	2008-10
Algernon Percy	1976-82
Josceline Percy	1979-84
Julian Perkins	1985-90
Robert Phillips	
Sarah Phillips (née Talbot Rice)	1969-97
H. J. Pitman	1970-5
Lt Col J. H. Pitman OBE	1943-8
M. N. Pitman	2006-11
G. W. Pitman	1946-51
G. E. Pitman	1972-76
Jack Pitman	1977-82
T. E. Pitman	1977-80
W. H. Pitman	1973-8
Clare Pollard	1997- (Staff)
Daniel Ponomarenko	2012-
Benjamin Porter	2012-
Dominic Price	1998- (Staff)
Gareth I. J. Price	2001- (Staff)
F. C. M. Prickett	2011-
Willy Pryor	1947-52 (OS), 1969-99 (Staff)
J. A. S. Pugsley	2000-9 (Staff)
Christopher Purchas QC	1951-7
Merrick Rayner	1963-8
Cailan Reddy	2008-13
Stephen Remington	1955-60
J. J. C. Richardson	1931-5
Louis Rifat	2007-13
Alexander Robarts	1981-86
Charles Robarts	1979-84
Allan Roberts	1958-63
Derek Robinson	
Charles Rooth	2013-
Tobias Rooth	2014-
Nicholas Rowley	1972-6
Alasdair Russell	2000-05
Angus Russell	2012-
Ethan William Richard Russell	2010-14
Louise Russell	1999- (Staff)
Thomas Charles Martin Russell	2010-

Max Salata	2011-13
Melanie and Jean Salata	
Sebastian Salata	2013-
Sir Patrick Salt	1941-6
James and Annabel Salter	
Finn Salter	2006-10
Harry Salter	2008-14
Takanori Sano	2010-14
Nicholas Sansom	1963-8
Aidan Saunders	2013-
Denis C. L. Schmiegelow	1944-9
Ian L. Schmiegelow	1951-7
Justin Scott	1978-83
Mason Scott	1962-7
Otto Seymour	2012-
Dexter Simpson	2007-12
John B. Singer	1960-4
Gus Skinner	2010-13
Henry Skinner	2003-8
Thomas Skinner	2005-10
Sir Christopher Slade	1939-40
Andrew and Ann Snow	2012- (Staff)
Andreas Sohmen-Pao	1981-4
Tommy Sopwith	1944-6
Henry C. T. Soundy	2006-11
Mark W. Soundy	1972-7
Orlando H. T. Soundy	2010-
Mark Spiridonov	2010-
Joseph Standbrook	2013-
Augustus Stanhope	2013-
Christopher Stannard	2008-11
Richard Stark	1976-81
Charlie Steel	1993-8
Henry Steel	1997-2002
Christy Stewart-Smith	1978-82
David Stirling	2012-
Felix Stocker	2011-13
B. I. Straton-Ferrier	1932-7
Edgar Strugar	2012-14
Arthur Studholme	2004-9
Flynn Studholme	2010-14
Rafe Studholme	2007-11
John Henry Stuttard	1970-6
Dragon Sun	2009-14
Caesar Supple	2013-
Saxon Supple	2011-
Rupert Swallow	2006-9
Sebastian Swallow	2013-
Alexander Sweetnam	2010-
Thomas Sweetnam	2008-14
Chris Swift	2003- (Staff)
Helena Talbot Rice	1977-97

Nigel Talbot Rice	1965-75 (Staff), 1975-97 (HM)
Samuel Talbot Rice	1982-97
Gregory S. L. Taylor	2011-14
Harrison N. L. Taylor	2009-12
Spencer Taylor	2011-14
Alberic Teilhard de Chardin	2012-
Victor Teilhard de Chardin	2010-13
Matty Thavenot	1988-93 (OS), 2013- (Staff)
Harry Thistlethwayte	2008-13
David Theodore Thompson	1949-54
Sergei Tourian	2011-
Andrew Vaughan	1971-6
William Vaughan	1996-2001
James Virgin	1979-84
Freddie Vose	2012-
Gus Vose	2011-
Alex Waddington	2000-5
David Ward	1991-6
Jeremy Ward	1989-94
Jonathan Ward	1995-2000
Tom Watkinson	2007-10
Finlay Watt	2010-13
Xander Watt	2011-14
James Weaver	1977-82
Matthew Webber	1972-6
Tim Webber	1973-8
Alistair J. Welch	1951-6
Paul Wertheim	1999-2004
Denis and Alexandra Williams	
Edward Williams	2011-
Marcus Williams	2008-14
David J. M. Wilson	1955-9
Justin Wong	2010-14
The Woolley Family	2013- (Staff)
Poon Xuto	2003-7
Praj Xuto	2001-4
Boni Yin	2011-
Wei Yin	
Malcolm Young	1965-70
Tony Yu	2006-9
Santiago Zanini-Mazza	2013-
Steve Zhao	2013-

* Sadly Roddy Forman passed away on 26 January 2014

Index